"An ex-insider's thoughtful case for the proposition that since the end of WWII the U.S. Congress has effectively abdicated its responsibility to play an active, vital role in the nation's foreign affairs. . . . An estimable contribution to the quiet debate on an issue of genuine, if unappreciated, consequence for the electorate." —*Kirkus Reviews*

"The fashion today is to speak of an imperial Congress, even on matters of foreign policy. Not so, Weissman tells us, plainly and persuasively, with all the authority of one who knows Washington ways from the inside."—PAUL E. PETERSON, Henry Lee Shattuck Professor of Government, and Director of the Center for American Political Studies, Harvard University

"An experienced insider with a historian's grasp of pattern and a political scientist's gift for diagnosis, Weissman crisply tells the story of Congress's retreat from its foreign-policy responsibilities in the Carter, Reagan, Bush, and Clinton years. Rich in detail, sensitive to the human dimension, and based on revealing declassified documents and interviews, this book sensibly charts the road ahead for a congressional revival."—THOMAS G. PATERSON, author of *Contesting Castro* and Professor of History, University of Connecticut

"Anyone with an interest in Congress or foreign policy will find this well-written, well-argued book well worth reading."
—DEBORAH KALB, *The Hill*

"This is an important and useful book—one of those rare volumes that combines careful scholarship, skillful writing, and a wealth of first-hand experience. This book should be must reading for anyone who wants to understand Congress's tru
—JOHN T. TIERNEY, Professor

A CULTURE OF DEFERENCE

Congress's Failure
of Leadership in
Foreign Policy

STEPHEN R. WEISSMAN

BasicBooks

A Division of HarperCollins*Publishers*

Designed by Ellen Levine

Library of Congress Cataloging-in-Publication Data

Weissman, Stephen R.
    A culture of deference: Congress's failure of leadership in foreign policy
/ Stephen R. Weissman.
        p.   cm.
    Includes bibliographical references and index.
    ISBN 0–465–00761–9 (cloth)
    ISBN 0–465–00732–5 (paper)
    1. United States. Congress. 2. United States—Foreign relations—
1945–1989. 3. United States—Foreign relations—1989–
I. Title.
JK1081.W44 1995
328.73'0746—dc20   94–46263
                                          CIP

96 97 98 99 ◆/RRD 9 8 7 6 5 4 3 2 1

For Nancy . . . for all the reasons.

Contents

Preface

Looking at the old black-and-white photographs, I remember how intoxicated I felt. On a summer night in August 1979, I was reclining on a colorful North African carpet in a large tent deep in the Sahara desert. Through the open front of the tent, the stars were closer and brighter than I had ever seen them. Around me, in their long white *djelabas*, sat the young leaders of the Polisario Front, which was warring for the independence of the former Spanish Sahara against Morocco, an old U.S. friend. At my side was Congressman Stephen Solarz, who had persuaded me, a few months earlier, to leave academic life and join his House of Representatives Africa Subcommittee staff. A week of exciting and exhausting travel had taken us from the Royal Palace of Rabat, Morocco, where generals passed their time waiting to see the king like the hangers-on I'd observed at Jersey City Democratic clubhouses, to pro-Polisario, "revolutionary" Algeria, where the president greeted visitors in an airless room filled with ornate French furniture. Early that morning we had flown south from Algiers to the Polisario refugee camps near the oasis town of Tindouf. Trailed by a pitiless sun, 130-degree temperatures, and manhandling winds, we had visited refugees, conversed with vigorous-looking elders (some of the last African nomads), interviewed sad-looking Moroccan prisoners, and inspected captured American-made weapons. Now, as I looked up at the floodlit desert stage where Polisario women danced and ululated, Steve Solarz turned to me with a wry smile and asked, "Tell me, what are two Jewish guys from New York City doing here?" If I had managed to shake off my enchantment and reply in my sometimes overserious way,

I probably would have said, "We're trying to learn as much as we can to give Congress a basis for making a judgment on U.S. policy toward North Africa."

Like many others, I had come to Washington to gain influence. I had a liberal perspective on U.S. foreign policy interests in the Third World, and had hoped that my knowledge and passion for research could contribute to sounder congressional decision making. And during my twelve years with the Africa Subcommittee staff, two under Chairman Solarz and ten under his successor, Representative Howard Wolpe, I did have many opportunities to make a difference on issues ranging from famine relief to human rights to transitions from white minority rule. But life with Congress, including that memorable mission to the Maghreb, also taught me a lot about how the institution itself worked—and might possibly work better.

As a professor of American government, I was well acquainted with the age-old controversy over Congress's constitutional power in foreign affairs vis-à-vis that of the president. I was also familiar with fellow political scientists' studies comparing congressional foreign affairs committees with other committees along such lines as members' reasons for joining and their perception of the outside political environment. And I had read a number of detailed case studies of congressional decision making on "hot" foreign policy issues. But as a participant in the legislative process, I discovered that these approaches, though often enlightening, were in an important sense either too broad or too narrow. For beyond its legal framework and general predispositions, Congress has a special way of learning about foreign policy and an unusual way of acting on it.

And this peculiar approach cannot easily be captured by focusing on discrete and visible decisions. In the first place, the formal legislative agenda in foreign policy is relatively small: for example, the issue of arms sales to Morocco was never officially voted upon by either house. Then, even where there are votes, they are apt to be shaped by such hidden influences as private executive-branch briefings and phone calls, the competing priorities of members, the quality of staff work, occasional in-depth investigations such as the study mission to North Africa, and the quiet personal intervention of political fundraisers and lobbyists. One day I remember handing a busy Solarz a memo suggesting an ambitious course of action to influence an upcoming vote on military aid to Somalia. "That's fine," he said, looking up with steel in his eyes; "who's going to do it?" Finally, as in other areas of public policy, the act of passing legislation may be less important than its clarity of intent and its subsequent implementation. When Congress, for example, decided to ban imports of uranium and uranium oxide from the white minority regime of South Africa, my subcommittee and others failed to notice that small quantities of an intermediate compound called uranium hexafluoride were also being imported. That failure—a product of lack of time and a not uncommon casualness about making law—permitted the administration to create a significant loophole for South African uranium imports, one that Congress subsequently lacked the political will to close.

In stepping back now from the world of action and trying to render Congress's performance more comprehensible, I have a sense of the promise as well as the danger of the effort. The promise is the added insight an outside observer can gain from becoming a direct participant in events. The danger is that the provincial perspectives and political commitments that accompany such participation can spawn a skewed understanding of political reality. This is not a problem for many public officials who write memoirs with the express intention of recounting events "from my own perspective." Moreover, social scientists are the first to admit that values, emotions, and assumptions about how the world works inevitably influence the questions they pose and at least some of their bottom-line policy preferences. Still, the basic premise of social science research is that by adhering to tried and true methods of gathering and analyzing evidence, one can hope to arrive at some reasonable and testable conclusions about social reality.

Thus I have written this book with a special vigilance for political bias. Three methodological decisions stand out. One was to extend the range of analysis well beyond the African examples with which I was most involved. Only by looking at Congress's behavior in other regions could I tell whether the patterns I detected in Africa were typical. Another advantage of looking outward was the availability in certain cases of voluminous declassified documents that laid bare many elements of the executive-legislative relationship. This was particularly true for El Salvador, where a penetrating United Nations investigation of human rights violations during the long civil war had triggered a decision by President Bill Clinton to release related U.S. documentation. Previously, the Iran-contra scandal had resulted in the declassification of considerable information about U.S. intelligence activities in Nicaragua. And the persistence of investigative reporters like Raymond Bonner and W. Scott Malone in pursuing Freedom of Information Act (FOIA) requests had generated valuable documents on American policy toward the Philippines and on arms export controls—although this material sometimes did not arrive until after their books and articles had been published. (Indeed, after almost two years, most of my own FOIA requests to government agencies remain unanswered, despite my insider's advantage in being able to provide the names, dates, and numbers of many documents.)

A second important decision was to undertake approximately 130 interviews with key congresspeople and staff, executive branch officials, lobbyists, and other informed individuals. A good number were interviewed two or more times. Only a few insisted upon anonymity. These reflective conversations with informants representing diverse political views were invaluable, not least in forcing me to directly confront, and take account of, the variety of political perspectives on congressional actions. They transported me beyond my personal files and experiences—beyond even the valuable studies of other analysts.

Finally, I tried to look at issues arising during both Republican and Democratic administrations, and at ones that provoked legislative responses by members of both parties. This was not always easy, since the Democrats have held the presidency for only six of the last eighteen years and congressional Republicans have only recently begun to reassert their right (and, after the 1994 elections, enhance their capacity) to challenge the president on foreign policy. Nevertheless, the reader will find examples of Democratic presidents besieged by legislators from both parties and prominent Republican congresspeople confronting a Republican White House. I expect that my analysis and policy recommendations will be interesting and useful to people of various political stripes, both today and in the future.

Although I have tried to put forward a fair and balanced picture of Congress in foreign policy, I am not at all dispassionate about the institution itself. I share with many of my former colleagues and recent interlocutors a deep concern with and affection for the U.S. Congress, and a great respect for what it has been able to do at its best. If much of this book is critical of Congress's recent performance, it also demonstrates that Congress can do better. It is animated by the hope that Congress will do better.

A final assurance: while there are many revelations in this book about both Congress and American foreign policy, none of them comes from classified information that I received while employed by Congress and promised never to disclose.

Acknowledgments

I am deeply grateful to the Ford Foundation, especially Vice President Susan Berresford, for the two years of general support that made this book possible. I also very much appreciate the assistance of the Carnegie Endowment for International Peace. President Morton Abramowitz was not only willing to host my project; he (and his staff) did everything possible to facilitate it.

For the experiences that formed the basis of this study, I am enormously indebted to two former chairmen of the House of Representatives' Subcommittee on Africa. Stephen Solarz brought me to Washington and trained me for two years until he left to assume the chairmanship of the Asian and Pacific Subcommittee. His successor, Howard Wolpe, employed me for the next decade. Working over the years with such serious and committed individuals was a great privilege. The respect with which they treated their staff was gratifying. Although I know that they suffered me at times, they never failed to support me and my colleagues when necessary. I am also grateful to my colleagues over the years on the Africa Subcommittee staff, who provided the professional skill and personal friendship that helped me navigate the perilous and frenetic torrent of congressional business for so long. I felt as if I had a family at work. Its members included Mickey Harmon, Adwoa Dunn, Steve Morrison, Salih Booker, Johnnie Carson, Anne Forrester, Priscilla Newman, David Frank, Sarah Lisenby-Tucker, Mark Quarterman, and Anne-Marie Griffin.

In contemplating this project, I was buoyed by the encouragement of Crawford Young, René Lemarchand, Herb Weiss, Dave Wiley, Ray

Bonner, Jane Perlez, Mickey Harmon, Chris Chamberlin, and Bill
Swing. Helen Winternitz supplied me with sage advice on getting published. My agent, Gloria Loomis, believed in the book and skillfully
guided me into making it happen. Once embarked, I benefited from
the help of many people. In particular I would like to thank all of the
people I interviewed. They were willing to take the time to think about
and discuss their past activities, sometimes with an old political foe.
Their reflections provided much of the empirical core of this study.
Cynthia Arnson gave me the benefit of her deep understanding of
Congress's role in El Salvador and Central America generally. She also
provided thought-provoking and extremely helpful comments on relevant portions of the draft manuscript. Stanley Karnow generously
shared his valuable files on U.S. policy toward the Philippines, and
took time out from his current project to discuss them with me. Kenneth Mokoena, Peter Kornbluh, and Linda Davis of the National
Security Archives patiently took me through the mechanics of using
the Freedom of Information Act (FOIA) and facilitated access to the
Archives' vast collection of FOIA releases (including Ray Bonner's files
on the Philippines). Stephanie Plasse provided invaluable research
assistance on Congress's response to the Yugoslav crisis of 1991–94,
which contributed greatly to the discussion of Bosnia in chapter 1.
Michael Van Dusen, Chief of Staff of the House Foreign Affairs Committee, helped me get an important committee briefing on El Salvador
declassified. Jennifer Little, the librarian at the Carnegie Endowment,
collected research materials from around the country and even watched
out for relevant studies as they appeared. Olga Luck, from the State
Department's Freedom of Information Office, did everything possible
to enable me to make my way through the endless volumes of released
documents on El Salvador.

At Basic Books, President Martin Kessler helped me to clarify the
basic ideas behind this work, encouraged me to expand the range of
my research, and made me think about how to tell my story in the
most interesting way. His successor, Kermit Hummel, became my editor. He continued to probe for my essential themes, helped me think
through the organization of the book, and, most important, alerted me
whenever he thought I was in danger of losing the forest for the trees.

Whatever deficiencies remain in this work, I know that I have gained greatly from the quiet and efficient mentoring of these two professionals. I am also grateful to my copyeditor, Ann Klefstad, who helped make this a more readable book.

It would take longer than I have here to total up the contributions of my wife, Nancy Weissman, to this volume. She discussed virtually all of the substance, as well as various creative approaches, with me and she succeeded in persuading me to discard a number of bad ideas. She encouraged me to think again. She was also the first editor of all my drafts, a sharp critic within a framework of overall intellectual support. Watching her edit, I felt myself becoming a better writer. I know too that I was often saved by her solid political judgment. And it was Nancy's unselfish support and love that helped me to get through the two years of intense and hermitic labor this book required. I also want to thank my son, Daniel Weissman, for his enthusiastic support and love, and for his many insightful comments and suggestions during the final editing of the manuscript.

1

A Congressional Culture

In September 1993, a powerful U.S. senator offered his colleagues an ominous lesson from classical history:

> In the late summer of 29 B.C., Octavian came back to Rome after the Battle of Actium in 31 B.C. The Roman Senate gratefully—gratefully, gratefully—ceded its powers to someone who would plan and take responsibility and lead, because the Roman Senate had lost its will to make hard decisions. It had lost its will to lead. It had lost its nerve. It had lost its way.[1]

Robert Byrd (D.-W.Va.), the seventy-six-year-old former majority leader of the Senate and its second longest-serving member, had been provoked by President Bill Clinton's support for a United Nations operation in the African country of Somalia. After a glorious entrance as warriors against starvation, U.S. and U.N. troops had become mired in a bloody conflict with a local Somali military faction and its civilian supporters. "No Senator," Byrd complained,

> has gone on record by voting any commitment for the course we are now pursuing in Somalia, and under the Constitution, Congress is not bound to uphold any such commitment by the President—not until it votes to do so. And we have run from the issue up to this point. We have preferred to be left out of tough decisions. All we have to do is to look at a bit of Roman history and see exactly where we are going.

From the other side of the aisle, Republican senator William Cohen of Maine joined in Byrd's self-criticism: "We have used words to abdicate our responsibilities in so many ways."[2] Three weeks earlier, Carroll Doherty, a reporter and seasoned observer of Congress, had remarked, "Legislators don't know what role they're supposed to play [in Somalia and in Bosnia]." In the latter case, televised pictures of genocide

> seemed strangely detached from the business of the Congress. There has been no formal debate in either chamber—only a series of floor speeches by interested lawmakers. The foreign policy committees have not conducted detailed hearings on the conflict, mostly for fear of putting on public view the wide variance of opinion.[3]

Perhaps, Doherty suggested, temporary circumstances helped account for the congressional default. The Democratic Party, which controlled Congress, was disposed to give the new Democratic administration a "suitable honeymoon" to establish its foreign policy. And the emerging post–Cold War world was "uncharted," with new and daunting problems like "failed states" and "rampant nationalism." Still, like Senator Byrd's rhetoric, Doherty's analysis pointed to more fundamental factors at work. Congress seemed uninterested in helping the president outline a new foreign policy: it had yet "to engage the Administration on perhaps the most politically explosive issue of the post–Cold War era—whether the U.S. role in the world should be cut back in the light of the new geopolitical climate and increasing fiscal constraints." Also, he noted, "Most Americans already want their representatives to pay closer attention to domestic issues."[4]

The truth, as I discovered in my twelve years with the staff of the House of Representatives' Foreign Affairs Committee, is that Congress—Democrats and Republicans alike—has largely lost its will to co-determine American foreign policy with the president. This is the painful and continuing legacy of fifty years of world war and Cold War. Since the last days of the Vietnam War, Congress has on occasion displayed real initiative, as in the 1980s when it facilitated a democratic political transition in the Philippines and imposed economic sanctions against South Africa's apartheid regime. This sporadic activism, however, has represented the efforts of a few individuals and the tem-

porary admixture of a post-Watergate "class," not the characteristic thrust of the institution. It is not too much to say that Congress has substantially ceded its fundamental constitutional role in foreign policy. The executive branch has been the main beneficiary of Congress's default, but narrow-based special interests have also gained.

Congressional acquiescence in foreign affairs is not the result of a series of individual decisions. It is the product of a powerful set of internal norms and attitudes, customs and institutions, a veritable culture of deference. Even the demise of the international threats that first nurtured these habits has not greatly disturbed them. They persist as well because of the general absence of broad-based political constituencies pressing Congress to abandon its lassitude. And Congress, enmeshed in its culture of deference, does little to stimulate the growth of such constituencies.

Congress's retreat from foreign policy is not just a remote legal or constitutional issue. American diplomacy has had, and continues to have, a direct impact upon the American people, not to mention people in the rest of the world. Even in the post–Cold War era, developments abroad can have major effects at home. A politically unstable Russia retains the capacity to destroy America with a nuclear blow. With the growth of a global economy, international trade has risen to 25 percent of the gross national product. The spread of militant nationalism in Europe or the eruption of major war in the Middle East or Asia could seriously affect U.S. markets, supplies, and jobs. It could also divert resources needed for domestic investment to national defense. Worldwide environmental problems, such as the destruction of the ozone layer, the depletion of tropical forests, and possible global warming, threaten everyone's health. And a collapse of the fragile hopes for economic development and democratization in parts of Africa, Asia, and Latin America would send an onslaught of disturbing images into American living rooms, add to the flood of desperate refugees around the world, and produce heavy claims on U.S. resources.[5] Rwanda, Haiti, and Cuba have given us a taste of this bleak possibility.

Greater participation by elected representatives in decision making cannot, of course, guarantee a sound foreign policy. But in principle at least, an indifferent Congress makes it harder to achieve good decisions.

The great nineteenth-century political theorist John Stuart Mill provided the classic defense for wide-ranging political debate: "The steady habit of correcting and completing [one's] own opinion by collating it with others, so far from causing doubt and hesitation in carrying it into practice, is the only stable foundation for a just reliance on it."[6] In a broader contemporary formulation, Morton Halperin has argued for congressional consultation in foreign policy because of "the great uncertainties in the world, the impossibility of constructing a hierarchy of values for the nation as a whole, and the virtue of process as a means of determining 'truth' for a democratic society."[7] Reflecting upon the course of American diplomacy, Arthur Schlesinger, Jr., concluded, "History had shown that neither the President nor Congress was infallible and that each needed the other—which may well be what the Founding Fathers were trying to tell us."[8]

As the Watergate and Iran-contra scandals reminded us, presidential aggrandizement in foreign affairs can not only produce bad decisions, it can also threaten the rule of law and democratic institutions themselves.

President Ronald Reagan's secret diplomacy—trading arms for hostages in Iran and aiding contra rebels in Nicaragua—was a foreign policy disaster from almost any political perspective. The United States armed Iran but failed to reduce the number of American hostages or to moderate the revolutionary regime. And it "opened itself to blackmail by adversaries who might reveal the secret arms sales." It "undermined [the United States'] credibility with friends and allies by undertaking secret operations that contradicted its public policies." It "lost a $10 million contribution to the contras by directing it to the wrong bank account," and enriched private intermediaries with arms sales profits that were supposed to benefit the contras. It circumvented the law to help the contras, but the inevitable exposure of this effort helped undermine congressional support for the insurgency.[9]

These policies also constituted a significant assault on American democracy itself. Numerous laws were broken; secrecy and lying were rampant; and high officials made extraordinary claims for a virtual presidential dictatorship on "national security" matters. The majority report of the congressional investigating committees delivered this judgment:

> The common ingredients of the Iran and Contra policies were secrecy, deception, and disdain for the law. A small group of senior officials believed that they alone knew what was right. They viewed knowledge of their actions by others in the Government as a threat to their objectives. They told neither the Secretary of State, the Congress, nor the American people of their actions. When exposure was threatened, they destroyed official documents and lied to Cabinet officials, to the public, and to elected representatives in Congress. They testified that they even withheld key facts from the President.[10]

Recently congressional deference has played an important if little noticed role in three additional U.S. foreign policy failures. In Somalia, Bosnia, and Iraq, the executive branch acted alone, adopting what were later acknowledged to be mistaken or questionable—and ineffective—policies. Only when the political fallout from these policies became sufficiently dense did Congress belatedly react. But it scarcely acknowledged its own complicity in having left the initiative to the president. And it continued to hesitate to insert itself meaningfully into the policy-making process.

SOMALIA

Soon after Senator Byrd's warning, eighteen American soldiers were killed in a military clash in Mogadishu, the capital of Somalia. This incident was the culmination of four months of increasing conflict between the cooperating American and United Nations forces and followers of Somali faction leader General Mohamed Aidid. Responding to a surge of public concern, President Clinton offered his *mea culpa* to the *Washington Post*. "Where I think we erred," he said, was in not "keeping the political dialogue going after June with all the factions while we did our job with the United Nations." Other mistakes acknowledged by the president and his advisers were allowing U.S. soldiers to serve under U.N. command without adequate concern for their security, failing to enlist the nation in the debate over America's role in the post–Cold War world, and just plain inattention.[11] The United States had been spending approximately $44 million a month on an admittedly mistaken policy; eighty-three international peace-keepers (including twenty-six Americans) had been killed, as had an estimated six thousand to ten thousand Somalis.[12] Perhaps the biggest cost of the Somalia policy was an intangible one: the shadow it cast over future U.S. support for international peacemaking interventions in such turbulent places as Bosnia, Haiti, Rwanda, and the former Soviet republics.[13]

Emboldened by expressions of public discontent, Congress voted to cut back U.S. support for the U.N.'s expanded mandate of nation-building: disarmament, political reconciliation, reconstruction, and democratic institution-building. U.S. forces were restricted to self-defense and maintaining open lines of communication for supplies and relief operations. All funding for U.S. troops was to end on March 31, 1994, unless the president requested, and Congress authorized, new monies. The Republican opposition excoriated the administration for allowing the U.N. operation to stray from President Bush's original goal of providing humanitarian relief. Democrats acknowledged the administration's previous mistakes.[14]

Yet for nearly a year, Congress itself had consciously avoided taking any policy decision at all on Somalia, leaving the problem to the executive branch. When President Bush began introducing over 28,000 U.S. troops into war-torn Somalia in December 1992 to battle the starvation that had killed hundreds of thousands of Somalis, he failed to consult members of Congress; they were simply notified. Nevertheless, congressional leaders of both parties, including House speaker Thomas Foley (D.-Wash.), quickly endorsed the effort without insisting upon broader deliberation.[15]

In February 1993, without a single public hearing, the Senate passed a resolution supporting the U.N.'s deceptively narrow objective of creating a "secure environment for humanitarian relief operations." The resolution, described as "pro forma" by Senate majority leader George Mitchell (D.-Maine), was the subject of only brief and per-functory debate that scarcely touched upon the emerging issues of political reconciliation, disarmament of militias, and coordination between the U.S. and U.N. forces.[16]

The House of Representatives did not act until May. Following a spirited and partisan debate, the Senate resolution was revised to accomodate an expanded "nation-building" mission being undertaken by the United States and the U.N.[17] Then, as Senator Mitchell related, he requested Senate consent for a conference with the House to reconcile the two resolutions, but a single anonymous Republican senator objected. As a result, said Mitchell, "The Congress has not acted with respect to this matter."[18] However, key staff members from the House Foreign Affairs and Senate Foreign Relations Committees confirmed that there was almost no pressure from the Democratic majority in either body to proceed.[19]

Even when its hand was finally forced by the public outcry (and a partisan opportunity for the Republican opposition) Congress proved itself a reluctant policymaker. For while it moved to extricate U.S. troops from Somalia, it failed to establish any political direction at all for the hundreds of millions of dollars it continued to pour into the U.N. operation. How should the United States and the U.N. recast their priorities for Somalia now that U.S. troops were departing? How might they influence the situation to avoid the return of the civil war and resulting mass starvation that triggered their initial intervention? By neither asking nor answering such questions, Congress implicitly returned power over U.S. policy to the President.

BOSNIA

Since 1991 the violent disintegration of Yugoslavia has posed an intimidating challenge to European and American policymakers and indeed the entire international community. At its center has been a sometimes genocidal struggle among Serbs, Croatians, and Muslims in the new state of Bosnia-Herzegovina. The conflict has been particularly fueled by rival Serbia, and its victims have mainly been the Bosnian Muslims, the largest group in the state. According to estimates, as many as 200,000 people have died and 2,000,000 have been rendered homeless, often as a result of Nazi-like "ethnic cleansing" operations. Although many countries and international organizations have intervened with humanitarian relief, diplomacy, peacekeeping forces, and even limited military action, "The ongoing conflict has been viewed as a failure of the international community to respond effectively to the prolonged fighting, and a dangerous precedent for other regions in Europe and Eurasia."[20] An official who was deeply involved in U.S. policy making on Bosnia recently concluded, "We must see that America's interests and values, its credibility and self-respect, have been damaged in the former Yugoslavia, and we must thus recognize the face of failure."[21]

No one has yet established that different Western policies would have avoided the worst developments, or that an alternative American approach would have been accepted by the Europeans. But it is significant that a number of former and current U.S. officials have expressed serious second thoughts. For example, top Bush administration policymakers have indicated that a "relatively modest collective intervention by the United States and European countries, backed by threat or use of force," in the earlier Serbia-Croatia conflict during the summer and fall of 1991 "might have headed off the later disaster."[22] Others, including the former U.S. ambassador to Yugoslavia, believe a more aggressive Western military and political response to the outbreak of the Bosnian war could have promoted a viable, if not ideal, political settlement.[23] The early Clinton administration was sharply criticized by foreign service professionals for its counterproductive "indecision" and "policy swings," especially in Bosnia.[24] After "rethinking" in early 1994 the administration's previous "hands-off" stance, Secretary of State Warren Christopher acknowledged, "I am acutely uncomfortable with the passive position we are now in, and believe that now is the time to undertake a new initiative."[25]

Although many members of Congress spoke out on Bosnia and journeyed to the region, Congress was unable to make any significant contribution to American policy.[26] Sometimes this was for lack of even minimal action. For instance, the major foreign policy committees held no specific hearings on Yugoslavia during the critical spring, summer, and fall of 1991. And a raft of early 1992 resolutions encouraging recognition of the former Yugoslav republics were never even debated or voted on by the full House and Senate. Sometimes one chamber moved without necessary support from the other, as in June 1992 when only the Senate passed a resolution calling on the president to urge the U.N. to prepare a plan and budget for enforcing its resolutions for a cessation of hostilities in the republics. Even when Congress passed some legislation, notably that relating to the lifting of the U.N. arms embargo against Bosnia, its initial inclinations were to urge rather than to bind the president.

Congress became somewhat more energized following widespread media coverage of concentration camps and human rights violations. But it was consistently unable to create a majority consensus in favor of any coherent policy. In this connection, it is significant that most of the legislation it considered did not emerge from detailed hearings and patient, bipartisan legislative coalition-building by the foreign policy committees, but rather from individuals offering amendments to extraneous bills on the Senate and House floors.

The most important illustration of Congress's failure to make policy was its narrow preoccupation with unilaterally lifting the U.N. arms embargo against Bosnia. Certainly the embargo, in practice, discriminated against the militarily weaker Bosnian government forces. And making its elimination the major thrust of Congress's activity had the political virtue of avoiding potential controversy over possible American military involvement. Yet lifting the embargo was not a complete or coherent policy by itself. As most of its leading proponents recognized, it formed part of a larger policy fabric that remained to be woven, one that might include such threads as U.S./NATO air strikes, measures to protect or evacuate U.N. peacekeepers, a vision of an acceptable political settlement, an information or propaganda policy toward Serbia, preventive diplomacy to ensure that the conflict did not spread elsewhere, and other measures. Without a firm sense of how unilaterally lifting the embargo fit into a larger policy framework and was related to other objectives, some members of Congress could find themselves caught between conflicting priorities. That is precisely what happened in 1994 when the Senate twice publicly humiliated itself by simultaneously voting for a unilateral lifting *and* for administration recommendations to temporarily postpone such lifting while authorizing air strikes or pressuring the Bosnian Serbs to make peace. "In my 14 years in the Senate," commented Senator Arlen Specter (R.-Pa.), "I have not seen such inconsistent resolutions passed."[27] The confusion stemmed not only from the Democrats' desire to defend their president but also from the Senate's (and House's) failure over a period of years to create a compelling majority consensus for either existing policy or a coherent alternative.

Of course, Bosnia was a particularly difficult issue for Congress. It brought together the complex mysteries of the ancient Balkan conflicts, delicate military calculations, and a web of preexisting obligations to the European allies and the U.N. On the other hand, the human consequences of the conflict were catastrophic and its political fallout, in Europe and elsewhere, potentially serious. One might have hoped for a stronger congressional effort to guide the president while allowing him necessary tactical flexibility.

IRAQ

In the aftermath of Iraq's invasion of Kuwait and the resulting 1991 Persian Gulf war, President George Bush's administration wasn't making any excuses to Congress for its prewar policy. "We recognized that there was a potentiality of a very serious opponent here," testified Under Secretary of State Lawrence Eagleburger,

> We felt it was also important because of a desire to try to maintain some stability in the Persian Gulf that we had to try to bring him to a more reasonable position. It is clear that policy did not work. It is not the first foreign policy of the United States in a number of administrations that didn't work. We tried and we failed.[28]

The immediate price of that policy failure was paid by the Kuwaitis who endured a brutal occupation, the Americans and their allies who spent blood and considerable treasure in Operation Desert Storm, and the Iraqis who suffered massive military and civilian destruction.

Historians and others will surely debate whether the administration's approach encouraged Iraqi president Saddam Hussein's aggression, and whether any alternative policy might have prevented it. As war receded and national elections beckoned, however, the Democrats who controlled Congress were most interested in dissecting the corpse of the Bush policy. Didn't official U.S. statements imply that we would not necessarily defend Kuwait's borders? Didn't so-called dual-use exports, which could serve either civilian or military purposes, contribute to the Iraqi military machine? Didn't U.S. government loans for agricultural and other exports free Iraqi foreign exchange for nefarious purposes? What did the government know about massive private loans to Iraq from the Banca Nazionale del Lavoro office in Atlanta?[29]

What almost no one mentioned was that "Congress's own record on Iraq was one of compromise and inaction." The bottom line was inaction. In September 1988, a Senate Foreign Relations Committee staff mission produced evidence confirming allegations that Iraq had used chemical weapons against its dissident Kurdish minority. Congress seemed to be on the verge of passing a modest, bipartisan economic sanctions bill that curbed certain dual-use exports and international loans and threatened more substantial restrictions. But the measure was lost when it became a pawn in turf struggles among various congressional committees, and a bargaining chip in one senator's attempt to advance a minor amendment.[30]

The following year a new bill threatening future sanctions against Iraq and other chemical weapons users, and their foreign suppliers, foundered amid another turf battle between two Senate committees. In late 1989 and early 1990, renewed efforts to legislate immediate sanctions were stalled by opposition not only from the Administration but also from relatively narrow-based economic interests. Companies concerned with trading with Iraq helped defeat a proposed Senate prohibition on U.S. Export-Import Bank loan guarantees. And a pending House of Representatives ban on government financing of agricultural exports was gutted by the affected interests, even as Iraqi troops massed on Kuwait's border.[31]

HURDLES

"Can you tell me who is fighting who in Ishmaelia?"
"I think it is the Patriots and the Traitors."
"Yes, but which is which?"
"Oh, I don't know that."

—Evelyn Waugh, *Scoop*

To a certain extent, Congress's lethargy in foreign policy stems from its well-known deficiencies as a legislative institution. Today's members of Congress are "independent entrepreneurs, each with an autonomous electoral base, who will not allow other members, even leaders, an excessive degree of control over their careers."[32] It can be a challenge to assemble a majority behind anything that is not minimally required or unanimously felt. Working in Congress sometimes feels like being in the middle of a newly disturbed anthill. Each inhabitant hurries along in accordance with his or her unique set of political priorities and ambitions, major financial backers, subcommittee, committee, and leadership positions, and personal concerns and relationships. In addition, frenetic schedules—the result of crushing committee responsibilities and the relentless pressures of modern political campaigning—leave too little time for the patient discovery and pursuit of common legislative interests. As a staff member of the House Foreign Affairs Committee, I discovered that one of my most important and anxiety-provoking tasks was simply to locate and round up presumed supporters for crucial committee votes.

Traditionally, political parties organized Congress to debate and make public policy. Their contemporary efforts are hindered by members' growing individualism and the current era of fiscal constraint, which discourages new initiatives requiring spending. Moreover, insofar as the congressional parties do manage to produce policies, they are often strongly influenced by the powerful modern president, who has become both chief of party and chief legislator. Also, in recent years, control of the presidency and at least one house of Congress by different parties has helped produce a measure of gridlock. The new 1995 Republican congressional majority appeared relatively united, at

To Floyd Fithian, who was a Democratic member of the House Foreign Affairs Committee and subsequently served as a top Senate aide,
foreign affairs are "more exciting" than domestic ones, but "politically, a downer."[42]

Finally, on controversial subjects, the hidden nature of foreign policy and the dearth of political constituencies provide the executive
branch with a powerful temptation to manipulate Congress and public
opinion through various forms of deception. Perhaps the classic modern formulation is that of Elliott Abrams, who was a high State
Department official during the Reagan administration:

> We were at war, we and the Democrats in Congress, or so we
> thought and they thought. There were sometimes hearings where
> they asked fair, decent, intelligent questions whose purpose was to
> find out the truth. Hearings on Haiti, Jamaica, earthquake aid, or
> religious freedom in Cuba. But on Central America, hearings were a
> form of combat. Questions were weapons, and answers were
> shields. So when I was asked for information that might help them,
> might give them more ammunition, I tried to deny it to them. I tried
> to figure out how I could give them the least information possible.[43]

Democrat Richard Moose, who has been described as "the most
publicly frank individual to serve as assistant secretary for Africa,"
nevertheless makes a somewhat similar point. "Yes, people in the
executive branch tend to have a desired outcome in mind, and present their case in such a way that it supports the argument they make
or the outcome they want."[44] I happened to be in the room when
Moose did just that as President Jimmy Carter's administration
launched America's tragic relationship with Somalia in 1980. Questioned about the Somali government's assurances that it would not
send its forces into neighboring Ethiopia's Ogaden region, Moose
publicly assured the House Africa Subcommittee, "I do not believe
that there is any *significant* body of Somali regular forces in the
Ogaden [emphasis added]."[45] An hour or so later, Moose sat quietly
in a secret session of the subcomittee as a Central Intelligence Agency
colleague estimated that elements of three Somali battalions were in

the Ogaden. "Although the estimates were hedged," the *Washington Post* reported, "subcommittee members emerged with the conviction they had heard two conflicting reports."[46] Looking back at his testimony, Moose acknowledges, "I was trying to make as plausible and clear a case as I could without perjuring myself, believing nothing in the Ogaden was very clear. . . . I was enormously uncomfortable [with the policy] but had to put the best face on it."[47] What Moose reluctantly did was more than looking at an agreed body of facts and saying the glass is half full rather than half empty, more even than simple advocacy. It was, consciously or unconsciously, shading the facts to achieve a desired outcome.

Nor is the temptation to deceive Congress confined to the politically appointed honchos of the national security bureaucracy. It is part of the repertoire of career diplomats and other functionaries as well. It is "probably true," says former American Foreign Service Association president Lannon Walker, that "a different dialogue" occurs with Congress than within the State Department, and there is "a danger that if Congress [is seen as] the enemy, you could even eventually be lying."[48] Former U.S. ambassador to Somalia Frank Crigler admits, "I was less sanguine about creating paradise than the State Department might have been in public presentations."[49]

At the extreme, Elliott Abrams and some of his colleagues in the Iran-contra affair demonized Congress and ended up being prosecuted and convicted for telling it clear-cut lies. Their conduct fulfilled Saint Augustine's definition of lying: "Every liar says the opposite of what he thinks in his heart, with purpose to deceive."[50] More commonly, officials employ other forms of deception such as "evasion or the suppression of relevant information."[51]

Notwithstanding these hurdles, Congress has the potential to play a much more significant and thoughtful role in foreign policy making. It could learn a lot more about the world and the impact America has on it. It has the tools to hold officials accountable for misleading it. By exerting leadership, as the Founding Fathers expected it would, "to refine and enlarge public opinion,"[52] it could help address the problem of weak political constituencies for foreign affairs.

ANATOMY OF A CULTURE

Congress normally approaches foreign policy through what might be called a culture of deference: a distinct set of norms and beliefs, customs and institutions, that confine it to the margins of power. It is a bipartisan culture, setting limits to the normal competition between Democrats and Republicans. Although its original basis—the Cold War—evolved and ultimately disappeared, the culture persisted, recalling Karl Marx's reference to the "albatross of tradition" in political life. In its halcyon days, when the culture was at maximum strength, it was legitimated by the myth of presidential superiority in foreign affairs. And although buffeted by Watergate, Vietnam, and Iran-contra, this culture of deference has largely survived, protected by the revised myth that 535 members of Congress are mainly incapable of constructive action. For many influential members, the maxim "We shouldn't make foreign policy" dating from the early Cold War years has gradually been replaced by "We can't make foreign policy, at least most of the time." An important congressional player in foreign affairs, former Representative Matthew McHugh (D.-N.Y.) put it this way: "There's a certain deference to the President and the State Department. Part of it is ingrained custom. . . . Even in the reaction, like post-Vietnam, it was difficult if not impossible to play a significantly larger role."[53]

The culture of congressional deference in foreign policy has several key postulates:

(1) *Congress gives the president leeway to unilaterally undertake new and urgent initiatives which imply a future commitment of legislative support.*

> The Congressional mentality when dealing with a foreign policy initiative by the executive is timidity.
> —*Wyche Fowler, former Democratic senator and representative from Georgia*[54]

In 1823, an American president pronounced the Monroe Doctrine, dictating European nonintervention in the western hemisphere. But for decades this foreign policy was actually just a statement of presidential preference, backed by nothing but the compatible interests of Great Britain and its powerful navy. In 1978 President Carter diplomatically recognized the government of Communist China. This was an action that lay well within his exclusive constitutional power to receive foreign envoys. But a presidential decision to transfer military aid to a friendly government in the midst of a civil war, to launch a secret paramilitary campaign against an unfriendly regime, or to dispatch tens of thousands of American troops on a humanitarian mission to Africa touches directly upon Congress's constitutional powers to make laws and appropriate funds. Still, no matter who is president or which party is in power, Congress almost invariably comes up with the necessary money and political support. It should be noted that although the president generally invokes urgency or secrecy to justify his unilateral initiatives, a true emergency (like the Cuban missile crisis) or an operation requiring absolute secrecy (say, a counterterrorist strike against Libya) is relatively rare.

(2) *Congress declines to wield its weapons against executive branch deception.*

> These guys are too trusting. . . . I'd say to the [Subcommittee] Chairman, "They're lying to you." Sometimes he didn't want to hear it.
>
> —*A veteran Democratic staff member of the House Foreign Affairs Committee*[55]

Despite the executive branch's notable capacity to mislead Congress in foreign affairs, congressional custom does not promote the unmasking of official deception. For example, unlike many of their domestic counterparts, congressional foreign policy committees rarely swear in offical witnesses. If this occurs at all, it is usually a temporary reaction to a major public scandal. By not requiring an oath of truthfulness, at least in controversial areas, Congress foregoes the moral and political pressure of solemnization.[56] It also sacrifices a potential legal sanction—felony prosecution—against the most extreme form of deception, clear-cut lying.

More important, the committees rarely oblige the executive branch to produce relevant information that could undermine official deceptions. This information exists primarily in the form of classified cables, reports, memoranda, and other documents. Some of it is also in the heads of members of American embassies abroad and other foot soldiers of diplomacy. This is the raw material by which one can judge the veracity of the administration's public statements and private briefings. It is largely unavailable to Congress on controversial issues even though all the members and many key staff possess high-level security clearances.[57] Occasionally, a press leak from the administration or a dramatic allegation by a seemingly credible source will embarrass the executive branch into sharing a few cables or confidences. But the committees are averse to requesting—and if necessary, subpoenaing—broad categories of policy-relevant information.

Nor have they established procedures to achieve the orderly declassification of portions of the secret briefings and reports they do receive. So even if a congressperson possesses official information that challenges the official story, he or she cannot discuss it publicly without violating a trust and risking the censure of colleagues. But without such a discussion, Congress and public opinion are unlikely to call the administration to account. A perverse reaction to this dilemma is to refuse an offer of classified information in order to retain the freedom to discuss credible press allegations. Michael Barnes, who was a Democratic chairman of the House Western Hemisphere Subcommittee, recalls:

> There were some members who would not look at the classified stuff because it would then limit what they could say. There were a couple of times when I took that position and wouldn't be briefed by the [Central Intelligence] Agency.[58]

Alternatively, if Congress had the will to press the point, there are certainly ways to publicly release the gist of relevant classified information, such as the corruption of a political regime, international arms flows, or progress in diplomatic negotiations, without disclosing sensitive "sources and methods of intelligence" or otherwise jeopardizing the national interest.

(3) *Congress does not deploy its resources to ensure that it develops an independent perspective.*

> The hackneyed lament that there are now 535 Congressmen aspiring to be Secretary of State is simply not true. Relatively few members spend the time and energy required to articulate comments on the myriad of daily international events.
> —*Senator Richard Lugar (R.-Ind.)*[59]

Considering the special challenge it confronts, Congress's apparatus for considering foreign policy is relatively thin. "I'd bet you," says former representative Solarz, "that most members of the House Foreign Affairs Committee devote less than 50 percent of their time to foreign affairs. . . . Also it is relatively rare to see a member exert influence and leadership on a whole range of issues."[60]

Of course, even the secretary of state has time to spend but a few minutes a week on a typical foreign policy issue. For the rest, he or she relies upon the corps of deputy and assistant secretaries, office directors, desk officers, intelligence analysts, and others.[61] The relatively few interested congresspeople often rely upon "staff," particularly the more numerous staff of the major foreign policy committees, House Foreign Affairs and Senate Foreign Relations. Staff from other committees, especially Appropriations (the Foreign Operations Subcommittees) and Intelligence, are also important. Considering the remoteness of many foreign policy issues and the dearth of broad-based constituencies, dependence on staff can be relatively heavy.

Despite the vaunted "staff explosion" of the 1970s and 1980s, their numbers are probably inadequate (especially after recent reductions) if Congress is to be a real force in foreign policy. As staff director of the House Foreign Affairs Committee's Africa Subcommittee, I and two or three other professionals were supposed to advise House members on U.S. policy toward the African continent, from Casablanca to Capetown. In addition, a single staffer represented the Republican minority. We had as many people working on *all* of Africa's 50 countries as a single executive agency, the State Department, had on its Washington desks for a single medium-sized nation. What is more, other executive-branch agencies were also involved in Africa. Of course, our executive-branch counterparts were responsible for the conduct of day-to-day relations as well as overall policy, but we also had obligations that went beyond policy advice: educating members and staff, pursuing a legislative strategy, engaging interest groups and the press in the legislative process. Still, we were well off in comparison with the single professional who comprised the Senate Africa Subcommittee majority staff or the three who covered the entire world for majorities on the House and Senate Foreign Appropriations Subcommittees! John Carbaugh, a former top foreign policy aide to Senator Jesse Helms (R.-N.C.), observes:

> I'm for more staff. They get 30 to 40 issues to know. If they're good, they'll know 10. You end up with a symbiotic relationship: the regulated, the administration, runs the regulators.[62]

Even more serious impediments to a larger congressional role lie in the kinds of skills congresspeople require of their staffs and the kind of role they expect them to play. First, it is an open secret that a significant number of committee staffers lack the policy competence, investigative talent, political aptitude, or diligence to do their jobs well. They may have other attributes, including political connections, but those do not, by and large, empower Congress. Second, among the qualified there is too high a proportion of (often bright) generalists. One longtime staff member of Senate Foreign Relations remarks, "If Congress is serious, it needs to have more people with academic or practical experience in specific fields."[63] Often the major foreign policy committees attempt to cover regions without anyone who even knows a local language. Last, many staffers describe their roles as "sifting" and "distilling," or "mediating," the views of the administration and the few active interest groups or experts.[64] Although this kind of activity is useful, it falls short of the investigative orientation and substantive mastery of issues that would most enable Congress to be a partner in policy making.

The main congressional format for foreign policy discussion also leaves something to be desired. In principle, public hearings afford committees an opportunity to seriously confront the issues by questioning administration policymakers and bringing in outside experts and interests. But the practice is usually quite imperfect. The administration generally disregards rules requiring its testimony to be submitted well in advance for review. Its witnesses testify first and decline to be questioned alongside others, spoiling the chance for a confrontation of opposing assumptions (they are often more accommodating to television producers). The few subcommittee or committee members who show up are sometimes more interested in making their own positions clear than in exchanging views, especially if television cameras are around. Rather than organizing the limited time to permit sustained questioning and discussion of key points, members proceed individually in apparent disorder. After an hour or two, the administration departs along with most of the press (who feel they have gotten their stories) and some of the members. It is now time for the academics, interest group representatives, and other "private" witnesses to testify and briefly field questions before the committee adjourns to more pressing engagements. Despite the growth of modern satellite and other communications, they are not employed creatively to bring a deeper understanding of remote political realities into the hearing room. Former House and Senate foreign policy aide William Woodward finds the whole process "mind-bogglingly obsolete." The purpose, he says, "should be to elicit dialogue based on facts."[65]

Travel also has great potential for strengthening congressional capacity in foreign policy. It can provide members and staff with valuable opportunities for firsthand discussions with key foreign figures and American officials on the scene. Most important, it can enable them to gain a deeper understanding of unfamiliar societies, including America's interests in them and impact on them. Yet while most travel by the relatively thin cadre of congressional foreign policy activists is ill-described by the popular epithet "junket," its empowering possibilities are usually underutilized. Too often trips are of the "if it's Tuesday, it must be Belgium" variety. But a brief one- or two-day visit to a country practically confines one's explorations to the capital, a handful of meetings with top foreign officials, and a formal U.S. embassy briefing. This kind of education can be awfully narrow, and can actually suppress important questions about U.S. policy.

(4) *Congress has a weak commitment to making and upholding clear and binding law.*

> You know how it is. Somebody writes it; it passes; no one reads the damned thing.
>
> —*Former senator Dick Clark (D.-Iowa)*[66]

Reflecting on the legislative process in foreign affairs, Senator Clark notes, "Unless you've worked or served in Congress, it's difficult on the outside to imagine how disorganized, chaotic, and incomplete it can be." As Exhibit A, he cites his best-known piece of legislation, the Clark Amendment prohibiting covert aid to the Angolan insurgents, the meaning of which was subsequently disputed.[67]

Vague legislation may spring from a realistic recognition of the need for executive-branch flexibility in changing international circumstances. Or it can be the necessary result of a political compromise. But often it is the product of a politically tinged casualness about the law. "I sinned in that regard," confesses Gregory Craig, a lawyer who was a top foreign policy aide to Senator Edward Kennedy (D.-Mass.). "I constantly went for political expediency to avoid arguments over capillaries rather than veins and arteries." In the world of foreign intelligence, says former House Intelligence Committee chairman Dave McCurdy, "Ambiguity is the norm and juridical issues are unclear."[68]

Once legislation is passed, Congress is supposed to oversee its proper implementation by the executive branch. There is considerable dissatisfaction among members regarding their effectiveness as overseers, especially in foreign policy. "We don't even scratch the surface," complains former House Foreign Affairs chairman Dante Fascell.[69]

The further question of how serious Congress is about legislating at all arises in such notable cases of inaction as Somalia, Iraq, and the missing foreign aid authorization bills. Twenty or thirty years ago, the House Foreign Affairs Committee, under Chairman Thomas "Doc" Morgan (D.-Pa.), proceeded from the premise that its job was to "help make good foreign policy by helping pass the President's foreign policy legislation."[70] Congress's recent reluctance to insist, over executive opposition, upon enacting major legislation raises the question of whether it has come very far since the days of "Doc" Morgan. Matthew McHugh comments,

It's very unhealthy not to have a foreign aid authorization bill. It tends to diminish the standing of the authorizing committee and demoralize its members. And if the fundamental problem is public understanding, it is one of the rare opportunities to publicly debate foreign policy.[71]

(5) *Congress is sometimes driven by relatively narrow-based special interests with access to a few key legislators.*

A $2,000 contribution can have some result, as can a particularly active constituent who has access or a following in the community, if there is no significant constituency on the other side. Presumably, this is the course of least reaction; people are human.
—*Former representative Matthew McHugh (D.-N.Y.)*[72]

It is widely recognized that ours is "an era of vigorous activity by organized interests in national politics."[73] In Congress, this trend has been promoted by such developments as increased electoral insecurity, the rise of political action committee financing, and the decentralization of the congressional power structure. In general, "narrowly interested and well organized" minoritarian groups do best. And in foreign policy, where members are disinterested and broad-based constituencies scarce, a single company, foreign representative, or small interest group is even more likely to have a major impact on Congress. According to former representative Solarz, "It is easier for an individual or a group to influence foreign policy by enlisting one or a handful of members than it is on domestic policy where, generally speaking, you have a much larger number of involved members."[74]

Money, in the form of campaign contributions and other assistance in fund-raising, can be one source of influence. Howard Marlowe, former president of the American League of Lobbyists, says, "I can't see how any member of Congress can put out of mind the effect saying yes or no will have on the funding of campaigns."[75]

Lobbyists also gain access to members and potential influence over them through political ties and previous business or personal relationships. "What I saw," relates Stuart Sweet, a former foreign lobbyist and Republican congressional aide, "were people who had long-standing friendships. They knew the members personally and through political contacts . . . like at the Republican convention. Partisan interests lead to friendship."[76]

Another important ingredient in successful lobbying is the strength of one's case and how it is presented to potential supporters. Paul Manafort, a partner in a major lobbying firm that has represented numerous foreign clients, talks of employing "the kinds of skills you develop in a political campaign: strategy, tactics, arsenals."[77]

(6) *Congress reviews some major executive-branch policies in almost total secrecy, further narrowing its access to critical information and limiting its choices.*

> The intelligence committees are dependent upon what the intelligence community says to the committees.
> —*Representative Lee Hamilton (D.-Ind.)*[78]

"Covert action" is defined as "activities of the United States government to influence political, economic, or military conditions abroad, where it is intended that the role of the United States government will not be apparent or acknowledged publicly." In the 1980s, major CIA covert actions were under way in Afghanistan, Angola, Cambodia, Nicaragua, and Iran at a reported cost of several hundred million dollars a year.[79] In Congress, these efforts were supervised and funded under the aegis of the House and Senate Select Intelligence committees.

When these committees approach the secrets of state, Congress's power appears to be at its lowest ebb. As Representative Hamilton, a past chairman of the House Intelligence Committee, explains,

> The intelligence committees operate in a way that no other committees of the Congress operate. By that, I mean that almost the sole source of their information is the intelligence community. Those committees have almost no way of counterbalancing that information. If we have somebody giving us testimony with regards to education or Medicare or foreign policy, we can always counterbalance that with additional information.[80]

ROOTS

In a time when the pundits in the press hardly ever call on Congress to take a foreign policy initiative, it is easy to forget that Congress has not always been so deferential. The development of a culture of deference needs to be understood in the changing context of American history.

However surprising it may seem from a current perspective, the authors of the American Constitution were concerned about the real possibility of congressional *domination*, which they had already experienced under the preceding Articles of Confederation. This was mainly why they insisted upon America's unique system of separating the legislative, executive, and judicial powers while endowing each branch with some means to check and balance the others.[81] The legal scholar Louis Henkin observes that "The Constitutional blueprint for the governance of our foreign affairs has proved to be starkly incomplete, indeed skimpy." But he is certain that "for the framers, Congress came first." Thus

> Congress has the power to tax and spend for the common defense and general welfare (including no doubt foreign affairs purposes), to regulate commerce with foreign nations, to define offenses against the laws of nations, to declare war. The President has the power to appoint ambassadors and to make treaties (with the consent of the Senate). The Constitution provides that the President shall be the commander in chief.

The last function, often cited by ambitious presidents, "appears to have implied no substantive authority to use the armed forces whether for war (unless the United States were suddenly attacked) or for peacetime purposes, except as Congress directed."[82]

From the beginning, though, presidents gradually augmented their real influence over foreign policy through their day-to-day management of affairs, growing control over military and other resources, and increasing prestige as party and popular leaders. Presidential initiatives helped create what Supreme Court Justice Robert Jackson would call a constitutional "zone of twilight" in which "the President and Congress may have concurrent authority or in which its distribution is uncertain."[83] In this new realm, activist presidents staked out important claims. There was the right to dispatch military forces, short of war, to protect U.S. citizens and firms, and even to advance broader economic and political interests. This was memorialized in President Theodore Roosevelt's famous boast, "I took the Panama Canal and let Congress debate," and embodied in a series of early-twentieth-century interventions in Central America, China, and Russia. There was the authority to develop major foreign policies via "executive agreements" with foreign governments, which, unlike treaties, did not have to be submitted to the Senate for approval. And there was the ability to withhold certain information from Congress in the public interest.[84]

Still Congress continued to be a vital and important actor in foreign policy until World War II. It played a major and independent role in the debates and decisions preceding American entry into the War of 1812,[85] the Spanish-American War,[86] and the two world wars.[87] In each case it adopted a declaration of war. It also rejected, for better or worse, many proposed treaties, including those providing for the annexation of Hawaii and Santo Domingo, a canal and protectorate in Nicaragua, and collective security through the League of Nations.[88] It passed extensive neutrality legislation in a vain attempt to escape the impending World War II.[89]

Throughout this period, congressional assertiveness was encouraged by relatively broad-based constituencies. For example, "sectional" economic interests, such as the expansionist dreams of western frontiersmen and the Atlantic trade of northeastern merchants, influenced congressional deliberations in the lead-up to the War of 1812.[90] In the late nineteenth century, public sympathy for neighboring Cuba's revolt against monarchical Spain contributed to congressional pressure for recognition of the rebels. It eventually fostered congressional support for war with Spain, as did an emerging consensus in the business community that expansion would help resolve domestic economic and social problems.[91] Momentous congressional debates over the Versailles Treaty ending World War I, and over American policy on the eve of World War II, were fueled by the preoccupations of large ethnic groups with events in their European homelands as well as by regional differences concerning U.S. interests in Europe and the Far East.[92]

It was World War II and especially the succeeding three decades of intense Cold War that fundamentally transformed Congress's role in foreign affairs. Congress continued to pursue its constitutional responsibilities, but in form more than substance. America's decision to assume global responsibilities in a battle for national survival against a global foe led straight to presidential dominance. Endowed by Congress with unprecedented military, intelligence, diplomatic, and economic resources, presidents from Franklin Roosevelt to Richard Nixon persuaded both Congress and the public that only the executive branch had the unity, speed, and information to meet the challenge. From Korea to Indochina to the Dominican Republic, Congress yielded the crucial decision to use force almost entirely to the president. The number of executive agreements mushroomed. The president sent his foreign aid bill to Congress, and after some carping and cutting, his priorities were approved. The executive branch also established a general secrecy system, undertook a large campaign of covert action around the world, and developed a full-blown doctrine of executive privilege to resist congressional inquiries. The resulting "uncontrolled secrecy," Arthur Schlesinger, Jr., wrote, "made it easy for lying to become routine."[93]

By the 1970s, however, disaster in Vietnam had punctured the myth that only "the best and the brightest" in the executive branch could be entrusted with American foreign policy. The Watergate scandal revealed the threat a swollen "imperial presidency" posed to liberty itself. Moreover, the rise of Soviet-American détente and the diplomatic opening to Communist China held out the promise of a less menacing world. Spurred by its own internal democratization movement, Congress recognized that foreign policy had become a hot political item and reclaimed a voice in policy making. It ended military aid to Turkey after the latter's invasion of Cyprus, pulled the rug out from under CIA aid to South African–supported insurgents in Angola, and forced President Carter to withdraw the SALT II arms control treaty with the Soviet Union. The trend toward legislative "ascendance" that some observers detected, however, was never realized.[94]

The principal thrust of legislative reform had actually been procedural; it was an effort to inject Congress into major foreign policy deci-

sions. Congress passed legislation enabling it to review executive decisions on the use of force, covert action, arms sales, and executive
agreements. It enacted laws requiring the president to give consideration to new congressional concerns for human rights and nuclear non-
proliferation.[95] But, as the following chapters will show, the promise of
these reforms has been largely unfulfilled. Part of the reason was the
continuation, in moderated form, of the Cold War. Another part was
the enduring culture of deference in Congress.

The disappointment of the 1970s reforms was perhaps epitomized
by the fate of the War Powers Resolution of 1973. This was an attempt
to address the problem of creeping presidential military escalation,
which had culminated in the Vietnam disaster, by establishing a mechanism to reinvolve Congress in all decisions to employ force in hostile
situations. After prescribed consultations, the president would formally report any use of force to Congress, triggering a 60- to 90-day
limit in the absence of further congressional authorization. But time
revealed "the unwillingness of both the President and Congress to
invoke the key operative provisions of the War Powers Resolution."[96]
The problem was not fundamentally a legal or constitutional one,
though many argued in those terms. It was only partly a reflection of
the enduring Cold War, since many of the occasions for invoking war
powers had nothing to do with the conflict with the Soviet Union. The
problem was largely one of congressional culture. As Representative
Norman Dicks (D.-Wash.) remarked, "The Congress simply does not
want to be seen as weakening the President. It's a political problem."[97]

The silence in Congress was lifting. That body was more aware of
what the executive branch was doing. And it was no longer bereft of
substantive influence, as its interventions on such issues as aid to Israel
and Turkey, sanctions against South Africa and Cuba, and its belated
debate on war with Iraq showed. But Congress was still not even a
junior partner in the overwhelming majority of important decisions.
"The fact of the matter is the President of the United States makes foreign policy," Representative Hamilton stated in 1991, little more than
a year before he became chairman of the House Foreign Affairs Committee.[98]

Congress's reticence during the different phases of the Cold War may have also been related to a long-term decline in the traditional political constituencies for foreign policy. Widespread ownership and control of property, which gave farmers and small businessmen a directly felt stake in many international political issues, had been superseded by a corporate society that centralized property and divorced ownership from control. Regional differences on foreign policy faded as expanding transportation and communications bound the country together. The old ethnics from the massive immigrations of the nineteenth and early twentieth centuries became increasingly assimilated, while their successors had yet to muster the same political force.[99] In recent years new constituencies began to emerge around such issues as arms control (notably the nuclear freeze movement), human rights, and environmental protection.[100] But their influence was limited by continuing Cold War concerns and the dampening effect of congressional culture.

The advent of the Clinton administration in 1993 coincided with a sea change in the international environment. The main political underpinning for presidential predominance, the Cold War, disappeared, although the president's military, diplomatic, and economic resources for conducting foreign policy remained considerable. Suddenly there appeared to be a lot more political space for an emerging post–Cold War agenda running the gamut from nuclear and regional security to humanitarian intervention. The administration's early foreign policy challenges were truly daunting, involving less familiar areas of the world, deep-rooted politico-ethnic conflicts, and untested prescriptions for broad economic reform. Still the new range of post–Cold War concerns seemed to harbor a promise of broader public involvement in foreign policy, especially as an ongoing revolution in communications was bringing much of the world into America's living rooms.

Congress did erupt, with notable effect, when pictures of starving Somalis appeared on the Cable News Network during the last months of the Bush administration, and when President Clinton committed a post-Vietnam no-no by threatening to place U.S. troops in a sustained line of fire in such seemingly out-of-the-way places as Somalia, Bosnia, and Haiti. But Congress had yet to take advantage of the liberating potential of the new circumstances. Nor would it until it fully confronted and transformed its cultural heritage from the long Cold War. It couldn't change the intragovernmental balance of power alone. It would also need the support of new, broader-based constituencies. But like the presidency itself, it could help galvanize and direct constituencies by leading in the discussion of foreign policy.

This book is about the congressional culture of deference as it manifested itself during the Carter, Reagan, Bush, and early Clinton administrations. It does not pretend that internal congressional practices and norms account for everything Congress does in foreign affairs. Obviously, any particular congressional action is the result of many important factors, including partisan divisions, interest group activity, broad constraints in public opinion, international events, television, and the popularity, resources, and tactical skills of the president. As the book will show, however, the culture of deference is a major underlying force in congressional decision making, and it is often a decisive one. It also helps determine whether or not Congress even attempts to make a decision. Precisely because the culture is so powerful, it has become part of the unseen architecture of policy making.

This book is also concerned with the unusual moments when Congress has managed to transcend its culture. Here one can see the forerunners of a potential new culture of participation and of real partnership with the president. Finally, it is about how Congress might realistically proceed if it wished to transform its culture and restore, under new conditons, the constitutional balance.

The focus is on what might be called classical foreign policy, the predominantly political relations among nations. International issues more directly affected by economic impulses—such as trade and certain defense policies—generate greater constituency involvement and are handled somewhat differently.

Chapters 2 through 4 present several significant cases that illuminate the policy impact of the culture of deference. Chapter 2 focuses on the experience of the congressional opposition to U.S. policy in El Salvador during the early 1980s. The El Salvador issue was an important and highly visible one, resulting in a substantial commitment of U.S. resources for more than a decade. It was a dramatic test of congressional capacity in foreign affairs because El Salvador policy provoked unusually strong opposition in Congress and among domestic constituencies.

Chapter 3 considers the less visible controversy over U.S. aid to Zaire during the Carter, Reagan, and Bush administrations. It highlights the influence of a succession of narrow-based lobbies in marshaling congressional support for the administration's policies. Zaire was also a hard case to test the influence of special interests because there was a committed congressional cadre that opposed the positions of the major lobbyists and the administration.

Chapter 4 presents two cases that fell under the jurisdiction of the secretive intelligence committees. These were the Reagan administration's circumvention of congressional prohibitions against assistance to the insurgencies in Nicaragua and Angola, and the subsequent Reagan-Bush covert paramilitary action against the government of Angola. Again, these were among the more controversial issues in Congress and therefore furnished a good test of Congress's potential strength.

Chapter 5 ponders three instances in which Congress, with considerable bipartisanship, transcended its culture of deference and played major and widely appreciated roles in U.S. foreign policy. These were the promotion of human rights and political negotiations in El Salvador in the early 1990s, and the democratic transitions in the Philippines and South Africa during the 1980s. These cases, also hard-fought, offer some useful models for an alternative foreign policy legislature. Finally, chapter 6 presents some overall conclusions, including suggestions for pragmatic congressional reform and revival.

2

Giving the President the Benefit of the Doubt: The Congressional Opposition and U.S. Policy Toward El Salvador, 1980–1984

When Congress takes up a foreign policy issue, it rarely starts with a blank slate. Normally, the administration already has a policy that it is quite prepared to defend. It can draw upon a formidable American presence abroad, which gives it access to a variety of relevant information. Finally, it has all the moral weight and political prestige of the modern national security state. No matter what its political party, it is at least believed to be concerned with the defense of "American interests." Its pronouncements of fact will be published by the newspapers without regard for their usual rule requiring confirmation by two independent sources.

For Congress to truly make up its own mind, then, it has to find ways of effectively exploring different policy alternatives. And if it wants to make its legislative will felt, it needs to keep a watchful eye on the guardians of national security. Yet as the El Salvador case shows, this paradigm of participation is regularly defeated by Congress's own culture. At many key turns, Congress tended to give the benefit of the doubt to the executive branch. When the administration requested leeway to undertake new commitments in "urgent" situations, it got it. When the "facts" that justified the president's policy were brought into question, Congress shied away from undertaking the kind of active inquiry that might have threatened the administration's rationale. And when the administration resisted the clear intent of the law, and even attempted to govern without restriction, Congress was surprisingly acquiescent.

A DEFINING MOMENT

On Tuesday, March 25, 1980, CIA headquarters in Langley, Virginia, received a cable bearing important news from the small Central American country of El Salvador:

> At approximately 1800 hours on 24 March 1980, Salvador's Archbishop Oscar Arnulfo Romero Galdamez was assassinated while celebrating mass in the chapel of the Devine [*sic*] Providence Hospital in San Salvador. While numerous accounts are circulating, most reliable appears to be that Romero was killed by a single bullet through the heart. . . . Presumable, Romero killed by a rightist assassination squad.[1]

As eyewitnesses later established, the archbishop was standing behind the altar facing the congregation, finishing his homily, when "a loud gunshot" came from a red four-door Volkswagen stopped "outside the open-doored main entrance of the chapel." He "fell to the floor, mortally wounded in the chest and bleeding profusely from the nose and mouth."[2]

Upon receiving the news, the CIA quickly produced a report that briefly and accurately analyzed the political significance of the murder. Calling Archbishop Romero "the most influential public figure in El Salvador," it warned that his assassination "could provoke widespread violence and further dim the Government's chances of survival." Then it insightfully portrayed the contending political forces. "Known as the champion of the poor," the archbishop "had been the nation's most articulate critic of repression and injustice; and had recently stepped up his denunciations of violence by the security forces and the right. He also came close to endorsing the alliance of extreme-left organizations as a political alternative." Reaction to his assassination "may split the coalition [military-civilian] government, already weakened by dissension over the military's failure to curb rightist violence. Regardless of guilt, the military will at least stand accused of having inspired the shooting, and the U.S.—because of a perceived association with the military—may also share the blame." Finally, "the ultraconservative opposition would view the possible collapse of the ruling junta as a way to drive the civilians from the government and engineer a restoration of repressive military rule."[3]

The assassination of Archbishop Romero would be a defining moment for American foreign policy. American aid to El Salvador had averaged only $11 million a year in the late 1970s, and virtually none of it was for the military. But in 1980, the United States provided $64 million, including $6 million for the Salvadoran armed forces. Between 1980 and 1990, the political leadership of this densely populated land of five million would receive more than $4 billion in American foreign aid, of which more than $1 billion would go to the military.[4]

For much of this latter period, Congress was intensely involved with the development of U.S. policy. Especially during 1981–84, the Democratic-led opposition in Congress waged a strong battle against the policy of the Republican Reagan administration. The opposition's influence was greatest in the Democratic-dominated House, but it was also a force in the Republican-controlled Senate.

This congressional challenge was bolstered by the post-Vietnam national mood of caution about American intervention in the Third World. As Thomas Carothers has written,

The U.S. public was extremely wary of anticommunist crusades in obscure countries where the United States was defending a government of dubious character and flirting with the possibility of an escalating military involvement. The constant reports of brutal political violence by the Salvadoran security forces, in particular the December 1980 murder of four U.S. churchwomen by members of the Salvadoran security forces, ensured an extremely negative image of El Salvador in many Americans' minds. The churchwomen were just four out of thousands of victims of right-wing violence in El Salvador, but the fact that they were American and that they were nuns gave the case a special visibility in the United States. The Reagan administration's initial cavalier attitude towards the case (Secretary of State [Alexander] Haig joked about it in testimony before Congress) and the Salvadoran government's long delay in solving and prosecuting the case galvanized liberal opposition to U.S. policy.[5]

The appearance of a significant religious constituency that opposed the administration's policy was also politically important. Rising Catholic activism was especially effective. Many leaders and members of the American Catholic Church had been influenced by their Latin American counterparts' new thrust on behalf of the poor and human rights. They were also deeply affected by the murders of Archbishop Romero and the four churchwomen. Through the U.S. Catholic Conference, the bishops communicated their concerns to Congress and the mass media. According to a conference staff member, their message also "flowed just kind of naturally" through the Catholic network of "social ministers" in each diocese, parochial schools, charities, and the religious press.[6] The congressional lobbying campaign mounted by the religious constituency and its labor-union, peace, and other allies (broadly coordinated by the Coalition for a New Foreign and Military Policy) ran the gamut from private conversations with church leaders to letter-writing, sit-ins, and mass demonstrations.[7]

There was a significant area of agreement between the Reagan administration and a broad bipartisan majority in Congress on *some* elements of U.S. policy. Neither wanted to see the Farabundo Martí National Liberation Front (FMLN) guerrillas, spearheads of the "extreme left," shoot their way into power—especially since their supporters in the Sandinista government of neighboring Nicaragua seemed to be moving in a more "pro-Cuban" and "pro-Soviet" direction. Both sides also favored an eventual "political solution" to the conflict. Toward this end, partly because of congressional pressure and the post-Vietnam mood, the administration agreed to support land reforms, democratic elections, and other measures to limit the power of the "ultraconservative right." Finally, the administration and Congress broadly agreed that the United States should furnish no more than fifty-five military advisers on the ground, and that the Salvadoran

government should investigate and bring to justice the murderers of
the churchwomen and of two American labor-union advisers.

But the administration and a strong opposition group in Congress
differed regarding two key aspects of the quest for a political solution.
First, Reagan officials deemphasized what the CIA report had called
"the military's failure to curb rightist violence." They ascribed much of
the killing to unknown assailants, clandestine private groups, traditionally decentralized rural security forces, and individual soldiers.
Thus they were prepared to furnish the government ample military
assistance as it continued its "slow and arduous" task of reforming the
military and taming the violence. The congressional opposition, bran-
dishing reports from various human rights organizations, maintained
that the military was responsible for most of the political violence. It
asserted that important elements of the military apparatus were systematically associated with extrajudicial executions, "right-wing"
death squad assassinations, and peasant massacres, and that the government basically condoned the killings. It was therefore willing to
threaten significant reductions in military aid unless effective reforms
were undertaken.

The second point of contention was the mechanism for reaching a
political solution. The administration opposed forcing the government
into broad political negotiations with the FMLN and its political allies.
It argued that a democratically elected government (elections were held
in 1982 and 1984, though without the left's participation) ought not to
be compelled to reach "power-sharing" agreements with unelected
guerrillas. The government should offer the latter nothing more than
the opportunity to participate in the next round of voting. The congressional opposition objected that such an offer might, in the prevailing violent circumstances, be perceived by the FMLN as a kind of
invitation to a beheading. Instead, it called for unconditional political
negotiations between the government and FMLN to achieve "an equitable solution." This would include free elections but could contain
other elements (such as security safeguards and military reorganization) as well.[8]

Already in the last months of the Carter administration, the congressional opposition, led by liberal Democrats on the critical foreign

affairs/relations and foreign operations committees, had asserted that
the Salvadoran government wasn't adequately controlling its armed
forces or seeking a negotiated settlement. It pursued the same themes
during Reagan's first term, usually by critiquing various "presidential
certifications" that Congress required for the release of American military aid. Particularly controversial were those Reagan issued declaring
that the government was "achieving substantial control" over its
armed forces to end "indiscriminate murder and torture of Salvadoran
citizens," and was demonstrating "good faith efforts to begin discussions with all major political factions" toward an "equitable political
solution."[9]

On these crucial issues, the congressional opposition largely lost. It
didn't lose because its facts were clearly wrong or its arguments inher-
ently weak. Indeed, leading students of Salvador policy have concluded that "strengthening the military inevitably clashed with the
goal of promoting democracy."[10] Furthermore, by 1990 the Republican Bush administration had embraced a concept of broad political
negotiations and compromise that "was anathema to the architects of
U.S. policy towards El Salvador in the 1980s."[11] When the U.N. finally
brokered a successful peace accord between the government and
FMLN, it included provisions for the purging of abusive and corrupt
military officers, the abolition or reorganization of three security
forces, a Commission on the Truth to investigate past human rights
violations by both sides, land transfers, and U.N.-monitored elections.
Although it is impossible to prove definitively that the congressional
opposition's policy of pushing harder for human rights and negotiations would have been more conducive than Reagan's to the eventual
solution achieved, in the light of history the reverse proposition
appears even more difficult to establish.

Nor could the opposition's defeat simply be blamed on the influence of a popular president and the appeal of his "hard-line" anti-
Communism, though these factors undoubtedly played a major role.
At key junctures, leaders and members of the congressional opposition
themselves failed to act early enough on their doubts about administration policy, failed to make politically effective arguments against the
administration's case, and failed to translate temporary political advan-

tages into clear and binding law. And while one cannot be absolutely certain that these lapses significantly undermined the congressional opposition's influence, there is a strong possibility that this was indeed the case. It was not any lack of brains, hard work, or political commitment that prevented the opposition from pressing its points home. It was, in significant respects, the weight of longstanding congressional customs in both the Democratic-controlled House and the Republican-controlled Senate, customs in which the opposition was itself enmeshed. Nothing would show this more clearly than the congressional response to the slaying of Archbishop Romero.

GIVING LEEWAY

On the day after the assassination, Carter officials appeared before a House Appropriations Subcommittee to seek approval for $5.7 million in "nonlethal military aid" to the Salvadoran junta. This soothing sobriquet referred only to the specific functions of the equipment (vehicles and communications gear rather than guns and bullets), which could certainly be used to support "lethal" operations. Robert White, the new U.S. ambassador to El Salvador, cabled the subcommittee that the purpose of the aid was to "strengthen the professionalism of the armed forces and reinforce their commitment to reform." It was his "best guess" that "as this government establishes its bona fides among the people, the human rights record of the armed forces will improve and incidents of excessive use of force will end."[12]

The legislators were also made aware of a letter Archbishop Romero had sent to President Carter the previous month. "Because you are a Christian and because you have shown that you want to defend human rights," he wrote,

> I ask you, if you really want to defend human rights, to prohibit the giving of this military aid to the Salvadoran Government. The brutal form in which the security forces recently attacked and assassinated the occupiers of the headquarters of the Christian Democratic Party in spite of what appears to be the lack of authorization ... is an indication that the Junta and the Party do not govern the country, but that political power is in the hands of the unscrupulous military

who only know how to repress the people and promote the interests of the Salvadoran oligarchy.[13]

Since the administration's request was technically a transfer to El Salvador of foreign aid funds already approved by Congress, it required only a nod from the two Foreign Operations Appropriations Subcommittees. The Senate side acquiesced without a public meeting. House "Foreign Ops" held an open hearing, listened separately to the administration and other witnesses (including representatives of churches and church-supported groups and the American Legion, as well as a former U.S. ambassador to El Salvador), and approved the request by a vote of 6 to 3.

What was striking about this first congressional step into the Salvadoran conflict was how much it was eased by an inclination to accept presidential initiatives in new and seemingly urgent situations. This tendency was publicly expressed by Representative McHugh (N.Y.), one of three liberal Democrats who supported the administration's appeal. Noting that "my own bishop" had called to oppose the request, and that he had been "effectively" lobbied by "people who clearly have a sensitivity for the people of El Salvador," McHugh stated, "I instinctively react negatively to this kind of proposal" because "our history in Latin America with respect to military aid is sorry." Even modest nonlethal aid "would be read wrongly by the people of El Salvador and the administration and this committee may come to regret the decision. There is no easy way to know for sure." Nevertheless, he concluded,

> I think in the end it is one of the situations where we have to give the administration and the people who have worked on it the benefit of the doubt. . . . [Although] in hindsight it would have been wiser [for them] to say they were supporting the Junta with economic assistance . . . *they have gotten into it; their credibility is on the line and we are in a box* [emphasis added].[14]

As McHugh later explained, "There's a tendency when the president comes to give him the benefit of the doubt, if one doesn't feel some degree of competence for lack of information. . . . There would be more opportunity to get information the longer it was on the table—through hearings, staff work, travel . . . Congress could be more confident then." In addition, "There was a separate issue of trust. I trusted Carter more than Reagan." Still, "even with the opposite party in the administration there's a tendency to give [the president] the benefit of the doubt."[15]

Another critical vote for the president was that of Representative William Lehman (D.-Fla.). "I do not think I have agonized over any issue more than this one," he confessed; "I have never voted for military aid to any country for counterinsurgency." Yet he dreaded the "virulent" and "infectious" Salvadoran left, which "could be much worse than what we are hoping to bring to bear with the present Government." Looking for a way to resolve his inner conflict, Lehman said, "I prefer a delay. . . . The level of violence is very high now. . . . I think that the [aid] would have less of an adverse effect if we could get the violence down and get some kind of stability there and then send in something to support the stability when it does become obvious." The subcommittee decided to proceed with its vote, however, so Lehman also gave the administration the benefit of the doubt, while conserving the hope that "we can step in if it is going the wrong way and do something about it."[16]

With the advent of the Reagan administration in 1981, the Foreign Ops Subcommittees were again confronted with a request for a "reprogramming" of military aid to El Salvador—this time $5 million in lethal as well as nonlethal assistance. Once more the discussion centered in the House subcommittee and congressional deference played a major role in the outcome.

By chance, the House hearing took place on the first anniversary of the archbishop's assassination. Ambassador White, recently dismissed by the new administration, now testified that "very little" progress had been made in curbing military repression. He attributed the majority of the more than 10,000 civilian deaths in the past year to government forces. He also informed the panel he had disagreed with President Carter's decision to renew military aid after having suspended it at the time of the churchwomen's murders, and denied the State Department's contention that the Salvadoran government was making progress in its investigation. Against White and other witnesses, Acting Assistant Secretary of State John Bushnell defended military aid as a necessary response to external Communist assistance to the FMLN and rejected the notion that the majority of civilian deaths could be attributed to government forces. A representative of the Federal Bureau of Investigation (FBI) expressed satisfaction with the ongoing Salvadoran investigation of the churchwomen case.[17] As before, and as would continue to be the case in all subsequent congressional hearings, the government and private witnesses appeared separately, so there was no direct confrontation of opposing assumptions.

When the subcommittee voted, the three Democrats who had previously backed President Carter now moved into the opposition. Thus Lehman noted that since his previous vote, "from testimony before our Committee and from the best information I could obtain I have seen a diminishing threat from the left. . . . On the other hand, the government we gave the assistance to has been unable to control its own excesses."[18] Nevertheless, the administration prevailed by a narrow 8 to 7 margin when the Democratic chairman and ranking Republican of the full Appropriations Committee availed themselves of their right to join the subcommittee, and voted for the president.

As Cynthia Arnson has observed, this vote in part "reflected an attitude of deference to the president in the conduct of foreign affairs among congressional moderates." Now instead of liberals deferring to Carter it was moderates deferring to Reagan. The new president had emphasized that El Salvador had become the place to draw the line against "indirect armed aggression by Communist powers."[19] And the Appropriations Committee leaders backed him up, albeit with strong expressions of doubt. As Chairman Jamie Whitten (D.-Miss.) explained, "I feel that this early in the term of office of our President to fail on this small transfer of funds would be misunderstood throughout the world. . . . I shall vote for the transfer on the narrow basis that we need to show the world that we too back up the President to this point." But he would not "rule out" future "reconsideration of our policy, whether it is not headed in the wrong direction, and whether we have to start feeding the people as against funnelling arms around the

world." Representative Silvio Conte (R.-Mass.) said he would also vote
yes, "simply because of what my Chairman said . . . [the] great concern that the failure to stand up to international terrorism and aggression will, I think, send the wrong signal." Yet he too reserved his
future position, indicating he would not support additional military
aid unless the investigation of the churchwomen's deaths was com-
pleted, and there were assurances that the military no longer "inflicted
violence on innocent civilians."[20]

Two years later, Whitten, like Lehman before him, appeared somewhat chastened by the consequences of his decision. Addressing Secretary of State George Shultz at a hearing, he recalled, "I cast the deciding
vote several years ago to give the President an opportunity. I have had
reports, and it looks like the situation is deteriorating rather than
improving." Invoking "long experience," he lectured the secretary,

> For you or me to feel that the people in those areas are going to get
> like us and are going to change their background, going to change
> their attitude, going to change their feelings about needing a strong
> man at the head of the government, however he may get there, to
> make them go through the form of an election to satisfy our public
> is not going to change their background.

Then it was Conte's turn:

> As you know, Mr. Secretary, I made it clear on that vote that Mr.
> Whitten just talked about . . . that I could not support additional
> security assistance to that government until meaningful and visible
> improvements are made in the area of human rights and in particu-
> lar the resolution of the cases involving the murder of American cit-
> izens. . . . [Concerning] the case of the nuns . . . there has been very
> little, if any real progress in that case.[21]

These first two congressional decisions on military aid to El Salvador were pivotal. If either vote in the House subcommittee had
gone the other way, the practice was that the administration would
not have proceeded. Since the Appropriations Committees have the
last word on foreign aid funds, that would have sent both Congress

and the administration a strong signal for the future. At the very least, it would have slowed the momentum for U.S. military involvement in El Salvador.

A habit of transcending doubts about policy and giving the president leeway to act in new or newly defined "urgent" situations appears to have contributed significantly to Congress's decisions. It was a tradition, however filtered by partisan or ideological lenses, that helped prejudice Congress's ability to put its own imprint on American foreign policy. And as Chairman Whitten suggested in another remark to Secretary Shultz, it was also a deeply rooted habit: "History shows, and I shall not give details, that if it takes an outbreak every 30 days to increase foreign aid, you will have it, not only here but you will have it elsewhere."[22]

LOSING THE ARGUMENT

The 1992 Salvadoran peace accord established a United Nations Commission on the Truth with the task of "investigating serious acts of violence that have occurred since 1980 and whose impact on society urgently demands that the public should know the truth."[23] According to estimates, 70,000 people lost their lives in the Salvadoran struggle, including 40,000 civilians.[24] In March 1993, the Commission on the Truth, consisting of three distinguished South and North Americans and a formidable team of consultants and researchers, issued its report.[25]

The commission's findings strongly vindicated the congressional opposition's perspective on the state's complicity in the violence. In analyzing 7,312 cases where it received direct testimony, the commission noted that members of the state apparatus were accused of participating in 66.8 percent of the murders.[26] It found that state-connected violence "originated in a political mind-set that viewed political opponents as subversives and enemies." Furthermore,

The death squads, in which members of State structures were actively involved or to which they turned a blind eye, gained such control that they ceased to be an isolated instrument or marginal phenomenon and became an instrument of terror used systematically for the physical elimination of political opponents. Many of the civilian and military authorities in power during the 1980s participated in, encouraged and tolerated the activities of these groups. . . .

The inhabitants of areas where the guerrillas were active were automatically suspected of belonging to the guerrilla movement or collaborating with it and thus ran the risk of being eliminated. . . . In the early years of the decade the violence in rural areas was indiscriminate in the extreme.[27]

Former representative Michael Barnes (D.-Md.), who chaired the House Foreign Affairs Western Hemisphere Subcommittee in the early 1980s, commented, "We believed that the things that we now know were true were true at the time. But had we had those facts, it would have made our case so much more compelling."[28] Representative David Obey (D.-Wisc.), a key member of House Foreign Ops during the period, said the report "simply verifies what a number of us knew all through the eighties, namely that our own government was lying like hell to us."[29]

Yet in examining the record, it is clear that the congressional foreign policy committees themselves missed many opportunities to uncover critical facts and unmask the administration's deceptions. Congress was not only manipulated; it also in a sense chose not to know. Two of the best examples of this process were the congressional responses to the assassination of Archbishop Romero and the December 1981 massacre of hundreds of peasants in and around the village of El Mozote.

THE ARCHBISHOP'S ASSASSINATION

The Commission on the Truth analyzed in depth over 30 specific cases which "either reflected the most shocking events of the conflict or formed part of a broader, systematic pattern of abuse."[30] It found overwhelming evidence that extreme right political leader Roberto D'Aubuisson, a former major, "gave the order to assassinate the Archbishop and gave precise instructions to members of his security service, acting as a 'death squad,' to organize and supervise the assassination." Among those involved was one Captain Eduardo Avila, then a leading figure in the National Guard Intelligence Section's death squad. The subsequent Salvadoran governmental investigation "was not only highly inefficient" but "plagued by political motives." The judge charged with leading the inquiry left the country within days following an attempt to assassinate him at his home.

At the time, D'Aubuisson was directing a number of death squads that linked "wealthy civilians who feared that their interests should be affected by the reform programme announced by the Government Junta" and "the intelligence network and operations of the S-II sections of the security forces." D'Aubuisson subsequently formalized his political power by founding and leading the rightist ARENA (Nationalist Republican Alliance) Party. In 1982, he was elected president of the National Assembly, where his chief of security "ran D'Aubuisson's death squad from his office." Prevented by United States opposition from becoming El Salvador's chief executive, D'Aubuisson's position nevertheless enabled him to exert significant influence on such policies as agrarian and judicial reform.[31]

Had the congressional opposition been able to expose this crime, or even cast a shadow of "probable cause" on the culprits, it would have challenged—in a dramatic case of great human interest—the administration's crucial assumption that leading elements of the state were *not* involved with the death squads. Furthermore, it would have opened a window on the continuing D'Aubuisson-related network of violence in the National Guard, police, army, and Armed Forces High Command. It would have also struck the politically potent chord of Congress's institutional interest in punishing administration deceit. But neither the congressional opposition nor the foreign policy committees made any effective inquiry into the archbishop's assassination.

During an April 1981 public hearing, former ambassador White gave the Senate Foreign Relations Committee a copy of a document seized when D'Aubuisson and his colleagues were briefly arrested for coup-plotting in May 1980. This was the diary of D'Aubuisson's personal secretary, former captain Alvaro Saravia. In it were details of arms, ammunition, and related transactions, and, White testified, "over a hundred names [many with phone numbers] of people who are participating both within the Salvadoran military as active conspirers against the government, and also the names of people living in the United States and in Guatemala City who are actively funding the death squads." (A number of these individuals were subsequently implicated in political murders and other human rights abuses.) White said he had given the diary to "three of the most skilled political analysts I know in El Salvador," who had all concluded "that there is, within this document, evidence that is compelling if not 100 percent conclusive, that D'Aubuisson and his group are responsible for the murder of Archbishop Romero."[32]

The Commission on the Truth later confirmed that the Saravia diary contained important pieces of information about the assassination, including the purchase and delivery of arms and ammunition of the type used in the murder, repeated mention of the names of people who participated in or covered up the crime, the name of the assassin's chauffeur, and gasoline receipts for his red vehicle.[33] The diary was also mentioned in a 1982 House Intelligence Committee staff report, which criticized the executive branch for ignoring it.[34]

If ever there was a smoking gun in a high political mystery, this was it. Yet, as Ambassador White later observed, "There was no follow-up of any consequence" by Congress to his Senate testimony.[35] Ironically, when a U.S.-funded Salvadoran investigations unit began looking into the assassination several years later, it used the diary to locate the chauffeur, who in turn implicated D'Aubuisson, Saravia, and others.[36]

It was not until almost a year after the ambassador's allegations that a high administration official was first publicly questioned in Congress about them. "We do not agree," Secretary of State Alexander Haig told a House subcommittee on the eve of D'Aubuisson's 1982 election as president of the National Assembly. Available information did not "definitively establish" who killed the archbishop.[37] A detailed State Department response to a similar query from Senate Foreign Relations Chairman Percy read, "We have received some information that could be interpreted as a possible link [with D'Aubuisson]. However, this information is limited and incomplete and no conclusion can be drawn from it." In a secret session of the House Foreign Affairs Committee, an administration official qualified the charges against D'Aubuisson as "rumors . . . which we cannot substantiate."[38] Following an April 1983

Los Angeles Times story revealing that "highly reliable" information in two 1980 and 1981 State Department cables supported the charges,[39] the Department's response to congressional inquiries was: "There is no hard evidence. . . . Available information is limited and inconclusive."[40]

In February 1984, right before the Salvadoran presidential election that D'Aubuisson nearly won, White told a House subcommittee that the two State Department cables contained an eyewitness account of the murder plot, proving that "from its first days in office, the Reagan White House knew, beyond any reasonable doubt, that Roberto D'Aubuisson . . . planned, and ordered the assassination."[41] But Assistant Secretary of State Langhorne Motley rejoined,

> These cables based on information from a "source of undetermined reliability" do not in any sense prove what Ambassador White claimed they did. . . . The charges were serious but the information was not definitive. In fact we have received various accounts of this assassination from different sources, and these accounts are at variance with one another."[42]

It is clear from interviews with U.S. officials and recently declassified documents that the administration's responses to Congress were deceptive. On the foundation of an elementary truth—that there could be no "conclusive" evidence in a country that lacked a functioning criminal justice system—the administration built an edifice of prevarications. The former assistant secretary of state for inter-American affairs, Thomas Enders, has acknowledged, "We all thought D'Aubuisson was guilty. But you don't go to Congress and say you think D'Aubuisson's a murderer. Congress will say: no more aid."[43]

In fact, even before its first congressional testimony on the subject, the administration possessed substantial evidence of D'Aubuisson's culpability. Beyond the leads in the Saravia diary, White had forwarded to Washington a privately circulated videotape in which, he said, D'Aubuisson "implicitly takes credit for the murder," referring "with contempt" to "the Ayatollah who has left us."[44] As White recalls, "We knew, the CIA knew, and the military attaché knew, because the whole conduct of the military told you they knew. We got feedback that his stock went up [because of the assassination] from the barracks room chatter."[45]

More significant evidence quickly followed. In November 1980, Carl Gettinger, a young political officer in the American embassy in San Salvador, was asked by a military colleague to meet with a Salvadoran National Guard officer who had dropped by for a visa. The Salvadoran was reputed to have good information on the depradations of the left.[46] The next day Gettinger sent a stunning cable to Washington relating their conversation:

> The source told poloff [political officer] that he participated in a meeting during which the assassination of Archbishop Romero was planned. He indicated that Major Roberto D'Aubuisson was in charge of the meeting and that it took place shortly—a day or two—before Romero was assassinated. According to the source, the participants drew lots for the task of killing the Archbishop. The "winner" was an ex–national guardsman. . . . The officer said that the cartridge used in the assassination was his own.

The junior officer told Gettinger that his brother and father had been slain by leftists, and that he had been a member of a National Guard death squad. He was, Gettinger wrote, "a badly educated," even "savage" individual, "whose reliability cannot be judged." But "as far as his participation in brutal activities is concerned, poloff believes the source was telling the truth."[47]

Over the next several months, the officer passed on further details about the assassination plot, including the names of other participants later confirmed by the Commission on the Truth.[48] Although he was described by the State Department to Congress in 1984 as a "source of undetermined reliability," a December 1981 embassy cable called him a "contact [who] has provided very accurate sensitive information in the past."[49] What had firmly established his overall credibility by the spring of 1981—and was withheld from Congress—was his crucial assistance to the embassy in solving another important case, that of the murdered churchwomen.

Recognizing a lack of serious investigation by the Salvadoran government, Gettinger had requested the officer's assistance. He told Gettinger, "He knew that he killed people but that he did so for a reason. He would . . . have no truck with an organization that allowed to go unpunished the killing of four defenseless women" who were "citizens of the country that is feeding us."[50] Using information communicated by this source during furtive phone calls and risky meetings, the embassy officer "broke the case." The perpetrators, also members of the National Guard, were arrested and, after three years of delays, convicted of their crimes.[51] A 1985 internal State Department memorandum confirmed that its source on the planning of the Romero assassination had "demonstrated his reliability by developing critically important information in connection with the churchwomen case."[52]

Nevertheless, the State Department had not only publicly referred to him as late as 1984 as a "source of undetermined reliability," it had also cautioned Congress that "various accounts of the assassination" were "at variance with one another." This last statement may have been accurate concerning certain details of logistics and personnel, but it was fundamentally misleading regarding the central issue of D'Aubuisson's complicity. By 1984 the U.S. government had obtained even more information about the assassination and who was behind it. Todd Greentree, an embassy political officer during 1981–84, remembers, "The leads were pretty clear. There weren't any other candidates [than D'Aubuisson] for it."[53] Ambassador Deane Hinton (1981–83) remembers that he "reached the conclusion [that D'Aubuisson was guilty]" about halfway through his stay "one night when he and I got drunk together. I put it to him and recall the impression that 'He doth protest too much'."[54] *All* of the recently declassified CIA cables from this period on serious assassination suspects explicitly state or strongly suggest D'Aubuisson's involvement.[55] Thus a March 1984 CIA memorandum to Vice President George Bush concluded that while there was "nothing that could be construed as hard proof," D'Aubuisson's "complicity" in the assassination was "credible."[56] Of course, everyone concerned knew that "hard proof" was a chimera in a situation where, as Greentree commented, "there was no Salvadoran FBI."[57]

Despite its notoriety and potential political importance—and relevant disclosures from a former ambassador and "leaked" cables—the archbishop's assassination failed to generate an effective congressional response. The Democratic-led opposition and troubled moderate Republicans, like Senate Foreign Relations Committee chairman Charles Percy (R.-Ill.), did not call for an administration investigation, much less attempt any of their own. "You'd learn a lot," Ambassador White later remarked, "by picking up the phone [to call the numbers in the Saravia diary] and sending someone down there to interview these people. A lot of them considered themselves pro-American."[58] In fact, Carl Gettinger used the diary with his source to help locate the family of an alleged participant in the murder, a man nicknamed "Musa" who had himself been found dead.[59] Gettinger believed that the key to unraveling the plot was "to find out what happened to 'Musa.' . . . If you had put somebody on this task in the same way as we were working on the churchwomen case, it's possible you could have developed this case."[60]

Nor did the congressional opposition take any meaningful steps to try to counter the "lying" leaders, like representatives Barnes and Obey later said they felt the administration was practicing. There was no effort to raise the potential moral, political, and legal price of withholding the truth by swearing in witnesses. Generally speaking, relevant cable traffic and reports from the State Department and the CIA were not requested or, if necessary, subpoenaed.[61] An exception was the House Foreign Affairs Committee's request for the two cables reporting the officer's story that had been already leaked to the *Los Angeles Times*.[62] These were duly provided, but without any reference to the dramatic events that had established the source's strong credibility other than a single indication of his past provision of "accurate, sensitive information."[63] And the two cables stood alone, without the mass of other supporting information from the CIA and State Department. Finally, they were provided in classified form so they could not be used publicly.

Had the Foreign Affairs Committee been able to obtain even a partial declassification of the cables that protected the source's identity, it might well have attracted interest and generated political pressure to provide additional information to Congress and the public. Yet this was the kind of initiative that the Committee took only during major public scandals. In normal times, even a modest effort to press the administration and challenge the rites of secrecy seemed out of bounds.

THE EL MOZOTE MASSACRE

According to the Commission on the Truth, there is "full proof" that, in December 1981 in the village of El Mozote, units of the American-trained Atlacatl Battalion "deliberately and systematically killed a group of two hundred men, women, and children, constituting the entire civilian population that they had found there the previous day and had since been holding prisoner."

More than a decade later, an exhumation and analysis of the skeletal remains of 143 bodies from a little building known as "the convent" revealed that most of the victims were children, with an average age of six years. Counting additional massacres in nearby villages and cantons during the same antiguerrilla campaign, there were altogether "more than 500 identified victims. Many other victims have not been identified."

The commission found that the Armed Forces High Command "received news of the massacre" but "repeatedly denied" that it had occurred. It "took no steps whatsoever to prevent the repetition of such acts, with the result that the same units were used in other operations and followed the same procedures." The minister of defense "initiated no investigations that might have enabled the facts to be established."[64]

Early reports of the massacres from church sources in San Salvador inspired a letter from the U.S. National Council of Churches to Ambassador Hinton.[65] Then, in late January 1982, the *New York Times* and *Washington Post* ran front-page stories on the killings. Government forces had withdrawn from the region, and the returning guerrillas had taken the *Times* reporter Raymond Bonner, *Post* reporter Alma Guillermoprieto, and *Times* photographer Susan Meiselas on a tour of death. In El Mozote, they reported on and photographed "dozens of bodies" beneath the rubble of burned-out houses and strewn over nearby fields. More than a dozen peasants, including three who said they were eyewitnesses, accused the army (the Atlacatl Battalion was specifically mentioned) of massacring several hundred people in El Mozote and nearby hamlets.[66]

Once again, had the congressional opposition come close to establishing the facts, it would have struck a strong blow at the administration's rationale that it was supporting a reform-minded military. And it would have done so in a case that attracted unusual press attention. Here was the first American-trained Salvadoran military unit committing mass murder and covering it up with the aid of the high command and the defense minister. Even more clearly than in the Romero case, exposure would have also brought into question the veracity of administration statements. But no investigation was even attempted.

Within days of the massacres, Assistant Secretaries of State Enders and Elliott Abrams testified before several congressional foreign policy committees. It was the time of the first required presidential certifications on military reform, human rights, and other matters. In response to questions about El Mozote, Enders and Abrams read or referred to the summary of a January 31 cable from the embassy. The cable reported on a visit by three embassy officers to "the area" of the alleged massacres, but not to the crime scenes themselves, which had been reoccupied by the FMLN. The summary was brief:

> Although it is not possible to prove or disprove excesses of violence against the civilian population by government troops, it is certain that the guerrilla forces who established defensive positions in El Mozote did nothing to remove them from the path of battle.
>
> Nor is there evidence that those who remained attempted to leave. Civilians did die during the operations, but no evidence could be found to confirm that government forces systematically massacred civilians in the operation zones, nor that the number of civilians killed even remotely approached the number being cited in other reports circulating internationally.[67]

The full "confidential" cable was given to the committees, again on condition that it remain secret.

It was only months later that a House Intelligence Committee staff report publicly disclosed that the body of the cable cast doubt on some of the summary's main conclusions. While the cable appeared to assume that "there was a fight rather than a massacre of noncombatants," "the only confirmation of this from any of the refugees the investigators spoke with was that a man from a town several miles away from El Mozote *'intimated'* that he knew of violent fighting in El Mozote and other nearby centers! The cable reported that he was unwilling to discuss the comportment of government forces." As for the certainty that the guerrillas did "nothing to remove [civilians] from the path of battle," this was "made less certain by the body of the cable, which reported that an aged couple from El Mozote (apparently the only refugees from El Mozote interviewed) as well as refugees from other *cantones* said that the guerrillas warned them of the impending military operation and urged them to leave because they were old."[68] Notwithstanding this public critique, the foreign policy committees made no attempt to declassify the cable and follow up on its contradictions.

In 1993, Mark Danner's extremely perceptive account of the El Mozote incident in the *New Yorker* showed the process through which the cable itself had become, essentially, a lie. From the "tremendous fear" they observed among refugees as well as the sullenness of the soldiers, two of the embassy's three investigators, political officer Todd Greentree and military attaché John McKay, had respectively concluded that "something horrible had happened at El Mozote," and "there had probably been a massacre." But there were political pressures on the embassy to write a "credible" report, one that distanced itself from allegations by leftist guerrillas and "biased newspapers," and which bolstered an administration policy under fire in Congress. So, in the absence of the definitive proof that was so elusive in a place like El Salvador, the final embassy-approved cable excluded "the very things that had most impressed the men who actually ventured into the war zone."[69]

That Ambassador Hinton and officials in Washington knew uncomfortable truths had been omitted from the report is apparent from two cables sent by the ambassador himself the following day. In the first, he recounted a dinner chat with the defense minister on the same day his investigators returned from seeking the facts about El Mozote:

I warned Garcia to be ready to respond to . . . massacre story . . . and added he would have to explain away details provided by correspondents. It might be possible—we were investigating and were grateful for his help—but he should bear in mind that something had gone wrong. Who did it, when, and in what circumstances was something else.[70]

The second cable was given an EXDIS label, meaning its distribution was very restricted within the executive branch. Here Hinton, irritated by a State Department message recalling him "denying" the earlier National Council of Churches report, stressed that things had changed since January when he wrote the Council he could "certainly not confirm" massacre reports. "Additional evidence strongly suggests that something happened that should not have happened and that it is quite possible Salvadoran military did commit excesses."[71] Since neither Hinton nor Deputy Chief of Mission Kenneth Bleakley recall what the "additional evidence" was, one can only speculate from various known ingredients. First, there were the impressions of the two embassy investigators, acknowledged though not supported by the third, Bleakley. Then there were the newspaper reports. Last, Hinton generally remembers that "my thought was to be skeptical of what was coming from the government and the military. I would not exclude excesses."[72] In fact, he was criticizing the defense minister at this very time for an army attack on a house where an American lived, an urban massacre, and propaganda attacks on the Jesuits.[73]

Neither of Ambassador Hinton's two cables was shared with Congress.[74] Nor was the congressional opposition aware of still another cable from the U.S. embassy in Honduras describing an early February visit by a political officer and a House Foreign Affairs Committee Republican staff member to a Salvadoran refugee camp. They interviewed "several newly arrived Salvadoran families" from villages mentioned in Bonner's *New York Times* story. The latter spoke of a December military sweep that "resulted in large numbers of civilian casualties and physical destruction, leading to their exodus." According to one family, "In past sweeps, a few civilian casualties had been registered; this time, they claimed, houses were burned and many residents killed." Another family said that "this had been the fourth sweep of their district and this time they fled for their lives." The embassy commented, "Most significant element in refugees' reports was their decision to flee at this time where in the past they had remained during sweeps. This lends credibility to reportedly greater magnitude and intensity of [government] military operations."[75]

Two of the most credible newspapers in the country had printed stories alleging a major massacre. The embassy's main cable on the subject, which was given to congressional committees, contained information that seemed inconsistent with its conclusions and the administration's public testimony. And the incident had arisen at the very moment that Congress was beginning a major review of Salvador policy. Yet Congress did nothing more than pose a few simple questions. El Mozote quickly disappeared from the mass media and no more would be heard about it until a decade later when the remains of the residents were exhumed.

Once again, the congressional opposition and uneasy moderates did not call for an administration investigation or propose any alternative inquiry. Years later, however, a State Department review panel would state:

> This was clearly a case where an extraordinary effort—possibly including pressing for a Salvadoran military operation to escort neutral observers to the site—was needed. The Embassy does not seem to have been inclined to press, and Washington preferred to avoid the issue and protect its policy then under siege.

Another form of investigation had actually been suggested to political officer Greentree by a representative of Socorro Juridico, a Catholic human rights office. A commission consisting of representatives from Socorro, the Mexican embassy, the U.S. embassy, the left-oriented Human Rights Commission, and the Baptist Church would go to El Mozote. It would enter "without the help of the Armed Forces" in the company of the International Committee of the Red Cross. Greentree ventured, "While such a commission was a good idea in general, it would be clearly unacceptable to the Government of El Salvador . . . and the Embassy."[76] Neither idea was discussed or proposed by congressional critics.

Despite all the contradictory reports and the general suspicion of the administration's candor, there was also no move to swear in administration witnesses, obtain testimony from the embassy investigators and the ambassador, or request, and if necessary subpoena, relevant and politically explosive cables and reports. One cannot be certain that such efforts would have compelled the administration to bare more of the truth. Significantly, however, foreign service veteran Greentree believes that if Congress had created "additional political pressure" on State Department professionals by swearing in officials or demanding cables, "it would have produced a more determined and credible investigation."[77]

SHEATHED WEAPONS AND MISSING RESOURCES

Why was the congressional opposition so ineffective in challenging the administration's perspective on official violence? Why was a Congress that required the president, before releasing military aid, to certify that the Salvadoran government was "achieving control" over military abuses so unwilling to probe the justifications for his determination? Why was a Congress that regularly reduced presidential requests for military assistance so unable to investigate the rationale for that assistance? Some relevant answers are suggested by a further illustration: the experience of an abortive House Foreign Affairs Committee effort to investigate the death squad phenomenon.

In late 1983, Representative Gerry Studds (D.-Mass.), a leading critic of American policy, asked Committee Chairman Clement Zablocki (D.-Wisc.) to establish a task force on so-called right-wing death squads. This proposal reflected in part the judgment of key staffers, William Woodward from Studds's personal office and Robert Kurz from the Western Hemisphere Subcommittee, that "if you could prove there are death squads from the government, you could undermine U.S. policy."[78]

Actually, the U.S. by then had substantial if incomplete evidence of official complicity in death squad activity. Ambassador Hinton believed there were "two governments" in El Salvador, "the government and the military," with the latter "far stronger." "Most" of the death squads were "connected" to the military. The minister of defense "knew," but "had to cover up."[79] Declassified CIA cables included significant reporting on a death squad in the National Police commanded by the chief of investigations and an ARENA Party death squad headed by the chief of security of the Constituent Assembly. A late 1983 CIA Special Intelligence Analysis reported that "death squads in the Army and the three security forces apparently operate out of urban military headquarters and rural outposts. They [deleted] are led by senior enlisted personnel and junior officers, and they may function with or without the knowledge of immediate superiors."

A subsequent House Intelligence Committee staff report commented, "The staff was somewhat surprised at the significant nature of the post-1982 intelligence reporting on death squads. In part, this surprise results from the limited distribution of such reporting due to its sensitivity."[80]

Chairman Zablocki agreed to the establishment of a "Working and Study Group" on death squads. It was headed by the subcommittee staff director, Victor Johnson, and essentially staffed by Kurz and Woodward. After interviewing reporters and other knowledgeable people, the group quickly ran up against a stone wall. It identified some foreign service officers, such as Greentree, who were informed about the subject, but the State Department denied them permission to talk about it. It discovered, from inside sources, the numbers of some relevant embassy cables, but the State Department refused to divulge them. It sought information from the CIA, which replied that it had only to report to the secretive intelligence committees, which almost never communicated classified information to other foreign policy committees. The FBI, which was assisting in the investigations of the murders of two American labor advisers by a death squad, was similarly uncooperative. "We'd have to subpoena things," the staffers decided.[81]

It was not long after this realization that the inquiry effectively collapsed. As Kurz later explained,

> We didn't know if we had the votes in the committee. . . . We practiced what we called preemptive capitulation. . . . Our people weren't very strong. The number of people who knew about this

was small. There was a problem of the chairman refusing to sign subpoenas. Zablocki or [his successor] Dante Fascell [D.-Fla.] wouldn't help. . . . If you had the votes, they would go along with you. [But Subcommittee Chairman] Barnes had not been around a long time; he had very limited political capital in an old boys' seniority system. You needed senior Democrats like a Hamilton . . . but they would only go so far. The members did not want to take on the president.[82]

The investigation foundered during a period when the Democratic-controlled committee was approving tightened presidential certification requirements for El Salvador, a procedure for congressional disapproval of the president's determinations, and a reduction in military aid. Clearly the major constraint on a more aggressive approach to the administration was not that the committee had bought its policy justifications. "Old boy" Democrats, including the chairman, endorsed substantive policy changes. But they "would only go so far"; they were reluctant to "take on the president."

Victor Johnson emphasized the broader significance of this reluctance: "There's a culture in the place like there is in any organization. Issuing subpoenas and putting witnesses under oath were the kinds of things most of the time we didn't do. You held hearings to expose the issues. You took trips." For those who wanted to venture further, the burden was heavy. Regarding subpoenas, Johnson remembers, "It was always a problem if you knew enough reliably to go down this road. You'd better have your ducks in order, be prepared to rebut opposition."[83] Representative Fascell, who succeeded Zablocki as chairman in January 1984, says he conveyed the following cautionary message to subcommittee chairmen considering subpoenas: "If you can't generate the kind of interest required to pursue it to its ultimate, definite conclusion [including a possible House floor vote for contempt of Congress against noncooperators], you're going to be out there by yourself, my friend."[84]

Another factor in the failure of the death squad investigation was how "small" the opposition cadre was. Leadership on this important issue was largely left to two junior members (Barnes and Studds) and three staffers (Johnson, Kurz, and Woodward). With such limited troops, it was not going to be easy to overturn some deeply ingrained committee traditions. If this was the situation even in the Democratic-controlled House Foreign Affairs Committee (moderate Republicans, naturally more solicitous of "their" administration, controlled the Senate Foreign Relations Committee), it is little wonder that Congress as a whole did not deploy its weapons against executive-branch deception in the Romero and El Mozote cases.

Moreover, the self-consciously small opposition core lacked the human resources to undertake even milder initiatives that did not require the committee chairman's specific approval. Regarding the El Mozote massacres, Johnson noted that his staff—three professionals covering the entire Western hemisphere—was "greatly overextended . . . working 80 hours a week," and therefore largely confined to "getting mileage on press reports."[85] Kurz adds that the committee did not provide funds for special consultants and the subcommittee staff was "very inexperienced in investigations. We were learning as we went along." The problem went beyond the subcommittee: there was no repository of committee expertise on investigations to tap because that was not what the Foreign Affairs Committee characteristically did.

Looking back, Kurz summed up the plight of the House Foreign Affairs Committee opposition this way: "We were a small group without institutional levers or clubs."[86]

Would significant, or even partial, exposures of state-sanctioned violence have enabled the congressional opposition to mobilize enough congressional and public support to achieve a change in U.S. policy? Not, it would seem, if one is talking about a total cutoff of military aid to an anti-Communist government under attack in the hemispheric backyard. Once the administration had succeeded in defining El Salvador as a crucial Cold War front, many Democrats felt they would be politically vulnerable or personally uncomfortable with an exit option.[87] Yet there was a strong possibility that a *series* of exposures would have produced a more limited and heavily conditioned aid program. This is the retrospective judgment of a key State Department official as well as a number of activists in the House, where the challenge to the administration was strongest.

The former assistant secretary, Thomas Enders, believes that if

Congress had adopted the kind of tough investigative approach it subsequently did in the case of the 1989 Jesuit murders (see chapter 5), it "probably would have cut aid. . . . [But Congress] never pressed its point home." As previously mentioned, Enders feared that revelations of D'Aubuisson's role in the Romero assassination would have caused a major problem with congressional support. He generally thought that Congress's "human rights demands" had to be "part of the framework" or "Congress would interrupt aid for increasingly long periods."[88]

Representative Barnes also believes that if some of the key findings of the Commission on the Truth had been known, it would have "put the administration in a much more defensive posture," "changed the dynamic of the debate," and "might have" altered the outcome.[89] Staffer Kurz is convinced that "if the administration had come clean on El Mozote, Romero, and the churchwomen investigation [belatedly acknowledged to have been hampered by a government cover-up], the impact would have been dramatic on two groups: public opinion, the determinant in the end, and the 'swing group'[of moderate Congressmen]." His staff colleague, Victor Johnson, is more cautious: new information would have to be "dramatic. You could make a case if it were like the Iran-Contra revelations, in the headlines. . . . You can't predict when that critical mass will be achieved."[90] Representative McHugh thinks new facts "might have" made a difference, since "this was the kind of information relevant to the swing group due to what it reflected about those in power."[91] Finally, Representative Solarz thinks exposure of the El Mozote massacre in particular "would have had an impact" on members because of the "uncertainty" about what had happened there. Other revelations would have been less shocking since they were already widely believed. But even they might have had an impact "by virtue of the media attention they got which is the sort of thing that compels a response [especially] if it were on the front page."[92]

The thrust of these judgments is strongly reinforced by evidence of the fragility of congressional and public support for U.S. policy in El Salvador in the early 1980s. An April 1982 National Security Council (NSC) paper stated, "We continue to have serious difficulties with U.S. public and congressional opinion which jeopardizes our ability to stay the course."[93] At the time, bipartisan congressional leaders made it clear that their concept of promoting democracy excluded the putative domination of a new provisional government by D'Aubuisson and the right.[94] In May 1982, Senate Foreign Relations Chair Percy warned, "If the Salvadoran Government is reneging on the land reform program, then . . . not one cent of funds shall go to the government of El Salvador." A number of congressional committees moved to back up the threat.[95] The administration was also aware that a continued failure to successfully prosecute the churchwomen case would "erode political support for our El Salvador policy."[96] Indeed, in 1983 Congress passed an amendment proposed by Senator Arlen Specter (R.-Pa.) withholding 30 percent of U.S. military aid pending a trial and verdict in the case.[97]

During the spring of 1983, the Senate Foreign Relations and Foreign Ops panels tried to persuade the administration to stiffen conditions for military aid.[98] A new NSC paper cautioned, "The present U.S. policy faces substantial opposition at home and abroad; an increased effort would have to surmount even greater opposition."[99] Vice President Bush journeyed to San Salvador in December to persuade the government to reassign several military and civilian officials "linked with death squads" to posts abroad. Bush told the Salvadorans they should act within a month:

> If we cannot get this done by that time, when the Congress comes back, the Congress will take the initiative.
>
> I am also President of the Senate and I know the views of the Senate and the House of Representatives. All who support us know we cannot get done what must be done to increase our support for you if you are not able to help yourselves in this way.[100]

Congress continually demonstrated that its backing for the Salvadoran government was conditional. In fiscal years 1982 and 1983, it granted less than half of the administration's military aid requests (though the administration used "emergency" authorities to make up for part of the shortfall). It became more generous in 1984 following the election of the reform-minded Christian Democrat José Napoleón Duarte as president, and the long-awaited convictions of the church-womens' murderers. Still, a quarter of the administration's request was withheld.[101] Even at the height of the Duarte euphoria, an effort on the House floor to tighten significantly the certification requirements failed by only four votes.[102] A better-organized, better-timed campaign, or one that defined the compromise necessary to switch as three votes, would probably have succeeded. Concerning this May 1984 vote, Arnson has written, "Greater truthfulness [about 'government complicity in brutal acts'] might have altered the balance."[103] The same might well be said for the entire period, a time when Congress, beginning with its foreign policy committees, declined to weigh in effectively on behalf of the truth about El Salvador.

A RELUCTANT LAWMAKER

When it wrote the law governing U.S. policy toward El Salvador, Congress was sometimes unnecessarily loose in its expression. And when President Reagan exploited the confusion to evade the clear intent of the law, Congress failed to bring him strongly and rapidly to account. Congress was also willing to countenance long periods when the executive branch made policy essentially without any congressional guidance at all.

The language of legislation regulating complex and changing areas of activity is necessarily broad and flexible. This is as true for foreign policy as it is for domestic economic and social regulation. In addition, the necessities of political compromise often account for vague law. For instance, the words of some of the congressionally mandated presidential certifications, such as the one requiring the Salvadoran government to be achieving "substantial control" over its armed forces, constituted a carefully chosen middle ground between those who had higher and lower expectations of Salvadoran government performance. Both sides fully expected to carry on their political argument over state-supported violence when they evaluated the president's application of the language to circumstances in El Salvador. Anticipating the debate that arose over the president's human rights certifications, Senator Jesse Helms (R.-N.C.) told the House-Senate Conference that wrote the law:

This is laden with subjective words. What does "consistent" mean? Who is going to define it? What does "substantial" mean? Who is going to define it? You know Lewis Carroll wrote *Through the Looking Glass* and had a character named Humpty-Dumpty. He said when I use a word it means precisely what I intend it to mean, nothing more or less.[104]

Yet this ambiguity was the price of amassing sufficient political support to enact some kind of law that would constrain the executive branch and keep Congress involved in the issue.

The situation was quite different regarding the all-important certification language promoting political discussions to end the conflict. The House-Senate Conference decided that before providing military aid the president had to certify that the government:

has demonstrated its good faith efforts to begin discussions with all major factions in El Salvador which have declared their willingness to find and implement an equitable political solution to the conflict, with a solution to involve a commitment to:

A) a renouncement of further military or paramilitary activity; and
B) the electoral process with international observers.[105]

As the transcript of the conference shows, there was only one Humpty-Dumpty on this issue. The conferees clearly envisioned a two-step process beginning with unconditional political discussions between the government and the guerrillas, to be followed by their exploration of a political solution that involved at least elections and a renunciation of force. As the main author of the language, Senator Christopher Dodd (D.-Conn.), told the conference:

We are not saying that to sit down and discuss you have to either lay down your arms or agree to an electoral process. We should not place a priori conditions on a willingness to sit down and talk. But if in fact you are talking and you express a willingness to achieve a political solution, then as part of that solution you have got to understand that you have to renounce military activity and agree to an electoral process. So it is, in effect, a two-stage relationship. . . . If we say, in effect, that even before you sit down and talk you have to agree to that, we never get to the table, possibly.[106]

Yet the administration would consistently deny that the law meant what the lawmakers said it meant. According to Assistant Secretary Enders, the Salvadoran government fulfilled the certification requirement when it invited the guerrillas to "participate in the elections after an advanced dialog on the ground rules." To defend this position, Enders cited a phrase in the law that preceded the negotiations language, "[The government] is committed to the holding of free elections at an early date; and to that end." He claimed that since "the end" of the negotiations was government elections, they should also be the sole purpose of the talks.[107] Gone was the conference's vision of a two-step process beginning with unconditional discussions. The administration was manipulating a superfluous phrase to obfuscate the issue. It was language from the earlier Senate version of the bill that had been retained—presumbably for cosmetic reasons—when the conference revised the Senate bill in accordance with Dodd's conception. But the effect of leaving the words in was to give the administration an excuse to evade the law.

For eighteen months, the administration routinely violated the law by sending Congress recurrent certifications of the Salvadoran government's "good faith efforts to begin discussions with all major factions" on the sole basis of its invitation to the FMLN to participate in elections. This certification was a requirement for the release of any U.S. military aid. The congressional opposition reacted, but without great consequence. Basically it complained at a few public hearings and vainly tried to enact new legislation (over a potential presidential veto) that would tear away the administration's verbal fig leaf. But in the end, the opposition, and Congress as a whole, were willing to tolerate a president who flouted the law. There seemed to be no strong feeling that it was incumbent upon him to immediately cease and desist. Thus Congress did not use its resources and weapons (such as high-profile publicity, and the holding up of funds, nominations, and legislation) to force the issue. Instead, it assigned itself the burden of discovering, and pushing through a lengthy legislative process, a new way to present the law to the president. This kind of response sent a signal that there would be no real cost for breaking the law.

Congress's reluctance to stand strongly behind its own legal constraints in foreign policy is highlighted by an even starker El Salvador-related example, this time with a reverse partisan twist. It has a special significance for the contemporary political scene, in which a Democratic president confronts a Republican Congress. In 1980, Representative C. W. Bill Young (R.-Fla.) succeeded in persuading the House to pass legislation making aid to the Sandinista government of Nicaragua conditional on a presidential certification that it was not "aiding, abetting or supporting acts of violence or terrorism in other countries." By September, when President Carter made that certification, "the intelligence community reached, and communicated quite clearly, a view that did not support the administration's position." A CIA review concluded that there was a "very strong likelihood" that "training, transit, material and arms" assistance was flowing from Nicaragua to the Salvadoran FMLN and that "they represent official policy."[108] But Carter wanted to send Nicaragua aid in hopes of moderating the regime. So he certified, telling Congress, "We did not find conclusive evidence of Nicaraguan Government support for acts of terrorism in El Salvador."[109] The president acted as if he was being required to certify the Sandinistas were not "conclusively" helping the FMLN rather than to certify they were not aiding them, as the law read. Since the intelligence concerning the Sandinistas' probable conduct precluded him from doing the latter, he in effect rewrote the law.

When a House Foreign Affairs Subcommittee convened a hearing on the certification, Representative Young showed up to complain: "I think the security of the United States is in jeopardy when its intelligence community is either ignored or completely misinterpreted." But when Representative Benjamin Gilman (R.-N.Y.) asked him whether, if the evidence did not justify the certification, there was now "some procedure that the President should follow," Young retreated to a position that seemed to elevate the president above the law:

> Mr. Gilman, I have a little problem with that. The President as Commander in Chief and the one person responsible for the secu-

rity of our Nation, has to be given considerable flexibility and quite a bit of discretion in decisions that he makes relative to the national security. I would hate to see a President put in the position of not being able to exercise that flexibility when it was necessary.[110]

"Fortunately," Young recalls, "the voters took care of this because [within weeks] they elected Ronald Reagan [who cut off the aid]."[111]

Congress was also an infrequent and, on occasion, indifferent lawmaker on Salvador policy. Normally, the House Foreign Affairs and Senate Foreign Relations Committees set foreign policies and funding targets, while the Foreign Ops Subcommittees determined actual appropriations. While the latter inevitably shaded into the area of "making policy," an overall division of labor was at least broadly accepted. But during the 1980s, when the foreign affairs and foreign relations committees confronted, for the first time since Vietnam, an executive determined to have his own way, they practically stopped legislating. In 1982 and 1983, neither committee brought the major foreign policy bill—the foreign aid authorization—to the floor for full House or Senate consideration. In 1984, only the House acted. Thus virtually the only bills passed by Congress affecting El Salvador after 1981 were appropriations measures containing precious little policy guidance.

The disappearance of the foreign aid authorization had serious consequences for the congressional opposition. When it seemed strong— say from late 1982 to early 1984—it missed the chance to lead public and congressional debate, tighten aid conditions, establish precedents, limit funds, and guide the appropriations process. Even when it appeared weak—as Salvadorans visibly trooped to the polls in the spring of 1982 and 1984, for example—it missed the opportunity to influence public opinion and assert a continuing jurisdiction over American policy.

My own perspective on this inaction, as a staff member of House Foreign Affairs at the time, was conveyed in a series of memos to my subcommittee chairman and his predecessor. In mid-1983 I wrote,

The general issue . . . is [Chairman] Zablocki's increasing unwillingness to bring foreign aid bills to the floor. It is clear that the big obstacle is not so much that the foreign aid bills will lose but rather that Zablocki lacks the stomach for a fight. . . . Liberal Democrats will lose influence over foreign affairs issues if they are afraid to pursue their policies on the floor.[112]

By September I was noting, "There is no pressure from committee members on the leadership to schedule the bill."[113] The committee finally did get to the floor in May 1984, where it suffered its narrow four-vote defeat on Salvador policy. My memo a few days earlier gave the impression of a fainthearted and ill-timed process that had become oddly disconnected from the committee's general legislative goals on El Salvador:

Due to the inability [until now] of the committee to publicly establish a position on Central America, the lack of organizing among members in favor of the [Democratic] Caucus compromise, and the likely election of Duarte on the eve of floor debate, the outlook for the bill at this time is not auspicious.[114]

The various elements of the culture of deference had a cumulative effect on the congressional opposition's capacity to deal with a difficult political issue. As each theme played itself out, the remaining ones became more and more important. Giving leeway to the president to initiate new commitments in El Salvador increased the burden on the opposition to deploy its resources and weapons to make a politically effective argument. Limited success in that endeavor made it all the more imperative to consolidate gains through clear and binding law.

With its legislative defeat in May 1984, the congressional opposition virtually disappeared until the end of the 1980s. Its decline was facilitated by the Salvadoran military's improving fortunes, and a partially related drop in political violence. The State Department charted eighteen politically related deaths a month in 1988, far less than the hundreds it estimated during the early 1980s. Still, as Carothers pointed out, eighteen political murders a month in little El Salvador was the proportional equivalent of the U.S. army and police, in addition to fighting a dirty civil war, "targeting and assassinating *every day* twenty-seven labor leaders, human rights activists, student leaders, university professors, and other persons involved in political activity of a populist bent. Such a level of repression . . . would be considered . . . horrifying, not the triumph of democracy."[115]

The Salvador issue would return to Congress's attention in 1989, in much the same way as it had originally appeared. As the left undertook its "final offensive" in the streets of San Salvador, a detachment from the Atlacatl Battalion entered the University of Central America and assassinated six Jesuit priests, a cook, and her sixteen-year-old daughter.

3

The Politics of Lobbying:
U.S. Policy Toward Zaire,
1979–1990

It is not news that well-organized interest groups exert a disproportionate influence over Congress. But their impact on foreign policy can be particularly dramatic, producing some rather startling political conversions.

As in domestic affairs, lobbies employ a variety of techniques to get what they want from Congress. Prominent among them is the use of money. Financial aid, such as campaign contributions, honoraria (only recently prohibited), and gifts, has built a foundation for many of the "personal relationships" between members of Congress and lobbyists. In addition, monetary resources allow lobbyists to hire the staff, conduct the research, and make the contacts necessary for the selling of their policies. Beyond money, foreign policy lobbies try to make their way in Congress by skillfully using partisan, personal, and other business ties and by marshaling a modicum of constituency support in particular districts or states.

Whatever their assets, the lobbies also depend upon the political predispositions and personalities of the representatives and senators themselves. Not every congressperson has the time or inclination to listen to a particular interest, even if there are no counterbalancing voices to heed. So lobbies customarily direct their efforts toward those most likely to respond.

But what most distinguishes foreign policy from other lobbying is

the enormous influence that a single person, company, or other relatively narrow-based interest can have on congressional decisions, even
if it targets less than a handful of members. This is a direct result of the
general absence of broad-based constituencies in foreign policy and of
Congress' relatively weak efforts in this area.

A tendency to yield to the narrowest of special interests is therefore
an important component of the congressional culture of deference. Usually it complements other elements of the culture favoring executive-
branch predominance. The typical setting for the exertion of lobbyist
leverage is one in which an issue is receiving only modest attention
from the administration and little at all from the public. The resulting
partial vacuum is rapidly filled by narrow-based groups that help
move Congress one way or another—most often in the direction the
administration wishes.

The recent history of U.S. policy toward the Central African nation
of Zaire furnishes a particularly good illustration of this phenomenon.
Zaire, the ex-Belgian Congo, is the second largest country in sub-Saha-
ran Africa and the third most populous. It is endowed with what the
Belgians liked to call a "geological scandal" of important minerals:
copper, cobalt, diamonds, tantalum, and others. In contrast with El
Salvador, recent U.S. administrations have assigned Zaire a secondary
priority, and no significant domestic constituency has emerged. For
more than a decade, the narrowest of special interests have endeav-
ored to fill the gap. During the same period, the Zairian regime has
evolved from a corrupt and repressive Cold War ally to a looming
post–Cold War "failed state"—a Somalia waiting to happen. Congress's relation to this tragic evolution cannot be discussed without
considering the long and colorful saga of the Zaire lobbies.

A CIA LEGACY

President Mobutu Sese Seko has dominated Zaire since his coup d'état
of November 1965. But he was already the power behind the throne
when he made his first coup as a twenty-nine-year-old colonel in September 1960. Mobutu is the last remaining survivor of the "successful"
CIA "anti-Communist" political and paramilitary operations of the

1960s. "Agency support," under such covert-operation cryptonyms as Projects WIZARD, WIANCHOR, WITHRUSH, and WIARES, helped build his personal wealth and political influence over a decade.[1] Overt U.S. military and economic assistance was also considerable. As President John F. Kennedy's assistant secretary of state for African affairs once remarked, "There was talk of sending troops. . . . In 1961 the Congo was as big as Vietnam."[2]

After a brief period of economic and political stability in the early 1970s, plunging copper prices and political unrest renewed a period of seemingly interminable crisis. The Zaire government developed into a notorious "kleptocracy" where officials, led by the president, diverted much of the foreign exchange and most of the budget to their own purposes. Although political killings were not as numerous as in, say, Idi Amin's Uganda (partly because organized political opposition had been destroyed or driven into exile), arbitrary arrest, torture, and extortion by unpaid soldiers were widespread. Under these conditions, French, Belgian, and American military intervention was required to enable the regime to defeat lightly armed Zairian exiles who "invaded" from neighboring Angola in 1977 and 1978.[3]

The Carter, Reagan, and Bush administrations all favored modest military and economic assistance to Zaire. For Mobutu, military aid was symbolically useful in menacing a potential opposition that looked back at two decades of Western military intervention in his behalf. And economic aid helped open the more generous coffers of the International Monetary Fund (IMF) and World Bank, whose officials were uneasy about institutionalized corruption, which they euphemistically labeled "mismanagement." For the executive branch, Mobutu was worth supporting because he was a "pro-Western," "anti-Communist" force in an economically important country adjacent to turbulent Southern Africa. He dispatched troops to Chad to provide an African fig leaf for joint French and American intervention against Libya. He lent his territory to an American-supported insurgency in neighboring Angola. He was the first in Africa to reestablish relations with Israel (which he'd led Africa in breaking on the eve of the 1973 Yom Kippur War). He was helpful in supporting certain U.S. diplomatic positions in international forums like the United Nations and the Organization of African Unity. Whatever dangers internal decay posed for him would, it was hoped, be obviated by Western-sponsored economic reforms, limited military tutelage, and CIA intelligence sharing.[4]

Critics in Congress (mainly liberal Democrats but also some Republicans) stressed the risks of continued economic and political deterioration, of "one day reaping the anti-Americanism and unnecessary strife that it is in our interest to prevent." They were not convinced that Zaire's diplomatic assistance was so important that human rights and other values should be set aside. They were skeptical of international economic and other reforms that paid "scant attention to the political system that sustains Zaire's corruption and economic mismanagement."[5] (Privately, administration aides often conceded this point. In 1983, for example, a State Department official told me and a visiting Zairian that when Mobutu's relative and business partner, "Uncle Litho," had recently died, he possessed a foreign bank account of approximately $1 billion. The previous year an Interagency Intelligence Memorandum noted, "Mobutu continues to add to his impressive personal fortune as the Zairian standard of living spirals downward." And a 1990 State Department intelligence analysis indicated, Mobutu "continues to siphon off as much as 30 percent of total government revenues.")[6] Decrying the burden to American taxpayers of corrupt and ineffective foreign aid programs, the critics wondered why substantial Belgian and French aid wasn't sufficient to protect Western foreign policy interests.[7] They favored an alternative policy of ending American "overidentification" with Mobutu by gradually decreasing military and other "security" assistance while continuing a U.S. role in Zaire through well-monitored economic development and humanitarian aid and the encouragement of "stabilizing political reforms."[8]

But the foreign policy bureaucracies, and even the most liberal Democratic policymakers, found it difficult to contemplate a policy that even suggested the prospect of Zaire without its longtime ruler. As Assistant Secretary Richard Moose argued in 1980:

> No one has been able to demonstrate or to describe how basic human rights might be assured during a period of abrupt and complete change of government; how vital economic and political interests of

the United States would be safeguarded during that process. Indeed it requires an act of intellectual and logical ju-ju to posit a situation of the sort which is described by the critics and to accept that as a basis for rational foreign policy.[9]

Slowly, haltingly, Congress adopted the critics' approach and modified U.S. policy. By 1989, military aid had descended from nearly $20 million annually to $3 million; economic aid was reoriented to more developmental and less security-related support. In 1990, as the Soviet empire collapsed and Mobutu attempted to repress a growing democratization movement, Congress cut off aid to the government altogether. Subsequent congressional resolutions called upon Mobutu to step down and allow a democratic transition. But with backing from his Israeli-trained, 5,000-man Presidential Guard, Mobutu hung on even as Zaire's economy crumbled, unrest mounted, foreign governments evacuated their citizens, and international aid disappeared.[10]

The country's rapid decline appeared to validate many of the congressional critics' concerns. But it was also possible to take a hard-nosed realpolitik position that the United States had long continued to draw a net profit from its relationship with Mobutu, although the Cold War might have ended just in time to save the diplomatic balance sheet.

As in El Salvador, it was the political process in Congress that resolved the intellectual debate about policy. Here the ultimate outcome was somewhat unusual, given the normal advantages of the administration and the culture of congressional deference. Three special conditions helped account for the progress, however slow, made by the critics. First, administrations do not have unlimited political resources, and Zaire was generally considered to be a foreign policy priority of the second or even third order. Second, Zaire's embarrassments could not be concealed as easily as those of militarized El Salvador or many other countries. Zaire's economic and political crisis had gone on too long. Too many other countries and financial institutions were involved and knowledgeable. Too many American officials had begun to talk openly concerning their doubts about U.S. policy. Too many private Americans—academics, missionaries, Peace Corps volunteers, even Mobutu's personal physician—had lived and worked in the country and become estranged from the policy. And too many former members of Mobutu's revolving political elite had stories to tell. Last but not least, a small but significant group of legislators and their staffs pursued the issue vigorously for more than a decade, assembling information, conducting investigations, traveling to Zaire, and publicizing their findings. As the staff member principally responsible for Zaire on the House Africa Subcommittee, the author of a book on U.S. policy in the 1960s, and a former professor at a Zairian university, I was one of them.

Despite this confluence of factors favoring a more independent congressional role, it was remarkable how much influence narrow-based interests managed to exert on Zaire issues. Before tracing the history of this lobbying, it seems worthwhile to focus on perhaps the most illuminating episode of all, the Zairian odyssey of the late congressman Mickey Leland.

INCIDENT IN KINSHASA

> That is the dumbest single human rights violation by a government that I have ever seen.
> —*Elliott Abrams, Assistant Secretary of State for Human Rights and Humanitarian Affairs*[11]

Our congressional delegation had arrived in Kinshasa, Zaire's capital, during a twenty-day fact-finding mission to Africa in August 1983. The seven representatives and their staff were briefed upon arrival by U.S. embassy officials who talked up a recent government amnesty for political prisoners as a step toward liberalization. On a sunny African morning, we met in our hotel with ten prominent ex-parliamentarians, ex-cabinet ministers, and businessmen. They had been negotiating with President Mobutu for recognition of a second (non-Mobutuist) political party, a constitutional conference, and free elections. The congresspeople made it clear to their visitors that they could not officially recognize their organization, the "Group of 13," named after legislators imprisoned for advocating a nonviolent democratic transition.

As the Zairians left the hotel, they were greeted by close to one hundred sympathizers in the front parking lot. Three banners welcomed the American delegation, proclaimed "Victory," and carried the name of the projected second party. The delegation departed for other appointments, but one representative, Mickey Leland (D.-Texas), unexpectedly returned because he had forgotten his wallet. Thus he accidentally became an eyewitness to a part of Zairian political reality that official visitors rarely glimpsed. As he later recounted,

> Several men were wielding large cinder blocks to destroy a car in the parking lot. Standing near me was an American hired by the U.S. Embassy to handle transportation for the delegation's visit. He said that I should ignore what was happening, dismissing it as "typical African behavior." Suddenly people were running in the parking lot and about twenty men emerged from jeep-like vehicles and began to kick and beat several people. I saw one man being whipped by three men. Another was grabbed by two or three men, thrown to the ground, and beaten with what appeared to be chains. I did not understand what was going on or who was being beaten until I noticed one of the victims being yanked by his necktie and slammed to the ground. . . . It was one of the ex-parliamentarians we had just met. Blood was pouring from his forehead and soaking his shirt. I headed down a ramp from the hotel entrance to help him but the Embassy employee grasped me and warned that I might be beaten or killed. I asked him where the police were and he pointed out a policeman who was watching the beatings without interceding. I then checked with Embassy personnel in the control center set up in the hotel to coordinate the delegation's visit and found that several of them had witnessed the destruction of the automobiles and the beatings. I hurried to the Embassy where the American Ambassador attempted to dismiss the beatings by characterizing them as behavior which "happens all the time." He told me that this was a different society from ours and I did not understand it. I went back to the hotel where I waited until the rest of the delegation had returned and told them what I had seen. Later we learned that six of those we had met with had been beaten and imprisoned.[12]

Whenever I think about that incident, I run through a kaleidoscope of emotion-filled memories: the quiet state of shock of the delegation as it listened to Leland, and penned its letter of protest to Mobutu requesting the immediate release of all those arrested; my own sadness the following day when I had to ask the liberated dissidents, their heads and faces cut, horribly swollen, and bandaged, to strip down so that we could duly record their other wounds (a U.S. Army doctor reported that their lacerations, edemas, fractured ribs, contusions, and bruises "do not appear to be life, limb, or vision threatening, but will be painful"); the vainglorious insecurity of President Mobutu as he sat across from the members of Congress on his yacht on the Congo River, coaxing them to reconsider their decision to boycott lunch ("Try my pineapple juice, from my own farm"), and fretting over the small group of men his security forces had continued to beat in a secret prison near his residence ("They carried signs saying 'Victory.' Victory over whom?").[13]

And I also think of Mickey Leland who died, along with members of his staff, other Americans, and Ethiopians, in a 1989 plane crash as they tried, in doubtful weather, to fly to a refugee camp for Sudanese boys. Leland's humanity had almost pushed him down that hotel ramp in Kinshasa. His distaste for the Zairian regime had been so strong that he had even questioned the plan to visit Zaire. Afterwards, he told the press, "The arrogance of Mr. Mobutu about our concern about human rights was despicable."[14] And over the next three years he joined in a number of congressional letters asking the State Department to help assure humane treatment of imprisoned and harassed members of the Zairian opposition.

So I was surprised to learn, in August 1987, that Representative Leland had just spent a week in Zaire, traveling, fishing with President Mobutu, and inviting him to come to the United States to meet other members of the Congressional Black Caucus. According to the Zairian press, he had also made some statements favorable to Mobutu and increased private and public American aid to Zaire.[15] To be sure, there was a slender basis for political hope in a just-concluded agreement under which political dissidents would again be freed in return for backing down from their demand for a second party, pending "reform" of the government party. Leland later said that he had returned to Zaire as chairman of the House Select Committee on

Hunger to "communicate with Mr. Mobutu about the problems of hunger, population explosion, and AIDS."[16] But the atmosphere and aftermath of the trip belied any attempt to rationalize it as consistent with the congressman's past position. He did not bring back any message from the Zairian opposition about their political expectations and how Congress might continue to be helpful. He did not take other members or staff of the Hunger Committee with him. Indeed, the latter were never informed of the details of his visit. And when the repression shortly resumed, his name was conspicuously absent from the rapidly growing list of congressional protestors. Nearly all of his twenty-two colleagues in the Black Caucus eventually endorsed a bill to end U.S. military aid to Zaire; Leland was one of three who declined.

It appears that part of the explanation of Leland's new stance on Zaire lay in his relationship with a wealthy and politically connected New Jersey businessman. As he later explained to a Zairian visitor, one of the beaten ex-parliamentarians, "I was urged to go [to Zaire] by a businessman named Grover Connell, to go there and talk [to Mobutu]. Because of my relationship with Mr. Connell I acceded to the invitation and went."[17]

Grover Connell was chairman of Connell Rice and Sugar, a leading commodity trading firm with additional interests in real estate and equipment leasing. His wealth had been estimated at $350 million. Best known for his cultivation of political contacts to advance his rice-exporting business, he was indicted for conspiracy, fraud, and perjury in the "Koreagate" congressional corruption scandal of the late 1970s. But the charges were dropped when South Korean influence buyer Tongsun Park changed his testimony.[18]

Connell was a significant financial supporter of Leland. From 1986 to 1988, Leland received $6,000 for three visits to Connell's company to discuss legislative developments with his executives.[19] In addition, Connell and his wife, Patricia, contributed $2,000 to Leland's 1988 congressional campaign, half of which came in a month after Leland's return from Zaire.[20] The Connells were also leading financiers of the Democratic Party in Congress. In the mid- to late 1980s they donated roughly three-quarters of a million dollars for honoraria,[21] campaign contributions,[22] and a media center for the Democratic Congressional Campaign Committee, headed by their friend Representative Tony Coelho (D.-Calif.).[23] Leland was close to Coelho and other Democratic Party leaders who had appointed him to head a special House Task Force on Africa.

Connell also had significant economic interests in Zaire and close personal ties with its ruler. His firm had sold rice to Zaire for many years, much of it through a U.S. government PL-480 food aid program, which had resumed in 1987 after a six-year lapse.[24] Three months after Leland's visit, Connell's company became the exclusive purchasing agent for certain U.S. supplies for Zaire's state mining corporation, Gécamines. Mobutu's son Manda facilitated the deal as an "interpreter."[25] In a 1990 interview, Connell said, "I consider Mobutu a personal friend and I admire a lot of what he's done. He created a nation. . . . I don't think Zaire has a severe human rights problem. I think he's being falsely accused. And corruption is a problem everywhere in the Third World."[26]

If one side of the lobbying equation was Connell's financial support and whatever personal charm he and his roguish friend Mobutu could muster, the other side was Mickey Leland's special personality. As Representative Howard Wolpe (D.-Mich.), a collaborator with Leland in Congress's successful efforts to triple famine relief to Africa and impose sanctions against the apartheid regime in South Africa, recalls, "Mickey always saw some good in someone. He loved everyone. He had a tendency to try to narrow distance. And to be responsive to people. He could respond in a personal way to some of the lobby types and forget their side of a broader, perhaps hidden agenda."[27]

Leland's longtime staff aide, Randy Katsoyannis, says, "I'd say he thought he could turn [Mobutu] around . . . and anyone who came to him, he'd think of a way he could help."[28] Wolpe and Katsoyannis maintain that Leland's very openness limited any particular influence. For example, after they questioned his return to Zaire, he "minimized the significance of the interaction [with Mobutu] that had occurred," and subsequently "did nothing" to advance Mobutu's cause.[29] On the other hand, following the Connell-inspired visit, an important congressional voice against American policy in Zaire was effectively stilled.

While it may be impossible to completely fathom all the elements of Leland's dramatic turnabout, there is little doubt that an important catalyst was his relationship with a single influential lobbyist.

As we shall see, it was a common occurrence for congressional policy on Zaire to be influenced by narrow-based lobbies. Almost always they pushed Congress in the same direction as the administration. In the early years, they helped slow the momentum in Congress toward disassociation from the regime. Later their efforts fell short, partly because of changing Zairian and international circumstances, but these efforts still appeared threatening to the critics. The lobbies' resistance to an unusual burst of congressional activism offers many indications of the actual and potential leverage of such lobbies over Congress. Targeting just one or a handful of members, they contributed to reversals of position that equaled or surpassed that of Representative Leland. It all began in 1979 with the first major congressional challenge to U.S. policy in Zaire.

THE RICE WAR

During a January 1979 visit to Kinshasa, Representative Solarz (D.-N.Y.), the new chairman of the House Africa Subcommittee, heard the U.S. government's PL-480 Title I food aid rice program was "shot through with corruption."[30] Soon, expert testimony before the subcommittee confirmed that "wealthy and powerful business-bureaucrats operating with the cover of state authority" sold U.S. rice aid at "four to eight times the established prices." They also diverted some of the rice to the country next door, Congo-Brazzaville, to obtain scarce foreign currency. As a result, "A 100-pound sack of Title I PL-480 rice, when available, costs as much as 250 Zaires, which for the average working Zairian citizen represents up to eight months' salary."[31]

The U.S. government rice program in Zaire had fallen victim to a system of public administration in which, "in a word, everything is for sale, anything can be bought. . . . He who holds the slightest cover of public authority uses it illegally to acquire money, goods, prestige, or to avoid obligations." The author of that insightful 1977 description was President Mobutu himself. In an earlier 1976 speech he had cautioned officials, "If you want to steal, steal a little cleverly, in a nice way. Only if you steal so much as to become rich overnight, you'll be caught."[32] Citing Western diplomatic sources, the *Los Angeles Times* reported in March 1979:

> Near the Kasavubu Market outside Kinshasa 12,000 bags of U.S. rice are hidden. The rice, a gift from the United States, will never reach the people for whom it was intended. The bill of lading has been changed and now bears the name of Mobutu's son Nywa.[33]

"American participation in this fiasco," wrote Professor David Gould, a Zaire expert, "demeans the American image, and identifies the United States in the public mind with the rapacious elite in power, as it aggravates the disparities between rich and poor in Zaire."[34] The Africa Subcommittee agreed, voting, on a bipartisan basis, to transfer the Title I government-to-government rice program to Title II so that American private and voluntary organizations and international agencies would distribute the food.

This recommendation did not please the administration, which hoped to reform the Title I operation in collaboration with the Zairian government, and which doubted the capacity of nongovernmental groups to fully implement a Title II program in Zaire.[35] Even more important, the subcommittee action did not sit well with Representative David Bowen, a Democratic member of the Foreign Affairs Committee from Mississippi.

Bowen's congressional district was one of the top five or six rice-growing districts in the nation.[36] He was a member of the Agriculture Committee's Rice and Oilseeds Subcommittee and chairman of its Cotton Subcommittee. Most of Bowen's financial backing came from national rather than local organizations, and included donations from many agricultural groups. "If I wanted to stay alive politically and do campaigns," he explained, "I had to work nationwide with commodity groups."[37] Among the major contributors to his 1978 and 1980 campaigns were the Rice and Soybean Political Action Committee, the American Rice Political Action Committee, the California Rice Fund, and Mr. and Mrs. Grover Connell.[38]

A graduate of Harvard and Oxford universities who had taught international relations and foreign policy, Bowen was admittedly "not that interested in agriculture." But he willingly took up the cudgels for Mississippi on the Agriculture Committee. When an opportunity arose for him to join the Foreign Affairs panel as well, he justified it to his Mississippi district in terms of the committee's jurisdiction over the PL-480 food aid program: membership would enable him to "better represent export agriculture interests."[39] This was particularly relevant for rice. Most of the crop was sold abroad, about 15 percent through PL-480.[40]

When he heard about the Africa Subcommittee's action, Bowen "got roused" by "the first real opportunity" to politically validate his foreign affairs role. He proceeded to "sound the alarm" by contacting "as many agricultural organizations as I could," including the Rice Millers' Association (the major lobby for both producers and agribusinesses), the California rice cooperatives, the National Farm Bureau, and "probably" Grover Connell (export agent for the California co-ops and the sole PL-480 rice supplier to Zaire). "They picked up on it pretty rapidly as a threat to export agriculture ... a bad precedent," he recalled. Bowen also networked with other members of the Agriculture Committee, arguing that what happened to the rice program in Zaire would set an example for other products in other places.[41]

In the ensuing debate in the Foreign Affairs Committee, Bowen received strong support from Representative Paul Findley of Illinois, the ranking Republican on the Rice and Oilseeds Subcommittee. Assuring Solarz that "I have been to Zaire before, and I would like to say that I agree with almost everything he said about the corruption in Zaire," Bowen warned, "There are 25,000 rice farmers in the United States of America who are concerned also about cutting off this large outlet for American rice." Backed by the administration and its promise of Title I reform, Bowen and his supporters narrowly defeated the Africa Subcommittee's recommendation.[42]

Undaunted, Solarz pushed on to the House floor, where he hoped to recoup with a coalition of human rights–oriented liberals and antiwaste moderates. Instead he was buried by the Rice Lobby. Speaking on behalf of Bowen's effort were Democrats from California, Louisiana, and Arkansas representing the three largest rice-growing congressional districts, along with others from districts or even states with rice farms. Representative Coelho, for instance, had little rice in his California district but thinks he was "probably" influenced by a request from his state's large rice cooperatives. Despite endorsements from Africa Subcommittee Republicans and a few liberal Democrats, the Solarz Amendment went down by more than two to one. Over 80 percent of the Democrats on the Agriculture Committee, including a number of liberals, voted "nay."[43]

Reflecting on the result, former representative Bowen emphasized the significance of his initial, political decision to become involved as well as the free field for lobbying by rice and other agricultural organizations. "Lots of times things get done because no one's geared up," he explained. "It was easy enough for people to say that Zaire got only a small part of the PL-480 rice [just 4 percent] and that Solarz was not changing the global total [so the rice might be sent elsewhere if a Title II program proved impractical in Zaire]. . . . I was at the right place at the right time . . . and was highly motivated to get everyone in gear and everyone mobilized across the country." From "conversations with agriculture sector people," Bowen concluded that without his intense commitment "we probably wouldn't have won." (It certainly seemed that way to me when Bowen descended from the Foreign Affairs Committee dais to quiz me about the fine points in Solarz's argument, rushed out to check my answers, and returned to deliver his rebuttals.)

Once the battle was joined, continued Bowen, supporting his position "was a no-lose vote for most members, [one] for America's friends and export sales." As a result of agricultural lobbying, "a congressman could get 30 or 40 letters against Solarz, with the issues laid out. And on the other side, there was zero."[44] Indeed, the only outside lobby expressing support for the Solarz Amendment was the small Interreligious Task Force on Food Policy, which referred briefly to the provision in a longer letter to House members.[45]

While a political process that seemed to favor relatively small rice-exporting interests over millions of U.S. taxpayers and hungry Zairians did not measure up to the democratic ideal, time would bear out the Africa Subcommittee's substantive concerns. Even as the House debate got under way, a Kinshasa newspaper reported that the administration's initial reform of Title I was "far from being implemented according to all the evidence." The rice was supposed to be sold in small bags to discourage hoarding and reselling at exorbitant prices, but "in several markets of the capital . . . the rice is everywhere sold in big bags. Moreover, the little 7.05 Zaire bag is resold in the same markets for 15 Zaires, even more."[46] A subcommittee-requested 1980 U.S. General Accounting Office (GAO) investigation concluded,

> The scarcity of complete and accurate records, and the limited U.S. monitoring . . . makes it impossible to measure how well or badly the agreed-upon distribution plan was adhered to at the retail level. GAO estimated . . . that 13 percent of the rice . . . was unaccounted for by the time it reached the major importers/distributors. Although thousands of persons benefited from sale at official prices, there were reported instances of where rice (1) was sold at much higher prices, (2) was improperly sold to government officials, and (3) was diverted to the black market.

The GAO also uncovered such new scams as $5 million in rice sales proceeds designated for support of U.S.-approved development programs but never remitted to the Zaire government, and another $1.3 million that the government illegally "lent" to seven officials for their "private agricultural holdings."[47]

As early as August 1979, only months after the House vote, the U.S. Embassy had begun to recommend the termination of the Title I rice program. In 1980 it launched a new Title II (nonrice) initiative.[48] Finally, in 1981 the State Department quietly interred the Title I rice program due to "a myriad of difficulties encountered by the [government of Zaire and the U.S. Embassy] in ensuring that the rice was sold at prices within the reach of the poorer segment of the population." The burial was so quiet that Representative Bowen does not recall hearing about it.[49]

A CONSTRUCTION COMPANY IN IDAHO

During 1979 Congress also debated the issue of U.S. military aid to Zaire. The House version of the foreign aid authorization bill contained a provision eliminating military assistance. At first glance, the prospects for similar Senate action seemed good. The new chairman of the Senate Africa Subcommittee, George McGovern (D.-S.D.) was a liberal's liberal. And the head of the Senate Foreign Relations Committee was Frank Church (D.-Idaho), a strong critic of American efforts to prop up right-wing dictators in the name of anti-Communism.

But when the committee took up the aid bill, McGovern, backed by his principal staff aide, Pauline Baker, accepted the Carter administration's request for $10.5 million in military aid "to bring about a more disciplined and responsible military force." He did insist on inserting hortatory "guidelines" for the administration into the committee report, emphasizing the need for "substantial progress . . . toward the development of a legitimate, disciplined, and respectable security force," and making plain the committee's intent that aid "not be used for equipment that is in any way applied to violate the human rights of Zairian citizens, repress local discontent, or contribute directly or indirectly to personal gain, graft or corruption."[50] Baker recalls that McGovern's position also reflected "realism" about "how hard politically you could push in the Senate."[51] Nevertheless, Chairman Church cast a sharp eye on the apparent tension between the money McGovern wanted to send and his anxious "report language." "We could add the Lord's Prayer to it for help," he opined; "We will need Divine intervention to see these objectives obtained. . . . Maybe we should consider doing what the House did."[52]

Yet when a House-Senate Conference Committee later met to iron out differences in their foreign aid bills, Church took an entirely different tack. He now asked the House to accede to the full administration request for Zaire because "we have American citizens at risk over there. It happens that I know of that because one company, Morrison-Knudsen Company, happens to have headquarters in my state." Responding for the House side, Solarz asserted that U.S. military aid had been "badly abused and misused" for private purposes. More fundamentally, he argued, "History teaches us that this is an armed force which is feared by its own people. I think it is in our interest not to be formally identified with it." Church responded, "I equate very easily with that argument because it is so familiar to the liberal concept of the world and what our role should be in it."

But he quickly returned to Morrison-Knudsen's concerns: "The company is pleading to have a continued show of American interest." In the end, the conference compromised at $8 million in aid and stronger hortatory language. That the Senate had done better than the usual norm of "splitting the difference" was in no small part due to Frank Church's persistence. It was also due to the fact that no other well-organized constituency was active that might have countered Morrison-Knudsen's influence.[53]

Morrison-Knudsen, the Boise-based international construction firm, was one of the top employers in Idaho. In the late 1970s and early 1980s, it was working in Zaire's unstable Shaba Province on an infamous $1 billion "white elephant" of international aid: an 1,100 mile transmission line to provide Zaire with electricity it did not need at a price it could not afford.[54] According to former aides of Senator Church, Morrison-Knudsen was "not that important" to him politically; he had "both supporters and detractors" in the firm.[55] "He was not in their pocket," agrees Church biographer Leroy Ashby, noting their strong differences over Vietnam policy. On the other hand, the senator "would compromise" with them[56] and "try to be helpful if there were merit."[57] Evidently Church, who was facing a tough reelection campaign, decided to be helpful to the most significant constituency he perceived on the Zaire issue—a single company.[58]

A HOSPITAL IN INDIANA

The debate over military aid resumed in 1980. The House Africa Subcommittee recommended reducing the administration's new request from $8 million to $4 million. Subcommittee leaders viewed the latter figure as a meaningful act of disassociation from the Zaire government that was also politically more defensible than a complete withdrawal of assistance. One of the members of the subcommittee, however, Representative Floyd Fithian, a moderate Democrat from Indiana, offered an amendment in the Foreign Affairs Committee to restore the money.

Fithian's activism had been stoked by a hospital in his congressional district. The hospital was concerned about future supplies of cobalt, which it used for medical purposes (half of American consumption of cobalt was met by imports from Zaire). I knew this because Fithian's staff aide had told me so. Initially, he had approached the subcommittee staff for information on human rights abuses in Zaire, but after speaking with Fithian, he realized that the congressman was viewing the subject "from a whole other angle." Recalling the episode later, Fithian thought the hospital was "probably" being pushed by a supplier. He added that, at the time, he was not opposed to military aid to "some regimes like Zaire's," although his perspective had subsequently "liberalized."[59]

Fithian's preoccupations were apparent from his comments in committee. After questioning whether the administration's aid request for Zaire was *high* enough, he told an administration witness, "As you know, it is in our security interest to have conditions prevail in Zaire as good as possible because of the cobalt source that they represent for us and for the medical implants industry and lots of things." Picking up on a GAO investigator's discovery that Zaire was using a U.S.-maintained C-130 military plane for the unanticipated purpose of flying cobalt exports to Europe, Fithian commented, "There is a very real economic reason, for example, for supporting a [military aid] program which would restore the C-130s and the rest."[60]

Fithian's final amendment to restore $2.5 million of the subcommittee's cut was supported by the administration and barely lost in committee because it received a tie vote. Had it prevailed, the political momentum of the previous year toward disassociation from the Mobutu regime would have been reversed. Once again, a single narrow-based lobby could exert leverage on an issue where it had no political competition, but now it was unable to swing the balance. Instead, a new House-Senate Conference compromised midway between the higher administration/Senate figure and the lower House one. This time

Chairman Church, a lame duck after his election defeat, did not mention Morrison-Knudsen and guided the conferees toward a speedy disposition.[61]

THE ISRAEL FACTOR

In 1982 the Reagan administration proposed significant increases in military and economic aid to Zaire, even though President Mobutu's stock in Congress had continued to fall. His deposed prime minister, Nguza Karl-I-Bond, had journeyed to Washington to testify about massive presidential thefts of foreign exchange; institutionalized corruption; and political repression, including his own electroshock torture.[62] A December 1981 House-Senate Conference confirmed the trend of reduced military assistance. And the news media were reporting that President Mobutu and an entourage of nearly one hundred had flown to the United States on the Concorde and spent nearly $2 million entertaining themselves, mostly at Disney World in Florida.[63]

A new bipartisan Senate Foreign Relations Committee staff report described a visit to the military airfield in Kinshasa where Zaire's two operable C-130 military transport planes were observed. One had been converted into the president's personal aircraft with "complete and comfortable presidential quarters." The other was loading a cargo of cattle, "probably to transport the cattle to Mobutu's ranch for improving the quality of his own herd." Noting that it was "widely accepted" that Mobutu "has managed to amass a legendary personal fortune at the nation's expense" while the average citizen's standard of living "plummeted," the report observed, "It is increasingly risky for the United States to expect perpetuation of the status quo." Skeptical of proposals for increased American aid, it warned, "It may be that the only effective impetus for serious reform in Zaire will be a credible indication of U.S. willingness to disengage entirely."[64]

In May, the House Foreign Affairs Committee reduced the administration's request for $20 million in military aid to $4 million, and rejected a new program of "security-oriented" economic assistance (ESF). Zaire promptly proclaimed that it was renouncing all American aid due to "insulting remarks made by some U.S. officials." Con-

demned for their "intolerable attitude" were "some American congressmen of the Democratic Party, especially Stephen Solarz."[65] Solarz
had told the Foreign Affairs Committee,

> Anyone who knows what is going on in Zaire knows that any Amer-
> ican ESF funds to that country will either wind up in the private
> bank accounts of the ruling elite, or they will free up indigenous
> resources for additional diversion to these accounts. In other words,
> it is a total waste of funds.[66]

Forty-eight hours later, Zaire announced that it had become the
first African state to restore relations with Israel. In short order, the
Israeli Embassy in Washington, an American pro-Israel lobby, and a
new Zaire government lobby led by a recent American consultant to
the governing Israeli party were all urging Congress—especially Jewish members like Solarz and Howard Wolpe—to thank Zaire with
more aid!

The most imposing of these groups was the American-Israel Public
Affairs Committee. AIPAC is the principal organizational vehicle of
the pro-Israel lobby, which is "generally considered to be the most
powerful foreign policy interest group."[67] By the early 1980s, AIPAC
had a relatively large and skilled research and lobbying staff, a membership approaching 50,000 including key contact people in every
congressional district, and influence with political action committees
distributing over $4 million to national political candidates in the
1983–84 campaign cycle alone (much of it to members of congressional foreign policy committees). It also had considerable sway with
the 3 percent of the electorate that was Jewish.[68]

As far as Zaire was concerned, however, AIPAC's political base was
far smaller. According to participants, it was actually the *Israeli
Embassy* that took the initiative to ask AIPAC to help Zaire in Congress
as a way of showing other countries the rewards of recognizing Israel.
Additional encouragement came from the Reagan administration. But
AIPAC officials were reluctant to get involved with the Zaire issue,
fearing it could detract from more central concerns. AIPAC therefore
decided to mount only a low-profile effort, situated outside its offices
and run by a consultant, former Senate aide Barry Schochet.[69]

Also active was the Hampton-Windsor Corporation, which had signed a two-year $1.2 million contract with Zaire to help develop "cooperation in every field with the United States." Hampton-Windsor's president was Zev Furst, a former official of B'nai Brith's Anti-Defamation League, a leading American Jewish organization. Furst had been working in Israel for U.S. political consultant David Garth on the election campaign of future prime minister Menachem Begin. There he met a "former Egyptian Jew with business interests in Zaire." As a result, Furst gained an introduction to Mobutu as someone "who'd won an election in Israel" and "as a plus may have access to congressmen. [Mobutu] was interested in that point to counter the negative reaction on the Hill."[70]

Five months before Zaire recognized Israel, Furst had arranged a meeting between the new House Africa Subcommittee chairman, Howard Wolpe (D.-Mich.), and President Mobutu at the latter's Washington hotel. With a longtime Israeli adviser at his side, Mobutu dangled the prospect of normalization of relations with Israel before the Jewish congressman.

Wolpe subsequently commended Mobutu for recognizing Israel, but resisted pleas by Furst and others to soften his stance on aid. In any case, the House Foreign Affairs Committee had already taken its decision to cut military aid and deny ESF assistance. In June, "low-key, pro-Mobutu" lobbying by AIPAC and the Israeli Embassy, and administration efforts, could not prevent the Senate Foreign Relations Committee from halving the military aid request. The new Senate Africa Subcommittee chairman, Paul Tsongas (D.-Mass.), a liberal veteran of the Peace Corps in Ethiopia, read his colleagues excerpts from the critical committee staff report. Moreover, Foreign Relations chairman Charles Percy was no favorite of AIPAC's.[71] Still the administration's new ESF program went unchallenged.

The lobbies made a stronger bid in 1983 and nearly won. They decided to focus on supporting the administration's proposal for $17 million in ESF funds; this was likely to be more palatable than military assistance. The House Africa Subcommittee spurned the request, citing a report by the German banker Erwin Blumenthal, the IMF's former principal adviser in Zaire, which concluded, "The corruptive system in Zaire, with all its wicked and ugly manifestations, its mismanagement and fraud, will destroy all endeavors of international institutions, of friendly governments, and of the commercial banks towards recovery and rehabilitation of Zaire's economy."[72] Barry Schochet, the AIPAC consultant, spoke with numerous members of the House Foreign Affairs Committee, however, and asked some of their campaign contributors who were also members of AIPAC to contact them. He made particular headway with "pragmatic" Democrats with "strong relations with AIPAC" including representatives Larry Smith (D.-Fla.), Robert Torricelli (D.-N.J.), and Tom Lantos (D.-Calif.).[73] As the critical vote neared, Wolpe, who was being pressed by some of his own contributors, was beckoned into a private committee room by an irritated Smith, who asked him to "talk [on the phone] to my contributor."

In the meantime, Hampton-Windsor's Furst had a personal meeting and half a dozen telephone conversations with Representative Torricelli concerning "U.S. relations with Zaire." Furst lived in Torricelli's district, considered him "a friend," and contributed $250 to his upcoming campaign.[74] During the committee debate, Torricelli was the only Democrat who spoke up for increased aid to Zaire:

> While we can all cite disappointment with that Government in some respects, we must nevertheless remember that in difficult moments in American foreign policy initiatives the Government of Zaire has stood with us and has been dependable. Most notably, as has already been pointed out, with the Camp David process and in the courage exhibited in recognizing the State of Israel.[75]

In the denouement, Smith, Torricelli, and Lantos voted with the administration; another Democrat resolved his cross-pressures by walking out just before the vote. Wolpe and his camp narrowly prevailed, 16 to 13, only because two Republicans joined them unexpectedly.[76]

AIPAC's interest in Zaire waned after the committee debate, in part perhaps because Schochet's contacts with contributors upset some of its congressional supporters. Zev Furst's contract expired, and he went on to other business ventures. When the Foreign Affairs Committee resumed debate on Zaire in 1985, Representative Torricelli rose to make an unusual confession:

> I feel some obligation to speak to members of the committee on this issue since two years ago I offered almost the exact same amendment now being offered. Let it suffice to say that I have seen the errors of my ways. It was a mistake. I offered myself an education on Mr. Mobutu, and Mr. Mobutu does not deserve any expanded assistance. . . . The facts are that American assistance to the country is being misused on a grand scale.[77]

Nevertheless, the precariousness of their victory over the lone lobby in the field had somewhat intimidated the congressional critics. "In order to achieve greater consensus," they were henceforth prepared to countenance some increases in "well-monitored" ESF aid.[78]

AN OUTBURST OF LOBBYING

By 1987, the administration and its congressional critics had reached a stalemate on Zaire policy. The former was constrained by congressional opposition and budgetary stringency from lavishing as much foreign aid as it wished on its Zairian client. It tried to make do by inviting Zairian counterinsurgency units to joint United States–Zaire military exercises and by influencing the increasingly disillusioned IMF and World Bank to keep their assistance flowing. On the other side, the critics lacked the political force to achieve the complete disassociation of the United States from the Mobutu government. Yet they had managed to dent the political symbolism of American support that was so important to the crisis-ridden regime.

Now three lobbies came forward to try to swing Congress in a new direction. One was Mobutu himself and some of those who swirled around him. Another, the first important anti-Mobutu lobby, came from the radical left. The last was the ubiquitous Grover Connell. All focused primarily on the House, where interest in and opposition to administration policy were greatest. And all illustrated the power of narrow-based groups to mobilize members of Congress and achieve at least potential leverage on an important foreign policy issue.

Mobutu Inc.

When the prospect of picketing prevented Representative Leland from fulfilling his promise to invite President Mobutu to the annual Black Caucus weekend in Washington, Mobutu invited caucus chairman Mervyn Dymally (D.-Calif.) to visit Zaire instead. Representative Dymally was a political "progressive" who had inquired of a State Department representative during the 1983 committee debate, "Would you just explain to me how does the chief honcho of corruption institute reforms?"[79] In January 1988, Dymally spent approximately ten days in Zaire as Mobutu's guest.[80] Upon returning to Washington he became one of the president's leading defenders.

In early February, Representative Robert Mrazek (D.-N.Y.) and forty-seven other members of Congress sent Mobutu a letter saying they were "particularly disturbed" by "reports" that opposition leader Etienne Tshisekedi and hundreds of his supporters had been "arrested and beaten for trying to hold a peaceful public meeting on January 17."[81] Dymally promptly wrote Mrazek, "I think you ought to hear the other side of the story." Noting that he had discussed the matter with Mobutu in Kinshasa, Dymally reported, "His response was that Tshisekedi's arrest had nothing to do with politics, but rather his was a violation of a local ordinance against demonstrating without a permit (by the way, he reminded me that some of our cities have such ordinance)." According to Dymally, "The facts as reported by both Zairian and U.S. officials" were that "*No one was killed. Hundreds were not arrested and beaten.*"[82]

Mrazek replied, "It is difficult to accept President Mobutu's statement. . . . Mr. Mobutu refuses to allow opposition parties to exist, refuses to allow freedom of political expression, so that no such permit would ever be granted." Mrazek also pointed out that while "no one is sure what happened in the chaotic events of January 17th," he had relied largely on the State Department, Amnesty International, and the press for his information.[83]

During his trip, Dymally had also suggested to "the Zairians," "You guys ought to look at the Japanese model in the 1950s . . . where they set up institutes to get their message across."[84] The result was the March 1 formation of the Zaire-American Research Institute (ZARI). One of its objectives was "to promote friendships, cooperation and improved relations between Zaire and the United States." Two of the three initial directors, including the executive director, were former staff aides or associates of Representative Dymally.[85]

In September, Dymally and ZARI issued twin press releases stating that the Congressman had succeeded in "his seven-month ongoing human rights plea" to Mobutu to release Tshisekedi. Mobutu's action was deemed "an effort to show that there is room for divergent opinions within Zaire."[86] Tshisekedi himself attributed his liberation to a hunger strike and action by members of his clandestine opposition party. He had met with Dymally shortly before his release, but had concluded, "The whole attitude of Mr. Dymally seemed directed towards his sole concern of pleasing Mobutu without caring about what Zairians think of his political direction."[87] According to the then-U.S. ambassador to Zaire, William Harrop, "Dymally didn't really have anything to do with Tshisekedi's release. Mobutu used his visit."[88]

And when the overwhelming majority of the Black Caucus endorsed Representative Ronald Dellums's (D.-Calif.) bill to end all but humanitarian aid to Zaire, Dymally demurred in order "to keep a 'dialogue' open with Mr. Mobutu."[89]

Dymally's political behavior, like Leland's and Bowen's, seemed to arise from the interaction between outside pressures and his personal political agenda. The external forces were essentially Mobutuist, and they flowed through the usual personal and financial channels. Most important was Mamadi Diane, an African-born American businessman who was close to Dymally. Dymally subsequently said Diane "fascinated me. . . . He was an African Muslim. My father was Muslim." Diane and his wife contributed $2,500 to Dymally's 1988 campaign, $2,000 of it shortly after the congressman's first trip to Zaire. According to Dymally, he would not have gone to Zaire and "probably would never have been involved in the issue" had Diane not pressed him to "see it for yourself." Diane was Dymally's interpreter and guide during that and subsequent visits.[90] Ambassador Harrop perceived him as "stage managing [Dymally] all the time."[91]

Diane was also the Zairian government's agent for the entire PL-480 program. In return for arranging the supply and transportation of food aid, he received 2.5 percent of the shipping costs.[92] His contract was renewable annually. Zaire had "twice asked the State Department to recognize him as honorary consul of its government in Alexandria, Virginia."[93] In addition, Diane was "in business" with Bemba Solana, a leading Zairian entrepreneur, a member of Mobutu's inner circle, and, according to press and diplomatic reports, an illegal exporter of coffee and partner of the president and his family in various commercial ventures.[94] Diane also became president of ZARI, the Zaire image-polishing venture, in which capacity he depended upon Bemba's largesse. For instance, at least $91,000 of the 1989 budget of $220,000 came from Bemba.[95] Through ZARI Diane arranged visits to Zaire by black mayors and members of Congress (the most infamous of which was the visit of the Illinois Democratic representative Gus Savage who was accused of assaulting a female Peace Corps volunteer on a night out with Diane and others), and otherwise attempted to counter "misinformation" about Mobutu.[96]

Another supporter of Dymally was Dick Griffey, the head of Solar Records and an Africa-oriented trading company. Dymally said he originally sought out Griffey "because he was the only black with a five-story building in Hollywood. I thought it would be good to meet him." Considered "one of the wealthiest black businessmen in the country,"[97] Griffey and his wife donated $1,750 to Dymally's 1988 campaign. Two employees of Solar Records gave another $2,000.[98]

In the summer of 1988, President Mobutu did Griffey and Representative Dymally a favor that, one imagines, neither could easily forget. At their request, he contributed $250,000 to Griffey's Coalition for a Free Africa.[99] The coalition's main activity was a Los Angeles telethon on conditions in Southern Africa, including an appeal for funds to assist Southern African children. All but $8,000 of the charity's funds were spent on worldwide travel and other costs of promoting the telethon, leaving little for the children of Africa. Its most important result may have been to promote Griffey's African economic interests by enhancing his image "as a businessman who is concerned about issues in Africa."[100]

An internal impetus for Dymally's activism seems to have been his genuine commitment to the advancement of black business. "Who in this country is going to help a black firm in trouble?" he asked. "A white Congressman from Louisiana? If a black member of Congress can't do it, who can?"[101] Dymally was not just a passive target for Mobutu and his clients. He actively solicited Mobutu's financing for Griffey's telethon. He admired Griffey as "the only black man I knew with a vision of Africa: he was for economic empowerment." Someone who lacked a strong ideological commitment might not have been willing to endure the sometimes withering press and public criticism Dymally received for his position on Zaire and for his heavy-handed efforts to advance Diane's business interests with the government of Uganda and Griffey's with the government of Angola. Inevitably, though, Dymally's devotion to the cause of black enterprise became tangled up with the particular business interests he championed. Responding to a story in the *Journal of Commerce* about his "pressuring Uganda" to "appoint a good friend and campaign contributor [Diane] as its PL-480 agent," Dymally said he believed there was "a conspiracy" with "racist motivations" to harm Diane because he had succeeded "in a white man's business."[102]

A Rainbow Appears

As the Mobutuist offensive began, the first significant anti-Mobutu lobby was chalking up some early gains. In September 1987, Representative Dellums and fifteen other members of the Black Caucus introduced their new bill indicting the Mobutu regime and cutting off most American aid. Following the attack on Tshisekedi and his followers, Representative Mrazek had initiated the letter to Mobutu from forty-eight representatives, warning, "It is difficult for Members of the United States Congress to continue sending U.S. military and economic aid in light of current political conditions." Other expressions of discontent had come from senators Nancy Kassebaum (R.-Kan.) and John Kerry (D.-Mass) of the Foreign Relations Committee.[103]

Behind this outpouring from members, many of whom had not previously shown much interest in Zaire, was a new organization called the Rainbow Lobby.

Originally established to push legislation to increase third parties' access to the ballot and to presidential debates, the Rainbow Lobby was a spinoff of the New Alliance Party (NAP), a "pro-democratic, pro-socialist, and anti-imperialist" group with an appetite for political controversy. The lobby had come upon the Zaire issue almost serendipitously through Serge Mukendi, a Zairian exile in New York who happened to be a member of the NAP. It decided to add Zaire policy to its portfolio as an extension of its thrust toward democratization, and as an illustration of the failure of the Democratic, Republican, and Communist parties to confront "apartheid's key ally" in the conflicts of Southern Africa.

In the annals of Zaire lobbying, the Rainbow Lobby was unique not only for its political orientation but also for its mode of operation. It didn't make campaign contributions, give out honoraria, associate with political action committees, or make friends with legislators. No member of Congress appears to have perceived it as representing a significant political constituency though a few may have considered it a potential political nuisance. Furthermore, its scale of operation was relatively modest. "We were a pipsqueak lobby," acknowledged Deborah Green, the political director. At its zenith, the Rainbow spent perhaps $300,000 a year on its Washington office, which researched, lobbied, and publicized a range of domestic and foreign issues. This was roughly equivalent to ZARI's budget, and less than half of what Mobutu customarily paid his other U.S. lobbies. And it paled in comparison to the resources of groups like AIPAC and the rice lobby. Money was raised by paid door-to-door canvassers and telephone banks discussing mainly domestic issues. About 30,000 contributors ultimately gave enough to receive a quarterly newsletter from the lobby. (According to former lobby officials, only a tiny percentage of the approximately 200,000 people who gave some money to the lobby over several years are likely to have ever communicated with their legislators about Zaire). Finally, while many pro-Zaire lobbies strongly attacked their opponents, the Rainbow and its NAP associates were particularly combative.[104] Much energy was consumed in an intense feud with Representative Dymally, with each accusing the other of fronting for different diamond dealers and practicing "slander" and "harassment."[105]

The Rainbow Lobby's political influence seems to have been largely based upon its skill in gaining access to potentially helpful members of Congress, the reliability of its factual information on Zaire, and the way its message fit into broader congressional agendas. It brought Serge Mukendi to Washington in 1986 and introduced him to Representative Leland, who was still smarting from the 1983 incident. Leland, with characteristic generosity, invited Mukendi to address the Black Caucus.[106] Later, the lobby approached Representative Dellums to follow up by sponsoring anti-Mobutu legislation. Dellums was receptive. According to his staff aide Bob Brauer, he was aware of Mobutu's bad reputation in and out of Congress, and looking for a way to politically "validate" his leadership of the movement to impose economic sanctions against the white minority regime in South Africa by demonstrating an equal propensity to sanction black tyrannies. Aware that the Rainbow Lobby "wasn't where we were politically," Brauer nonetheless worked closely with it on Zaire legislation while checking out its facts and political judgments with the Library of Congress's Congressional Research Service, human rights groups, and other congressional offices.[107]

Representative Mrazek had been "genuinely moved" by an hour's discussion with opposition leader Tshisekedi during a visit to the United States arranged by the Rainbow Lobby in November 1987. He told his staff aide, Stephen Goose, that he "wanted to get involved and stay involved." Mrazek, recalls Goose, was "stimulated by international issues" and "wanted to become more involved in . . . areas such as human rights and the arms trade." This was apparently the reason he surprised Goose by agreeing to meet with Tshisekedi in the first place. With encouragement from the Rainbow Lobby, Goose drafted Mrazek's February 1988 protest to Mobutu after checking the facts with the House Africa Subcommittee staff and others. Mrazek soon became a force for reducing aid to Zaire in the important House Foreign Operations Subcommittee.[108]

The Rainbow Lobby also increased critical attention to Zaire in Congress through its press statements; its workshops and conferences; its mobilization of human rights, church, and antiapartheid groups; and its demonstrations during Mobutu's trips to the United States. Its vituperative clashes with Representative Dymally, however, enabled him to virtually close off its access to the Black Caucus. And a series of critical reports (including one by the B'nai Brith's Anti-Defamation League) raised enough questions about its broader political orientation and style to put off some white members as well.[109]

Grover Connell (Again)

Connell Rice and Sugar's long business relationship with Zaire crested with its late 1987 supply contract with the state mining company. According to an investigation by *Wall Street Journal* reporter Edward Pound, twelve American firms were required to sell to Gécamines through the Connell firm, which collected "exorbitant fees for an intermediary," amounting to as much as $5 million a year.[110] Pound's story was "on the money, 90 percent or more" said a former high official of the U.S. Embassy in Kinshasa, who added that the Connell company provided "few aftersales services" on its supplies. Another high embassy official agreed, but thought Connell's annual profit was "more like $20 million."[111]

The embassy suspected the deal included a questionable arrangement between Connell and Manda Mobutu, the president's son. Connell told the *Wall Street Journal* that Manda Mobutu had served as an "interpreter" but "was not our agent and he was not paid by us. . . . He had nothing to do with our getting the contract."[112] But the embassy possessed copies of two bank drafts from Connell to Manda totaling over $2 million. The bank was the Morgan Guaranty Trust Company, which had approached the State Department for assistance after making the "extraordinary mistake" of transferring over a million dollars twice! When an embassy official went to see Manda about returning the extra million, the president's son calmly informed him, "Connell is wrong. He owes me $3 million."[113] The State Department subsequently referred the case to the Justice Department for investigation of violations of the Foreign Corrupt Practices Act. Under pressure from the World Bank, which was concerned about "excessive fees paid to agents," Gécamines finally canceled the contract in 1990. In November 1994, a Justice Department spokesman described the Corrupt Practices referral as still "pending."[114] (Connell declined repeated requests to be interviewed for this book.)

Connell's lobbying grew along with with his economic stake in the Mobutu regime. After arranging Representative Leland's 1987 trip to Zaire, he sponsored receptions for Mobutu in Washington in 1988 and 1989, getting about fifty of his numerous "friends" in Congress to attend each time. While American business interests in Zaire often paid tribute to Mobutu during his visits to America (diamond trader Maurice Tempelsman regularly took him for a yacht ride around Manhattan), this was probably the most access, however superficial, the Zairian leader had ever had to Congress. More important, in January 1990 Connell personally accompanied four notable House members, all beneficiaries of his honoraria and campaign contributions, to Zaire where they were guests of the government.[115] The U.S. Treasury paid for the representatives' transportation to and from Zaire, but, according to an informed source, "The agenda was set by Connell." The only major departure was the delegation's request to see opposition leader Tshisekedi (who had been under house arrest for nearly a year), which Mobutu rebuffed.[116] Ambassador Harrop remembers inviting the group for a briefing, but "when I was critical of Mobutu, Connell tried to shut me up. . . . [The legislators] really behaved in a numb way." Another embassy officer described the visitors as "one of the less serious [congressional] groups" that came to Zaire: "It was frustrating. They asked a lot of you and then wanted to relax with Connell."[117]

The visit seemed to have left more favorable impressions on the congresspeople. Representative Torricelli, who received at least $8,000 in honoraria and $5,000 in campaign contributions from the Connells in 1985–89, seemed to be reviewing his position on Zaire again, saying he detected "subtle improvements" in human rights policies. Congressional critic Mrazek ($2,000 in honoraria and $2,000 in contributions in 1989, followed by $5,000 in contributions for a Senate run in 1991–92) said he hoped "there will be some improvements" in this respect. Neither Representative Mike Espy (D.-Miss.), heir to Representative Bowen's rice-growing district, nor Representative Bill Lowery (R.-Ca.) offered public comments about their trip.[118]

What were the actual legislative results of this burst of lobbying? In the end, not all that much. In retrospect, Mobutu's campaign with the Black Caucus was probably doomed almost from the beginning on account of his tarnished reputation in and out of Congress and the Rainbow Lobby's timely launch of the Dellums bill. Nor was Dymally the kind of legislative powerhouse who could marshal Democratic support for a potential coalition with conservative Republicans.

The Rainbow Lobby could take some credit for Congress's 1989 reduction of the legal cap on military aid to Zaire from $7 million to $3 million. That decision had been spearheaded by Mrazek from his strategic perch on the House Foreign Ops Subcommittee. But the overall political battle had already been won earlier in the year when Senate Foreign Relations voted 12 to 7 (with Republicans Kassebaum and Lugar in the majority) to sustain House Foreign Affairs' typical $3 million limit. Furthermore, the administration was so short of military aid funds that it had voluntarily allocated Zaire only $3 million during the previous two years. All in all, the Rainbow Lobby's activity does seem to have had a modest, but not decisive, impact on congressional perceptions of, and actions toward, Zaire.

As for Grover Connell's offensive, it seems to have come too late to be effective. In early 1989, four conservative House Republicans, led by Representative Dan Burton (R.-Ind.), the ranking Republican on the Africa Subcommittee, visited President Mobutu at his home "village" of Gbadolite. They were shocked by what they saw: a rented Concorde on the airport tarmac, palaces and villas under construction, a $3 million cathedral, giant gold urns, $400 bottles of French wine, and luncheon guest Tongsun Park, the congressional "influence peddler of Koreagate notoriety."[119] Around the same time, a U.S. AID official acknowledged in congressional testimony that the World Bank was concerned about $400 million in "missing" Zaire government mining revenues.[120] And in 1990, political repression intensified as Mobutu sought to cope with a growing democratization movement, culminating in a widely publicized massacre of students at Lubumbashi University.

With the Cold War ebbing, and the IMF and World Bank on the brink of cutting aid, House Foreign Ops chairman David Obey (D.-Wisc.) publicly assured Wolpe and Solarz, who had come by to testify on Zaire, "No bill that bears my name will have any money for that turkey [Mobutu]."[121]

Partly because of Connell's interest, Torricelli explored the possibility of continuing economic aid, but found there was little political support even from Republicans.[122] A couple of new Zaire government lobbies vainly pushed an environmental assistance initiative that would be paid for by forgiving part of Zaire's debt to the United States. Before departing for Zaire with Connell, Representative Mrazek had reassured his staff aide that "there would be no sea change" in his position on Zaire. Given the political atmosphere in Washington, Mrazek "was never put to the test."[123]

Of course, all of the above represents 20-20 hindsight. From my vantage point on the Africa Subcommittee staff, each of these three lobbies had, at various times, an opportunity to greatly affect congressional policy. Had events developed differently in Zaire and internationally, their capacity to help move a small number of key members of Congress might have given them significant leverage in the contest between the administration and its congressional critics. As it was, the mere threat of the pro-Zaire groups, only partially counterbalanced by the Rainbow Lobby's effort, probably reinforced the critics' caution about moving too rapidly to end American assistance.

LOBBYING ZAIRE

As the Zaire drama shows, foreign policy lobbying is not a one-way, mechanical process in which the "fat cats" devour the "people's representatives." Whatever their clout, lobbies depend crucially upon the political predispositions of their targets. Representative Leland's passion for narrowing political distance, Senator Tsongas's background in Africa, the "pragmatic" bent of some pro-Israel members of the House Foreign Affairs Committee, Senator Church's impending difficult reelection campaign, Representative Dellums's eagerness to show he opposed black as well as white dictators in Africa, Representative

Mrazek's search for a human rights issue to pursue in his subcommittee—all illustrate the importance of the member side of the lobbying equation. Indeed, members of Congress sometimes mobilized lobbies themselves in behalf of their political objectives. Representative Bowen's interest in justifying a foreign affairs role to his Mississippi constituents helped provoke him to "sound the alarm" to the rice lobby. And Representative Dymally's dedication to the advancement of black business helps explain his soliciting of President Mobutu on behalf of his businessman supporter's telethon.

On the other side of the relationship, financial aid (campaign and party contributions, honoraria, gifts to member-favored charities) played a central role. There is no way of measuring its precise impact. Human motivation is complex, and members of Congress are naturally restrained in discussing the subject because of the tension between the laws permitting political financing and the laws prohibiting political bribery. From members' general discussions about the relevance of contributors, their sometimes dramatic changes of position following lobbying contacts, and their observed behavior in the presence of lobbyists, as well as appreciations by staff aides and the lobbyists themselves, it appears that financial factors were of great importance. Other pathways to influence included the lobbies' local constituencies (however small), personal and political party ties, material resources, and skills in gaining access to sympathetic congresspeople and furnishing them with reliable information.

But what also made the lobbies so effective with the few members targeted and with Congress in general was that, as Representative Bowen had said, "There was zero on the other side." Compared to many domestic issues, relatively few interest groups were involved and their popular base was especially narrow. The voice of a single $2,000 contributor, company, or "low-key" professional lobbyist could seem awfully loud to a member of Congress against a background of overwhelming silence on the part of potential constituencies, colleagues, and party leaders.

In the culture of deference, Congress yields much of its power to the executive branch and to narrow interest groups. Due to an unusual confluence of congressional activism and Zairian and international circumstances, Congress ultimately cut off nonhumanitarian aid to the government of Zaire. But this result was significantly delayed due to the efforts of the administration and the maneuvers of the "Zaire lobby." By the time Congress finally acted, Mobutu had bought valuable time to expand and strengthen his praetorian guard and Zairian society had virtually collapsed. Meanwhile, the Cold War—which had established the parameters of congressional debate on Zaire—had suddenly disappeared. In the emerging post–Cold War lexicon, Zaire was now "a failed state," and, as we have seen, Congress had barely begun to deal with that issue in Somalia.

4

The Secret Congress:
The Intelligence Committees and
U.S. Covert Action in
Nicaragua and Angola

"Covert action" has been a staple of American foreign policy from the CIA's support of centrist political parties in the 1948 Western European elections to its reported assistance to forces opposed to Saddam Hussein in Iraq in the early 1990s.[1] The number and cost of these publicly unacknowledged propaganda, "political action," economic, and paramilitary operations have fluctuated with international and domestic developments. Thus covert action consumed most of the CIA's budget at the peak of the Vietnam War, but reportedly declined to less than 5 percent of the total by 1980 with the postwar reaction and revelations of CIA assassination plots against foreign leaders and domestic spying.[2] Under the energetically anti-Communist Reagan administration, covert action increased from "a dozen or so small scale" operations at the end of the Carter years to "some 40-odd" programs in 1986, many described as "major undertakings." Their cost reportedly mounted to more than $600 million by 1986.[3]

Although the conclusion of the Cold War appears to have brought about a major decline in covert action, this weapon is unlikely to disappear. It continues to offer presidents an attractive "middle option" for situations "in which diplomacy is not likely to generate enough leverage to influence a foreign leader or problem" and "the use of military force carries grave risks." Recently, a task force of prominent Americans called for covert action to be "refocused" on such "new threats and challenges" as the spread of nuclear, chemical, biological, and long-range missile capacities, terrorism, international narcotics traffic, and aid to democracy movements struggling against tyrannical regimes.[4]

The lure of covert action is greatly enhanced by the special process of congressional oversight of these activities, centered in the House and Senate Select Intelligence Committees. The president can initiate covert action at any time without the approval of the committees. (They are only entitled to "prior notice" or "timely information.")[5] Their reviews and decisions concerning these activities take place behind closed doors, in the committees' specially secured offices— except for the rare instance when they themselves formally choose to disclose an operation to the full Congress. Thus the executive branch does not have to deal with 535 members of Congress as well as the public, as it must, potentially, on other foreign policy issues. It need only convince a majority of the 15 or so members of each Intelligence Committee of the merits of its case.

The current scheme of congressional regulation was established after the scandals and legislative investigations of the 1970s. It is unquestionably a great improvement over the nonsystem that preceded it. For the first time, Congress has a structure to regularly inform itself about covert action and ensure that the president takes responsibility for these projects. Its basic purpose is to reconcile the tension between secret foreign policies and democracy by delegating legislative power to a small, rotating group of members. Handpicked by party leaders, and representative of other relevant committees, the intelligence panels are supposed to discreetly supervise covert action, protecting beneficial programs and modifying or eliminating harmful ones. Although the executive branch has been subjected to new limitations, it has also gained the hope of stemming congressional "leaks" of secret information and forestalling sporadic congressional rebellions against worthy programs.

But the practice has been very different from the ideal. When Congress considers covert action it descends to the very nadir of its influence in foreign affairs. This is largely the result of a process that closets together a select coterie of officials entrusted with national security information, and a small number of legislators who have their own instincts and inclinations but are virtually isolated from the views and demands of colleagues, constituents, outside experts, and even other members of the administration. In these circumstances, members of the intelligence committees are even less inclined than their foreign affairs committee colleagues to challenge administration policy strongly, to demand information, to undertake serious investigations, and to make and enforce binding law.[6]

Also, while it may seem strange, narrow-based lobbies can have a major, indirect impact upon covert action. Administrations have learned from recent experience that certain kinds of programs, particularly large paramilitary efforts, bear a heavy risk of public exposure and are potentially controversial. In the Southern African country of Angola in 1975, and in Nicaragua in 1983, the unmasking of CIA-assisted insurgencies led to full-scale congressional debates and decisions to cut off U.S. assistance. In order to minimize such risks, the executive has resorted, with increasing purpose, to the so-called overt-covert program.[7] This involves a delicate operation to open the window on covert action just enough to defuse any future sense of shock and promote the general virtues of the effort in Congress without producing a full congressional debate and vote. The object is to create an overall political atmosphere favorable to keeping the real decisions in the more tractable intelligence committees. In this pursuit, the administration sometimes collaborates with professional lobbyists to promote public expressions of congressional sympathy. Members of Congress may be even more responsive than usual to these narrow-based lobbies since they bear no public responsibility for the actual covert-action decisions taken by the secret committees.

Two particularly good illustrations of these aspects of the culture of deference are the failure of the intelligence committees to detect the Reagan administration's violation and circumvention of legislative restrictions on covert action in Nicaragua and Angola in the early 1980s, and Congress's easy acquiescence to a new covert program in Angola during the latter part of the decade.

NICARAGUA: AN ABSENCE OF OVERSIGHT

In 1984, Congress adopted the Boland Amendment terminating a nearly three-year program of covert aid to the contra insurgents in Nicaragua. This decision was not simply the result of the intelligence committees quietly doing their job of separating the wheat from the chaff of covert action. Rather, it largely reflected a unique combination of external and individual factors.

The press exposed a politically unsavory counterrevolutionary project that went well beyond its original goal of disrupting Cuban/Nicaraguan support of guerrillas in Central America. The contras, many of them ex-henchmen of the former Nicaraguan dictator, were trying to overthrow the leftist Sandinista government. This spawned open congressional debate and pressure on the intelligence committees to respond. Put on the spot, the committees initially tried to protect the covert program, modifying it to make it more acceptable. But they were ultimately alienated by the transparent untrustworthiness of the CIA director, William Casey, who denied the clear implications of facts he himself provided and clumsily withheld other information that was already coming out elsewhere.[8] Also, the chairmen of the committees were unusual men, extremely proud and jealous of their reputations for public integrity. Representative Edward Boland (D.-Mass.) bitterly recounted his political deception to his colleagues: "A paramilitary operation, but a paramilitary operation that was going to be controlled, they tell us—controlled—and we believed them."[9] For Senator Barry Goldwater (R.-Ariz.), an enthusiastic supporter of the CIA, the crowning insult was more personal. He was embarrassed on the Senate floor after being less than fully briefed on the CIA's participation in the mining of Nicaraguan harbors, and, he protested, "lied" about and "bombed" by Casey and presidential national security adviser Robert McFarlane when he complained about it.[10]

The outcome was a law prohibiting U.S. intelligence entities from spending funds "for the purpose or which would have the effect of supporting, directly or indirectly, military or paramilitary operations in Nicaragua by any nation, group, organization, movement or individual."[11] Given their previous experience, one might have expected the intelligence committees to have been particularly vigilant when new press reports appeared in 1985–86 alleging that the National Security Council staff was violating or circumventing the Boland restrictions on covert action. After all, the slippery Casey had clearly represented the Reagan administration as well as himself. And accused NSC staff member Oliver North's boss was the same McFarlane who had leapt to Casey's defense against Goldwater. Yet in the absence of either definitive proof from the press or external political pressure, the committees, under new leadership, made only perfunctory efforts to uphold the law. "This is where the Committee really fell down," observed a veteran House Intelligence Committee staffer.[12]

The unfolding stories in such "prestige papers" as the *New York Times* and *Washington Post*, as well as in the *Miami Herald* and Associated Press, portrayed North as coordinating contra military operations following passage of the Boland Amendment. He was said to be facilitating logistical support, offering tactical advice, and orchestrating "private" fund-raising efforts in the U.S. and abroad. As time went on, more of his collaborators and agents (witting and unwitting) were specifically named. First, there was the retired general John Singlaub, who stated that he looked for "a signal" from North when he described to him specific fund-raising initiatives. Later on there was Robert Owen, reputed to be North's intermediary with the contras on arms supplies and training, and then Jack Terrell, Tom Posey, and John Hull—all thought to be involved in a contra military training scheme in Costa Rica. Sources for the reports included anonymous current and former administration officials and contra leaders, ex-contra official Edgar Chamorro, Nicaraguan Indian leader Teofilo Wilson, General Singlaub, Terrell, and Posey.[13]

The congressional committees and independent counsel who later investigated the Iran-contra affair confirmed the broad truth of these reports—and much more. They also presented convincing arguments that these activities constituted serious violations of the letter and spirit of the Boland Amendment and its successive modifications. In any case, they showed that, with its constitutional responsibilities for appropriating funds and overseeing programs, Congress had the right and obligation to know what the executive branch was doing to assist the contras militarily, particularly as administration requests for renewed contra aid were being acted upon by Congress throughout this period.[14]

Yet virtually the only thing the House and Senate Intelligence Committees did to follow up the press allegations was to ask the three prime suspects whether they were guilty. They submitted written questions to McFarlane and his successor, John Poindexter, and met with them. The House committee met once with North in the White House situation room. All three officials denied the news stories.

North later admitted that letters sent to Congress were "false" and that he lied to the House committee. McFarlane would only allow that his responses were "clearly too categorical." Poindexter acknowledged, " My objective all along was to withhold from the Congress exactly what the NSC staff was doing in carrying out the President's policy. . . . I thought that Colonel North would withhold information."

The chairmen of the committees said they were largely satisfied with the officials' responses. After the House panel met with McFarlane in September 1985, Chairman Lee Hamilton (D.-Ind.) told him, "I for one am willing to take you at your word." Following McFarlane's session with Senate Committee Chair David Durenberger (R.-Minn.) and Vice Chair Patrick Leahy (D.-Vt.), Durenberger said, "So we came away from the meeting feeling that from Bud McFarlane we're getting what he believes to be the situation with regard to his staff." And after the House committee's briefing with North, Hamilton "indicated his satisfaction with the responses received."[15]

What more could the committees have done to probe these serious charges? For one thing, they could have called in the others named in the press stories—Singlaub, Owen, Terrell, Posey, Hull, Chamorro, and Wilson—and questioned them under oath. They could have requested and if necessary subpoenaed their records. They could also have spoken with contra leaders, some of whom were sources for the journalists. In addition, the stories indicated, and subsequent investigations established, that elements of the NSC-directed operation were known to numerous U.S. officials (and strongly suspected by others) in Washington and Central America. The committees might have explored this field, including, as the former Senate committee staff director, Robert

Simmons, suggests, their own contacts in the military and other intelligence communities.[16] Finally, at some point they could have attempted to put McFarlane, Poindexter, and North under oath and could have subpoenaed their records. Considering the latters' positions in the White House, this would likely have provoked an assertion of executive privilege to refuse cooperation and a prolonged court battle. Yet that would have also raised the political stakes and increased pressure on others to come forward before the affair was exposed. In the end, there can be no guarantee that a serious investigation would have succeeded, but it might have. The committees, however, as one House staff aide put it, "were unwilling to go to the mat with the White House. . . . We asked the right questions, maybe of the wrong people."[17]

Some participants have indicated how they looked at the situation at the time. In public and in private, Chairman Hamilton has stated that he confronted a choice between "unsubstantiated allegations" and "direct flat denials from two national security advisers and North himself. . . . In that circumstance, I felt that I should rely upon the word of the National Security Adviser and Colonel North and I did."[18] Bernard McMahon, Chairman Durenberger's staff director, adds, "If we had assumed the White House was doing these things, or that they'd all perjure themselves [the outcome might have been different]. My conclusion is, it's hard to catch a criminal if they do it for the first time in a unique way."[19] Michael O'Neil, who was chief counsel of the House committee, agrees: "The Administration never made any secret they were fighting us . . . withholding information, but in hindsight we didn't feel they would directly perjure themselves."[20] Although these considerations clearly influenced the committees, there is a deeper level of explanation for their performance.

FORCED TO BELIEVE?

According to former members and staff, the committees' ethos included a very limited concept of their oversight responsibilities. Former representative McHugh (D.-N.Y.) evoked the pervasive influence of those who wrapped themselves with the prestige of secret information, and the resignation of their supposed regulators:

It was difficult to investigate beyond [our] administration witnesses. . . . It was in some sense peculiar to the Intelligence Committee in the sense that people you go to to ask questions are part of the
covert operation, part of the conspiracy if that's what it turns out to
be, or others who truly don't know or aren't supposed to know.
. . . Sources are more limited than other foreign policy committees.
You also know that sources to whom you go outside of those
appearing before the committee will feel some constraints. . . . It's a
crime to disclose covert action.[21]

"The only recourse we had," McHugh testified at the perjury trial
of the CIA deputy director for operations, Clair George, "was to ask
the people in government who know whether [the allegations] were
true or not. . . . When they denied they were involved, basically we had
no recourse."[22] This was the view of a liberal Democratic member of
the committee after whose chairman the restrictive Boland Amendment had been named. According to Dan Finn, who was counsel to
the Senate Intelligence Committee, "The director of Central Intelligence protecting his sources and methods was seen as tinged by executive prerogative," resulting in a "shying back from investigative
confrontations with the executive branch." This was reinforced by a
sense of "political vulnerability"; a sense that "if you went too far, you
could be accused of leaking secrets."[23]

The question, explained staff director McMahon, was, "To what
extent responsibility for oversight goes beyond the process of review
and interviewing in a dialogue. . . . Are we to investigate, subpoena,
hold hearings? We didn't view ourselves judicially; it was not our
responsibility to enforce the law. We weren't organized to do anything
else."[24] Indeed, each committee had only a handful of staff cleared to
examine covert action. Usually they had other responsibilities as well
(the committees' jurisdictions extended to all intelligence agencies and
activities) and, in any case, lacked investigative experience.[25] As former representative Robert Kastenmeier (D.-Wisc.) summed it up, "We
were very limited in our expectations and our capacity to follow
through."[26]

Another relevant feature of the committees' ethos was bipartisan
cooperation. The members realized that any effort to pursue an aggres-

sive investigation would incite fierce partisan conflict; such conflict was already rife in Congress as the administration sought to free itself from the Boland restrictions. Previous efforts by the committees to preserve bipartisanship on contra aid policy had collapsed under the weight of Casey's cynicism and outside political pressure. Now, though, the committees confronted only a *procedural* decision about whether to investigate—a decision that could be made in private. McHugh recalled:

> The [House] Intelligence Committee had a bipartisan tradition. The culture of working together had frankly broken down over this [contra aid issue]. . . . We lost confidence in the administration's veracity. . . . But there was still a presumption that this was a bipartisan effort. There was a reluctance to say the other side was partisan and the administration didn't tell the truth.[27]

The Senate Intelligence Committee had previously declared, "Partisan political concerns and activities are incompatible with the effective oversight of the Nation's intelligence activities."[28]

Ironically, the more combative the Republican advocates of the administration were, the more anxious Democratic critics were to appear nonpartisan. Kastenmeier remembers the House Intelligence Committee as "hopelessly divided. . . . Half would aggressively oppose this sort of investigation. . . . One problem was Republicans, especially [Representative Richard] Cheney [R.-Wyo.] and [Representative Henry] Hyde [R.-Ill.] constantly attacking Congress's ability to confront the administration. They were always suggesting we take lie detector tests though the question was who was lying to us."[29] The partisan divide was so deep that centrist Republican William Goodling had voluntarily left the committee because "The administration didn't need me questioning every move they made in Central America; they had the Democrats."[30] But ultimately the Democrats decided not to press the point. According to Representative McCurdy (D.-Okla.), "It was very difficult [to investigate]. . . . There was such polarity. . . . We gave the administration the benefit of the doubt."[31]

The presence of a large number of centrist Democrats on the Senate panel muted partisan divisions, but the norm of bipartisanship was still a factor. In the view of key staff aides, "If someone wanted to be literal on oversight, he would be seen as against Reagan in Central America," and "if it became public that we were investigating private people, we'd be seen to be taking sides."[32]

The paralyzing subculture of constrained oversight and bipartisan yearning was supported by the committees' insulation from day-to-day political pressures. "You didn't go to the floor if you were on the Intelligence Committee and tell your trusted friends. You were constrained in a public sense," McHugh observed. But this meant that the members did not have to account either to the public or to their own colleagues for their decisions not to pursue a careful investigation.[33]

In the end, many of the members of the committees almost sounded as if they had been forced, against their better instincts, into believing the National Security Council staff. McHugh was "skeptical" about what he was told, but "tended to accept the representations by our government officials that they were not violating the law, even though I was concerned about the allegations."[34] McCurdy "believed McFarlane more than North," but also led his colleagues in accepting North's falsehoods at their White House meeting.[35] Key Senate staff aides thought, "The members knew in all likelihood they were being lied to," and "enough [senators] knew or had reason to know that there was a rather well-organized private supply effort going on and that the trail seemed to lead to the White House."[36] Certainly Durenberger's and Leahy's further comments after the McFarlane meeting— "You cannot be satisfied" that "no one in any way involved was directing the effort [to aid the contras]"; "If the law had been broken . . . it will come out"—were in this vein.[37] The trouble, as McMahon pointed out, was that the senators could not "regard McFarlane as untrustworthy" without "creating an environmental switch in the way the members thought their relationship with the administration should be."[38] Apparently for many members of the committees the lurking truth could be admitted only by disturbing their whole *raison d'être.*

Members and staff also noted the dampening influence of the general political atmosphere: a popular president was gradually gaining ground on his contra aid proposals. Yet they maintained that the committees' culture was quite important. In this connection, perhaps the most revealing fact about these committees was the absence of any investigative push at all from members who were strong public critics of administration policy.[39]

In contrast, Representative Barnes (D.-Md.), the House Western Hemisphere Subcommittee chairman, came out of his corner swinging. Asserting his subcommittee's jurisdiction over "U.S. policy towards Nicaragua," Barnes wrote McFarlane requesting "all information, including memoranda and other documents" pertaining to contacts between Oliver North and Nicaraguan leaders. "Barnes is really a troublemaker," commented Poindexter, then McFarlane's deputy (neither intelligence committee ever requested any kind of documentation from the administration). Barnes's inquiry led McFarlane to conduct a document search, consider or direct alterations in six "problem" memos, and explore the possibility of claiming executive privilege. At a meeting in McFarlane's White House office, Barnes declined a hollow offer to rapidly peruse a "stack of documents" on McFarlane's desk, and subsequently insisted on "serious analysis" by "competent staff."[40] While Barnes found it "hard not to believe" McFarlane's outright denials, he also told his staff, "I think I just met a man who's afraid he may go to jail."[41]

At that critical point, Barnes suddenly decided to retire from the ring. His staff director, Victor Johnson, later wrote, "When it became clear that McFarlane would not respond adequately to our request in the absence of a subpoena, Barnes abandoned the quest because of the demands of his Senate campaign."[42] According to former subcommittee staff members, some of Barnes's advisers urged him on, saying that confronting the president would be a "dynamite issue." But others warned that the conflict, including court appearances, "will consume all your time." So it was decided to "punt to the Intelligence Committee."[43] Barnes remembers it differently: "I had no option. I was told they weren't going to give us all the information. It could only be provided to the Intelligence Committee."[44] In any event, Barnes wrote McFarlane suggesting he provide the documentation to the Intelligence Committee to "resolve any concerns about the security of the information."[45] Neither Barnes nor Hamilton seems to have inquired further into the matter.

What remains from this incident is the sense of a somewhat

stronger disposition toward real oversight outside the intelligence committees than inside them. A similar indication was provided by a 1986 "Resolution of Inquiry" introduced by Representative Ronald Coleman (D.-Tex.) at the prompting of House Democratic leaders and Barnes's subcommittee.[46] Based on the accumulating press allegations, the resolution directed the president to provide Congress with extensive documents and information concerning U.S. support for the contras. However, "because of the highly classified work of the National Security Council," it also wound up in the Intelligence Committee's court. Following the committee's August 1986 meeting with North, Hamilton relayed to Coleman his not entirely reassuring verdict: "It is my belief that the published press allegations cannot be proven."[47]

ANGOLA: THE UNKNOWN PRECEDENT

Although some participants stressed the difficulty of ferreting out a "unique" administration infraction, the intelligence committees' failure had an unknown precedent. Before the Boland Amendment there had been the Clark Amendment, which terminated covert assistance to two factions in the Angolan civil war of 1975–76. As in Nicaragua, press exposures had highlighted the warts of America's allies against the Soviet- and Cuban-supported de facto government. Not only were America's clients, including Jonas Savimbi's National Union for the Total Independence of Angola (UNITA), almost indistinguishable ideologically from their "socialist" Popular Movement for the Liberation of Angola (MPLA) rivals, but their other major sponsor was apartheid South Africa, anathema to the rest of the African continent. Caught in a political maelstrom of reactions to Watergate and Vietnam, the CIA scandals and the emerging U.S.-Soviet detente, the Gerald Ford administration sealed its fate by telling lies that could not last.[48]

Senator Dick Clark (D.-Iowa) wrote this recollection of the dramatic 1975 closed Senate Foreign Relations Subcommittee meeting that approved his amendment by a bipartisan vote of 7 to 0.

This meeting was a key to our success. [William] Nelson [the director of covert operations at the CIA] came in and reported what they were doing covertly and why they were doing it. [Secretary of State Henry] Kissinger did not come but sent the Acting Assistant Secretary for Africa, Ed Mulcahy, and he was scared to death. Kissinger had obviously told him not to say anything. Mulcahy had not been in the early meeting with Nelson. I asked him if our government was providing assistance to Savimbi when I was in Angola. He said, "No." I had a U.S. Information Agency ticker tape. . . . Mulcahy was quoted as saying we were not giving assistance to Savimbi. I pulled a copy of the statement out and read it to Mulcahy. I said, "You were lying when you said that." He said, "Absolutely not." I said, "This whole committee just heard Nelson, Deputy Director of the CIA, say we were giving assistance to Savimbi at that time." He was very shocked and upset. He said, "I guess we were giving assistance at that time." He was so upset, he said a number of other stupid things. At that point, Clifford Case (R.-N.J.) said, "You are a pretty slippery guy and you have admitted lying to the committee already."

At the end of the hearing, I said, "I would like to move for adoption of my amendment," and it got reported to the floor. It was just because of Mulcahy.[49]

The language of Clark's amendment was the model for Boland's, but in one respect it was even stronger. The Clark Amendment applied not just to the spending of U.S. funds but more broadly to "assistance of any kind" in "promoting" or "augmenting" military or paramilitary operations.[50] The provision was so starkly comprehensive that the Foreign Affairs and Foreign Relations Committees had to specifically point out that it did not prohibit U.S. aid to a country that became involved *on its own* in Angola unless the aid would "serve as a conduit for [U.S.] support of military or paramilitary activities" in Angola.[51]

Presidents chafed at this restriction. During the Carter administration, the CIA director and the deputy national security adviser tried in vain to persuade Clark to agree to an interpretation of his amendment that would permit them to supply UNITA with "defensive" Redeye surface-to-air missiles through France.[52] The United States had already secretly decided to "stop advising friendly countries against aid to Savimbi," a signal of sorts.[53] During his 1980 presidential campaign Ronald Reagan had said, "Frankly, I would provide [UNITA] with weapons."

Upon taking office, he asked Congress to repeal the Clark Amendment because it denied him "flexibility."[54]

Congress declined, but press reports suggested the administration was circumventing the Clark Amendment. In a January 1982 interview, Savimbi, just returned from meetings in Washington with U.S. officials and quiet visits elsewhere, declared:

> Material assistance is not dependent on or limited by the Clark Amendment. A great nation such as the United States has other channels. . . . As a consequence of having made a trip to the United States, . . . many African nations, many Arab nations, are now interested in giving us substantial aid that we need.[55]

UNITA soon claimed Savimbi had "never declared that the Clark Amendment had ceased to be an obstacle to American aid."[56] But by May 1983 *Time* was noting, "According to intelligence analysts, the U.S. . . . is suspected of circumventing the ban on covert operations in Angola in order to keep alive the anti-Communist insurgency there." In October *Newsweek* reported, "Training, arms and financial assistance are also given [by the CIA] to military forces . . . in Angola." According to the *Washington Times*, the CIA and State Department both "hedged their denials" of the *Newsweek* piece.[57] In 1984, Savimbi indicated that aid from close U.S. friends such as Saudi Arabia, Morocco, and Egypt had escalated to as much as $60 million to $70 million a year. Meanwhile, the administration acknowledged "reports of facilitative assistance" to UNITA from Zaire, which had been America's conduit for the earlier covert operation.[58]

Former Reagan administration officials have now admitted for the first time that the United States secretly encouraged American clients to support Savimbi (thereby circumventing or violating the Clark Amendment). Richard Allen, the president's national security adviser in 1981–82, stated:

> We were frustrated by the Clark Amendment. There was a willingness to have anyone else who would like to assist do so. Whatever made life difficult for the Cubans was OK. I don't think there was a presidential directive. I, [Secretary of State Alexander] Haig, and

Casey would have gotten together to encourage others to look to help just causes. Whatever else Bill Casey did I didn't know or don't recall.[59]

During the first half of 1981, according to a participant, the State Department sent a cable, under Haig's signature, to the chiefs of U.S. missions in several African and Middle Eastern countries including, among others, Saudi Arabia and nearby "Gulf states," Morocco, and Zaire. To ensure that as few people knew about it as possible, the cable was transmitted through "back channels" (CIA communications facilities). The message explicitly encouraged these countries to give aid to Savimbi.[60] Two former U.S. chiefs of mission had memories of either the specific cable or the policy it expressed.[61] Presented with this evidence Chester Crocker, former assistant secretary of state for African affairs, remarked, "It sounds about right to me. No doubt there were signals of encouragement, whether from back channels, the White House, or another agency . . . the general signal was, 'This is a different administration. We consider Savimbi legitimate. He needs support.'"[62] A former high official of the State Department's Near Eastern Bureau reluctantly acknowledged, "I guess I was aware we were encouraging other countries to support our policy; sure, we do it all the time, overtly or covertly."[63]

It was in this context that another message went out from Haig to various U.S. ambassadors in December 1981 to be delivered "by the most discreet and expeditious means available" to the chiefs of state of Morocco, Senegal, Ivory Coast, Gabon, and Kenya (all but Kenya were known supporters of UNITA). It said that the secretary understood Savimbi would soon be making "an unannounced visit" to their countries. Haig wanted them to know this: "After Dr. Savimbi's visit to the U.S., I am more than ever convinced that there is an important role for him in his country and in achieving peace and prosperity in Southern Africa. I know you share this view."[64] It was following these trips that Savimbi made his comment about the U.S. having "other channels" and certain African and Arab nations becoming "more interested in giving us substantial aid." (Haig declined repeated requests to be interviewed for this book.)

Former assistant secretary Crocker has written that he agreed to Savimbi's early 1985 request that he "step up our public references and private messages to African leaders signaling our support for the legitimacy of his cause." Meanwhile, Crocker found himself accused by CIA director Casey and South African officials of "discouraging support" for UNITA in Europe. "It was a cock-and-bull story," he protested; "We were in fact doing the opposite."[65] When asked by Representative George Crockett, Jr. (D.-Mich.), at a contemporaneous public hearing, "Has our government given any support, directly or indirectly, to UNITA?" Crocker replied, "No, Congressman, it has not; that would be against the law."[66]

Other sources, private and foreign, have suggested that Casey may have been doing even more to assist Savimbi through Morocco, Saudi Arabia, and Israel.[67]

The Angola gambit appears to have been a simpler version of the later scheme to circumvent the Boland Amendment by secretly enlisting foreign clients and employing agencies not normally involved in covert action. In Angola, the State Department was probably the prime channel; in Nicaragua it was the NSC staff. But in each case, the CIA seems to have been involved in the initial decision and ongoing support.

Still, with Angola receiving less press and public attention than Nicaragua, the intelligence committees initially ignored the reports concerning evasion or violation of the Clark restrictions. It was only in May 1985 that the House Intelligence Committee undertook an inquiry after a request from Africa Subcommittee chairman Howard Wolpe (D.-Mich.). Citing press and other reports that the United States "may be supporting military activities in Angola, either through the CIA or via other agencies," Wolpe wrote, "The Administration may be circumventing the law by encouraging third parties to aid the anti-Government Angolans with an implicit understanding that the U.S. will be helpful in return."[68] Hamilton replied only weeks before the first allegations against Oliver North surfaced. "Based on interviews of the appropriate intelligence officials," the committee declared there was "no evidence that any U.S. intelligence agency is directly or indirectly assisting UNITA or other anti-government Angolans."[69] With a timorousness that would be seen again, the committee had first narrowed the target from "the Administration" (in Wolpe's letter) to "intelligence agencies," and then interviewed only the "appropriate" officials. As in the case of aid to the contras, it seems to have "asked the right questions of the wrong people."

Yet here too a serious probe might have proven productive. After all, the major implementers of the policy in Angola were career State Department foreign service officers whose willingness to lie to persistent congressional investigators was probably less than that of Cold War zealots like North and veteran covert operators like Casey and Clair George. And had the scam on the Clark Amendment come out, it might have turned up pressure on Congress to examine closely the charges concerning the Boland Amendment. Perhaps it might even have given the administration pause in pursuing its secret policy making in the Iran-contra affair.

In retrospect, more effective oversight by the intelligence committees might also have hindered the administration's eventual success in obtaining congressional approval for both overt aid to the contras and the repeal of Senator Clark's barrier to covert assistance to Savimbi. In the case of Nicaragua, Arnson considers it almost certain that Congress would have "acted differently" had it known that the presumably "desperate" contras were in fact benefiting from "the administration's orchestration of an extensive private and third-country network of contra military support."[70]

As for Angola, the administration's critical 1985 House triumph over the Clark Amendment came by a somewhat larger margin than its narrow contra victories. Still, its most influential supporter, Representative Claude Pepper (D.-Fla.), had argued, "We are not advocating that we give money to anybody for anything. We are simply saying, let us remove the perception that the Clark Amendment gives the world that we washed our hands of Angola."[71] That perception would have been undone, along with Pepper's rationale, had the American role in mobilizing Saudi, Moroccan, Zairian, and other support been disclosed. Such revelations would also have weakened the administration's political credibility, and might have produced pressure for open congressional decision making on aid—as earlier exposures in Nicaragua and Angola had. Under such conditions, Crocker and others in the State Department who were then resisting immediate, *direct* covert aid to Savimbi[72] might have drawn strength from the tenuous situation in Congress. Even if Congress had voted for some aid to Savimbi, it might have looked very different from the administration's eventual package. Pepper, for instance, advocated "humanitarian assistance," not military support.[73]

A NEW "OVERT-COVERT" OPERATION IN ANGOLA

In mid-December 1985, less than three months after the repeal of the Clark Amendment, President Reagan notified the intelligence committees that a new covert action was about to begin in Angola. Earlier, Reagan had shone some light on the clandestine plan by telling the *New York Times*, "We all believe that a covert operation would be more useful to us and have more chance of success right now than the overt proposal that has been made in Congress." In February 1986, Assistant Secretary Crocker publicly stated that "appropriate and effective" assistance was on the way: "The decision has been made, and the process is in motion."[74] Reportedly, U.S. aid for the UNITA insurgency began at an annual level of $15 million in 1986 and rose to approximately $60 million a year by 1990.[75]

The long and tragic Angolan civil war, which may at last be ending, had been exacerbated by foreign intervention from the beginning. By the mid-1980s the major actors were the MPLA government, bolstered by 35,000 Cuban troops and Soviet military equipment and advisers, and UNITA insurgents, benefiting from large-scale South African support, including regular intervention by air and ground forces, and aid from U.S. client states. The stakes went beyond Angola. For the MPLA, the Soviets, and the Cubans, it was also important to back up the insurgents in neighboring Namibia attacking South Africa's illegal occupation. But UNITA and South Africa had vested interests in the Namibian status quo: UNITA because it was a secure lifeline for South African assistance, South Africa because it was a buffer against the spread of black majority rule southward.

The administration's decision to reenter the Angolan war was consistent with its emerging "Reagan Doctrine" of aid to "freedom fighters" struggling against foreign-supported Communist domination. America's objectives in Angola were twofold: to amplify pressure on the Cuban and Soviet military to withdraw and to achieve democratic "national reconciliation" among Angolans. Initially, the United States emphasized foreign withdrawal, attempting to broker a deal exchanging Cuba's departure from Angola for South Africa's relinquishment of Namibia. Once an agreement was reached, the focus shifted to persuading the Angolan government to submit to a political process acceptable to UNITA.[76]

As for Congress, it generally supported the administration's goals of removing foreign forces and promoting an internal settlement. But many Democratic liberals criticized the new military policy for inviting further Communist military intervention in Southern Africa, associating the United States with a despised apartheid regime under increasing assault at home, and supporting a dubious democrat (Savimbi had been trained in China and was a professed socialist until the early 1980s). They estimated that the fastest and surest route to a Namibian settlement and Cuban withdrawal was through diplomatic and economic pressure on South Africa. After all, it was the South Africans who were in the most offensive posture, illegally occupying one country and attacking another, while the Cubans (largely in defensive garrisons) and Soviets were mainly protecting the Angolan territory and regime. Regarding national reconciliation, the critics agreed that a diplomatic breakthrough removing foreign forces could encourage the Angolan parties to seek a political solution. Yet they thought the United States would best further this process through balanced diplomacy and economic incentives, not by joining the conflict.[77]

After almost eight years of persistence, the Reagan administration finally succeeded in brokering the December 1988 Angola-Namibia accord providing for the withdrawal of all foreign military forces. Nearly three years later, the Bush administration helped negotiate an

MPLA-UNITA agreement for peace and democratic elections (which subsequently broke down). In politics, success silences all previous debate, but one hopes that historians will discuss the many unresolved issues. Was the Angola-Namibia accord advanced, delayed, or unaffected by the addition of direct American military pressure on Angola? What was the impact of escalating Cuban military deployments and American economic sanctions on the South African side of the negotiations? Was the internal agreement facilitated more by U.S. aid to UNITA or by Soviet president Mikhail Gorbachev's retreat from expensive foreign commitments, the decline of Communism, and a late congressional threat to withdraw support unless Savimbi became more compromising?

On one point the critics seemed to have been tragically vindicated. Savimbi was not the democrat he pretended to be. Instead, he was a man credibly accused of complicity in the murder of his dissenting colleagues, one who ultimately returned to war rather than accept defeat in a negotiated free and fair election. One of his most devoted Washington representatives was "disappointed about how the whole thing has turned out . . . Savimbi for the good of the country should have come to terms with the fact that he lost a long time ago." Another erstwhile UNITA lobbyist went further. He now considered Savimbi just "a thug," complaining, "We were used."[78]

As elsewhere, the outcome of the policy debate was very much the product of the workings of the congressional process. Between 1986 and 1990, all congressional decision making on the "overt-covert" program in Angola occurred in secret meetings of the intelligence committees. A key feature of this process was the administration's ability to co-opt many of its former critics, poignantly illustrated by the experience of the House committee. Another important element was the capacity of pro-UNITA lobbyists, initially orchestrated by the administration, to foster an overall political atmosphere in Congress that deterred efforts to take the issue out of the secret committees. When Congress, in late 1990, openly debated U.S. action and adopted its own compromise policy, it was largely because some key members had become determined to confront the administration and the public relations experts, and abandon secret decision making.

CO-OPTING THE HOUSE
INTELLIGENCE COMMITTEE

By early 1989, Howard Wolpe, chairman of the House Africa Sub-committee and a longtime opponent of aid to UNITA, was increasingly disturbed about the drift of U.S. policy. Although the growth of the Cuban military presence in Angola had powered the drive to repeal the Clark Amendment, the Cubans' agreement to depart seemed to be accompanied by an *expanding* U.S. commitment to UNITA. Among the harbingers were a pre-inaugural letter from President-Elect Bush assuring Savimbi of continued assistance until national reconciliation was "achieved" and the shooting down of Herman Cohen's proposal (he was designated to be assistant secretary of state for Africa) for low-level U.S. representation in the Angolan capital.[79]

Following a subcommittee hearing on charges by former Savimbi supporters of UNITA human rights abuses, Wolpe approached two close colleagues on the Intelligence Committee. Representatives Bill Richardson (D.-N.M.) and Stephen Solarz (D.-N.Y.) were on record against aid to UNITA. Solarz, a new addition to the intelligence panel, had been active on the Angolan issue since 1975. Working with the subcommittee staff, the three came up with a legislative compromise designed to rebalance U.S. policy. In essence, the proposal maintained existing funding for UNITA, permitting further increases only if the military balance were threatened by external aid to the MPLA government. On the other hand, assistance could decrease if the Soviets agreed to negotiate a mutual reduction of aid, or as a means of promoting political negotiations and the observance of human rights. As a first step toward bringing their plan to the floor, Richardson and Solarz decided to test the waters in the Intelligence Committee. We later learned that their initiative was overwhelmingly defeated, and an emergency *increase* in aid to UNITA approved.

During subsequent conversations among members about possible Angola legislation, it became apparent that about half the Democrats on the Intelligence Committee who had voted against repeal of the Clark Amendment had quietly moved over to the administration's side. They included, among others, the chairman, Anthony Beilenson

(D.-Calif.), Representative Nicholas Mavroules [D.-Mass.], and Representative McHugh, who had taken a leading role in the Clark debate. McHugh volunteered that, in their almost private dialogue in committee, Crocker had won him over. He later recalled,

> I approached the issue with a fair degree of skepticism. But I was persuaded that Crocker was committed to a peaceful resolution. . . . He had expended a fair amount of effort and convinced me at least there was a reasonable prospect, if we kept to our current course, of a fruitful conclusion. I was willing to give him the benefit of the doubt.[80]

Two Senate Intelligence Committee aides also attested to Crocker's effectiveness in justifying the CIA program.[81]

Yet the power of the assistant secretary's argument was certainly enhanced by the claustrophobic structure of secret decision making. In the House Intelligence Committee, Representative Kastenmeier recalled, "Basically our sole source was the administration."[82] The Democratic staff aide who covered Angola was not a regional expert, but he made an unusually conscientious effort to contact other committees and interest groups to seek information from all sides. Undoubtedly, some of these facts cast doubt on the administration's assumptions. Yet it is virtually impossible for even expert staff members to weigh in effectively against official views when their principals do not hear diverse opinions from experts, colleagues, interest groups, and constituents, and do not have to justify their choices in public. There wasn't even much press coverage of Angola beyond battlefield reports. "The problem with secret programs," remarked the former chief counsel of the House Intelligence Committee, "is you don't have the benefit of public comment, private groups, and knowledgeable members of the House."[83] McHugh acknowledged, "[Administration officials] have a stake in covert operations. Even if they don't lie, it makes sense to talk with those with other premises."[84] It was not surprising, in these circumstances, to find McHugh and other members who voted on the House floor against aid to the contras, and for limitations on military assistance to El Salvador, approving, in secret, the unconditional tripling of aid to UNITA.

There is a mixture of truth and understandable subjectivity in Crocker's conclusion that "the quality of dialogue in the intelligence committees on the whole was the highest I experienced [in Congress]. It was refreshing to have matters discussed on their merits, with no microphones, no press relations, no principals with their new haircuts and blowdrys waiting for C-Span coverage, no playing to the galleries, no public charade or morality play."[85] The same might be said of Representative Richardson's contrasting reflection, "The Intelligence Committee is the perfect place where liberals can become conservatives to show [the administration] their responsibility on national security issues and get co-opted by the [Central Intelligence] Agency."[86]

PREVENTING OPEN DECISION MAKING

While administrations pursued their advantages in the intelligence committees, UNITA's Washington lobby built a wall of political protection around the secret deliberations. "We feared a public vote," recalled Christopher Lehman, a key UNITA representative. Not that a public debate and vote at the height of President Reagan's popularity would likely have been that damaging, but as a former Senate staff aide Lehman knew that "the trouble with Congress is that nothing is ever finished." The risks of future public votes were manifold: "They were too easy for the leadership to design [to skew things for their favored alternative]. . . . The State Department wasn't enthusiastic [about the covert program]. . . . The administration would have to get more involved, but the president has just so much time. . . . And the American public didn't like dirty covert wars," especially ones with the "odor" of South African involvement.[87] The lobbyists' concerns grew following the 1986 elections when the Republicans lost control of the Senate and had their ranks reduced in the House. Peter Kelly, a principal in UNITA's most important lobbying firm, Black, Manafort, Stone and Kelly (BMSK), worried, "If ever a large number of Democrats opposed UNITA, it could be a death blow."

To forestall such a development, the UNITA lobby worked to create a majority coalition of "the right" and "moderate Democrats" which could "vocalize" support for Savimbi and his democratic aspirations and opposition to the Soviet- and Cuban-backed Angolan dictator-ship.[88] Such expressions, usually in the form of resolutions, letters, or anti-Angola trade sanctions, would "buttress the intelligence commit-tees," "demoralize" the critics, and "deter" them from insisting on a public vote.[89] Thus the dangers of continually debating and actually voting on funds for a "dirty war" would be avoided.

McMahon, the Senate Intelligence Committee staff director, thought the quasi-public Angola program was "an abuse of covert action. . . . The government wanted funds but no debate on the floor. It was planned that way. Keep it in the committee, drum up support, avoid floor debate, plead secrecy."[90] In fact, there is little doubt that the U.S. government connived, at least in the beginning, to incorporate a public lobbying dimension in its covert program. According to a congres-sional intelligence committee source, "The White House colluded with foreign governments to give complete support to the lobby before there even was an official covert action."[91] McMahon agreed:

> It was Casey's project at his initiative, a coordinated effort by State, NSC and CIA to get [Savimbi] over here, approach Third World countries, and get publicity to cast Savimbi in a favorable light. At a certain point . . . the administration said to Savimbi we need to be more active, play a direct role and manage, not just give weapons—we can't without public support. Let's go to covert action and you get over here and we'll rehabilitate you. We don't want to screw this up like Nicaragua. Let's get a right-wing [lobby] group in who can support you.[92]

Assistant Secretary Crocker says he was unaware of third country support for the lobby, but, based on his experience, strongly suspects that Casey or his White House allies "dropped a name or two [of lob-bies]" to Savimbi.[93] BMSK president Paul Manafort stated he came by UNITA's interest in representation through an unidentified "lawyer-lobbyist." Like other UNITA representatives, he assumed that his compensation, which came from Europe, originated largely in Saudi Arabia and Morocco. He was verbally assured by UNITA that it did not come from South Africa.[94]

In one way, the UNITA lobby had a more difficult task than the pro-

Zaire one. Since it was attempting to create a pervasive political environment to stave off a new Clark Amendment or other legislative restrictions, it had to reach out and involve many more members of Congress.
And while standing up for freedom against the Soviets, Cubans, and
Angolan Marxists was a lot more appealing politically than upholding
"our son of a bitch" in Central Africa, there was the perceived problem
that "no one gave a shit about Africa except the foreign affairs types."[95]
Still, like its pro-Zaire counterparts, the UNITA lobby had the good fortune of encountering almost "zero on the other side." While pro-
UNITA forces spent approximately $2 million a year on a highly
professional operation, the Angolan government spent less than a sixth
as much in truly slapdash fashion.[96] And liberal Africa-oriented groups,
like the black American lobby TransAfrica and the church-sponsored
Washington Office on Africa, were relatively small and highly focused
on the concurrent effort to impose sanctions on South Africa.

Moreover, the UNITA lobby's special role in covert action gave it a
unique advantage. By and large, its job was to mobilize a public front,
not tangle with opponents over the actual legislative decisions, which
were made in secret. If it did its work well, it could avoid direct conflict, public hearings with diverse witnesses, and controversial votes.
When it got fourteen Democratic senators, including the liberal
Christopher Dodd (D.-Conn.), to sign a mildly pro-Savimbi letter to
the president, that was a victory. When it achieved an uncontroversial
cutoff of export credits to Angola until Cuban troops were withdrawn,
that could be trumpeted as a sign of the times. It seemed easier to marshal broad congressional support for the veneer of covert action than
for the thing itself.

For the most part, the UNITA lobby had no political constituency
beyond UNITA and its foreign money. BMSK was the leading actor and
the primary strategist for the entire effort. It was headed by three conservative Republican activists who were also principal consultants for
national and local Republican campaigns, and a major Democratic political fund-raiser. Another participant was TKC, a Democratic-oriented
firm headed by a former executive director of the Democratic National
Committee. The local UNITA office and its consultants also played a
role.[97]

The only part of the lobby that had a domestic political base was the Cuban American National Foundation (CANF), which weighed in at critical moments. Directed and financed by wealthy anti-Castro Cuban-American businessmen, CANF had a political resonance in the approximately one-million-strong emigré community concentrated in south Florida and northern New Jersey. Placing a high priority on bleeding and humiliating the Cuban military in Angola, CANF had contributed significantly to the repeal of the Clark Amendment when its president, Jorge Mas Canosa, persuaded Representative Pepper to lead the battle in the House.[98] As Pepper, whose Miami district was half Cuban-American, had explained,

> A few months ago I was not any more aware of what was going on in Angola except in a general way than one is aware of other parts of the world that pass in kaleidoscopic review from time to time before our mental and hindsight vision. But I was approached about this matter by the Cuban American National Foundation which is in Miami. . . . They fought the battle that free men fight, many of them offering their lives in the Bay of Pigs . . . but they told me something about the condition in Angola.
>
> Well, as far as I am concerned, I am just as strongly in favor of one part of the world being free as I am another.[99]

Energetically exploiting their Republican ties, the UNITA lobbyists provided the congressional right with a blizzard of information, draft letters, resolutions, and legislation, as well as meetings with, and visits to, a well-briefed and eloquent Jonas Savimbi. Even more important was their groundbreaking work with the critical "moderate Democrats." Utilizing political, financial, and personal ties, they strove to obtain serious hearings with sympathetic members of Congress. BMSK's Kelly, for example, had been treasurer and finance chairman of the Democratic National Committee, where he had initiated an effort to coordinate fund-raising with the congressional policy agenda. As a result, one lobbyist recalled, "All the senators knew Peter." As Kelly himself put it, "I was a centrist Democrat; I was active in the Democratic Party, around a long time, and knew these people well. I respected them and they respected me." Even while his firm lobbied for UNITA and other clients, Kelly assisted the House and Senate Democratic campaign committees with the "planning and operation" of fund-raising efforts. In addition to contributing about $40,000 each election cycle to individual and party campaigns, he "helped friends raise money—plan the activities, do the actual financing, the staff hiring." Asked if the friends he helped were also people he talked with about UNITA, he replied, "I'm sure there were some."[100]

As in all lobbying, the message had to be right for the member. Savimbi, said Kelly, "went from Chinese Communist to freedom fighter. That did not happen by accident. [It was] management of perception." The key was "enunciating our version of the facts" to a legislator, and "connecting it to his own style, his particular view of how foreign policy should be handled."[101] Moderate Democrats were attracted by an emphasis on Savimbi's commitment to democratic elections, and sometimes by the suggestion that they could help ensure that he kept that commitment.[102]

In these matters the lobby did its job very well. It is difficult to quarrel with Christopher Lehman's conclusion: "Without these people, you may never have had sufficient energy to crystallize sentiment for UNITA and a peaceful settlement."[103]

BMSK-inspired "Angola Task Forces" in the Senate and House were focal points for member and staff support of lobby initiatives. The Senate Task Force chairman was Senator Dennis DeConcini (D.-Ariz.), a conservative on foreign policy issues who had previously worked to lift economic sanctions against the outlaw white minority regime in Rhodesia. Kelly remembered the process of enlisting DeConcini:

> I knew Dennis from the role of ethnic organizations in the Democratic National Committee. I did fundraising for his 1988 race [Kelly also contributed $2,000 of his own in 1988–89]. . . . We talked in meetings about the need for someone to take leadership. He was identified. He knew a lot. . . . He immediately committed himself on the substance and needed to put this in his priorities—and he did.[104]

The choice for House Task Force chairman, Representative Dave McCurdy, was a harder sell. During the contra aid debate, McCurdy had emerged as the leader of a "swing" group of moderate-to-conservative

Democrats who were willing to pressure the Nicaraguan government for democratization, but were concerned about an overmilitarized administration approach. McCurdy appeared eager to exert foreign policy leadership in the House and perhaps beyond it. Kelly knew him from "centrist politics" and "may have" also given him "very little" fundraising assistance.[105] McCurdy was also close to CANF's Jorge Mas, with whom he had worked on the contra issue. Nevertheless, he initially declined requests from BMSK, CANF, and Representative Pepper to take the lead himself on Angola.[106]

According to Manafort, "He was busy and didn't see how the issue could be a winner at that time. Then we did the Senate Task Force. He saw how it could build value and influence policy in the Democratic Party, move it from left of center and enhance him politically in the institution."[107] A lobbyist close to McCurdy said, "He started the Task Force as a favor for CANF and Kelly."[108] McCurdy himself referred to "friends who were supportive and said I was in a position to make a difference, people out in the private sector: a lot of conservative Democrats, Peter Kelly, CANF."[109]

It was an exquisite irony of the "overt-covert" program that the two Task Force leaders promoting UNITA in public also happened to be members of the intelligence committees, where aid decisions were cloaked in secrecy.

As mentioned earlier, the lobby scored a significant success when Senator Dodd signed a May 1988 DeConcini-sponsored letter that included an expression of support for aid to UNITA. Dodd followed it up by accepting a BMSK invitation to attend a luncheon with Savimbi.[110] According to Manafort, he and Kelly knew Dodd from their common roots and previous political experiences in Connecticut. In addition, Dodd had received $4,000 in contributions to his 1986 campaign from Kelly and his political action committee, Kelly, Updike, and Spellacy.[111] Dodd had a few personal meetings and some other contacts with BMSK staff in the spring of 1988.[112] "We played to his intellectual interest in the foreign policy objective of democracy and the role he could play in persuading Savimbi and others [to democratize]," Manafort recalled.[113] (Dodd declined to be interviewed for this book.)

Representative Dante Fascell (D.-Fla.) was another increasingly active Democratic supporter of UNITA. The influential chairman of the House Foreign Affairs Committee was a longtime foe of Fidel Castro who remembered "writing the embargo law [against Cuba] before the Cubans became citizens [of the U.S.]."[114] But he also had a reputation as a moderate in foreign policy. Indeed, despite the presence of Cuban troops in Angola, Fascell had actually been the House co-author of the Clark Amendment and had voted against the Reagan administration's first repeal effort in 1981. As the proportion of Cuban-Americans in his Miami district climbed to about 20 percent in the mid-1980s, however, Fascell developed a close friendship with Jorge Mas, benefited from CANF financing (receiving nearly $15,000 from its political action committee and thousands more from individual members in 1985–90), and actively advanced CANF's legislative agenda.[115] Fascell "does not recall" whether there was a domestic political reason behind his new pro-UNITA activity.[116] But lobbyists and staff aides who knew him believed that "constituency pressure" from CANF was at least "a factor" in his political evolution.[117]

Finally, although the overwhelming thrust of the lobbying was toward the establishment of congenial public positions, the intelligence committees themselves received some attention. The TKC firm was "responsible" for four House Democratic members. One of them was Bill Richardson, who had publicly opposed the covert program. TKC vice president Art Roberts described himself as a "friend" of Richardson's, a former congressional staff colleague and past fundraiser. He thought of Richardson as an "ideological soul mate, liberal but wanting a more balanced foreign policy." Out of their discussions came a visit by the congressman and an Intelligence Committee staffer to Savimbi's headquarters in Jamba, Angola. The committee paid for the trip, but Roberts said he "may have helped put it together" and he met Richardson in Jamba. "He worked in a Democratic firm," Richardson explained. "There was a friendship with Art. . . . He wanted to look good with Savimbi. . . . I allowed him to come with us." Afterwards, Roberts came to believe that "my trip had a good impact on what [Richardson] saw. . . . I mollified him." Richardson said, "I came back willing to give Jonas Savimbi a little bit of a chance, but I was still very uneasy about him." Asked about Roberts's impact on his conclusion, Richardson observed, "He is a good guy and I respect his views. . . . Sure it's a factor."

Unfortunately for the lobby, the fragile seed that TKC planted was swept away by a passing TV show. "I was channel-surfing at home," remembered Richardson, "and all of a sudden I see Savimbi on Pat Robertson's program from South Africa praising the South African government. . . . I said, 'What a shit. I can't believe he's doing it.' I went bananas."[118]

OPENING UP DEBATE

After the decisive defeat of the Richardson-Solarz effort to limit covert aid in the House Intelligence Committee, Wolpe realized that the only way to advance his position was to counter the UNITA lobby and open up the political process. So he began a sustained campaign to mobilize "interest and political pressure within and outside the Hill." Over the next year, he contacted Democratic members of the House Foreign Affairs and Foreign Operations Committees, the House Democratic leadership, and the Congressional Black Caucus, stressing the need for "a more open and diplomatically balanced approach" to the achievement of national reconciliation in Angola. He insisted that the Democratic Party respond to the concerns of the black American lobby, TransAfrica, and associated U.S. civil rights leaders about Angola policy. Following a meeting with Randall Robinson, the TransAfrica director, Wolpe decided to co-sponsor a resolution urging modest steps to improve relations with Angola to serve as an organizing vehicle for outside interest groups.

In addition to the anticipated Democratic support, Wolpe personally persuaded a number of moderate Republicans to sign on. The subcommittee also held public hearings on Angola diplomacy and its staff critically examined the administration's position, drawing on visits to Angola and discussions with Soviet diplomats, Portuguese peace negotiators, and U.S. intelligence analysts. Wolpe continued to urge the Angolan government to be more forthcoming in the developing negotiations with UNITA.[119] In brief, Wolpe and his subcommittee, and the associated interest groups, began to behave as if covert action in Angola was another foreign policy issue like El Salvador or Zaire, not the private preserve of the secret committees.

By the fall of 1990, a new Solarz-Richardson Amendment nearly prevailed in the Intelligence Committee. Presently it was offered on the House floor, triggering the first open debate on the five-year-old, approximately $170 million Angola operation. In final form, the amendment provided for the suspension of the "lethal" portion of U.S. aid if the Soviets followed through on their promise to do likewise and the Angolan government accepted a cease-fire and proposed a reasonable timetable for free and fair elections. After a heart-stopping competition between Democratic activists and the UNITA lobby, the measure passed by a single vote, that of the speaker of the House.[120]

Senators Ted Kennedy (D.-Mass.) and Nancy Kassebaum (R.-Kan.) were moved to propose a similar amendment; but they withdrew it when Senate Intelligence Committee chairman David Boren (D.-Okla.)—who had been approached by Wolpe and Solarz—indicated he was essentially willing to accept the House position. Although the administration had strongly opposed the House effort, Assistant Secretary of State for African Affairs Cohen later judged that it "had a positive effect on both sides" of the Angola negotiations.[121]

Certainly changing circumstances had much to do with the specific outcome of the congressional debate. As the Cold War declined, the Angolan government was under increasing internal and external pressure to reach a political solution to the devastating internal conflict. With encouragement from its new U.S. lobbyists and Wolpe, its negotiating position had softened and become more politically saleable in Congress. Wolpe and Solarz were highly informed and brought unusual energy to the battle. And Solarz's strategic position on the Intelligence Committee, along with the strong commitment of Representative William Gray III (D.-Pa.), the House Democratic whip, were very important. But even if conditions had been different and the liberals had lost, the broader lesson of this Angola story is that Congress, under the current process for covert action, is inhibited from playing a meaningful role in a major area of foreign policy.

The attitudes, expectations, and norms with which Congress approaches covert action are only more extreme versions of the culture of deference inhibiting congressional participation in foreign policy making. Here the inclination to give the president the benefit of the doubt in a new and urgent situation hardens into a law enabling the president to undertake major initiatives with only "timely" notification to Congress. Here the reluctance of Congress to press the executive branch for the truth about hidden events, to conduct serious inquiries on its own, and to make and uphold the law is transformed into an almost abject obeisance to the secrets of state. And here a disinterested Congress's susceptibility to narrow-based lobbying interests is enhanced, since the political costs of complying with the lobbies can be displaced to secret decision-making bodies.

5

Transcending the Culture: Congressional Leadership and El Salvador, the Philippines, and South Africa

Precious and few are the moments when Congress is able to systematically consider and decide upon a major foreign policy issue without succumbing to the pleas and promises of the administration or the blandishments of narrow-based interest groups. Three such notable occasions were when:

- Congress pressed the Salvadoran Government to investigate the slayings of six Jesuit priests, their cook, and her daughter, and promoted a negotiated solution to the long civil war in 1989–91;
- Congress insisted that the beseiged Marcos regime in the Philippines embark upon military, economic, and democratic reforms in 1984–86; and
- Congress adopted limited economic sanctions against the white minority government of South Africa in 1985–86 to foster a democratic political solution to its conflict with the black majority.

Moreover, in each case there has been broad, bipartisan recognition that Congress's contribution to American policy was, on balance, useful. With regard to El Salvador and the Philippines, there was even significant cooperation between certain elements of the administration and Congress. Although all of these congressional initiatives were nourished by the Cold War conflict, they were at least partly motivated by such contemporary policy concerns as resolving political conflict, upholding human rights, and fostering economic and other reforms.

Several factors contributed to this congressional activism. Among the most important were changing international conditions, partisan ambitions, interest group pressures, shifts in public opinion influenced by the new power of television coverage of distant events, and the views and miscues of the president. Yet Congress's unconventional behavior cannot simply be reduced to the sum of these outside forces. A key element was *internal*—a willingness to abandon customary approaches to foreign policy. In varying degrees, Congress took steps to develop an independent perspective, make and uphold law, limit the executive's leeway in new and urgent situations, and resist domination by narrow-based lobbies. This recovered will to lead also helped Congress respond to—and expand—the influence of broad-based outside constituencies. In these unusual cases, one can discern the elements of an alternative congressional culture, one of participation and partnership in the making of foreign policy.

EL SALVADOR AGAIN

The cold-blooded murder of the Jesuits at the University of Central America in the early morning of November 16, 1989, shocked and outraged Congress and American public opinion. Legislators from both sides of the aisle wrote the administration that continued aid to the Salvadoran government, now headed by moderate ARENA party rightist Alfredo Cristiani, depended upon its ability to "bring those guilty to justice in order to satisfy the Congress that [the government] has the control over the judicial system and the military."[1] As this message from a moderate Texas Democrat indicated, Congress's reaction was more than a measure of the crime. The murders had crystallized a concern that, after ten years of substantial American assistance, El Salvador had not made the reforms required for a political solution to the war. After all, the army and conservative elite had long "viewed the Jesuits as the intellectual authors of revolution" even though they had supported President Cristiani's new initiative for negotiations with the FMLN guerrillas.[2] That history, together with the circumstances of the crime—a "naked execution in the middle of the capital with the armed forces nearby"[3]—suggested the continued vitality of El Salvador's tradition of right-wing and military violence.

Within days of the killings, the House overwhelmingly passed a resolution declaring that "a satisfactory resolution of this case is a pivotal test of El Salvador's democratic and judicial institutions and will be instrumental in determining continued U.S. support for the Government of El Salvador."[4] In this atmosphere, Tom Foley (D.-Wash.), speaker of the House, appointed a special task force of nineteen Democrats, headed by Representative Joe Moakley of Massachusetts, to "monitor the Salvadoran Government's investigation into that crime and to look into related issues involving respect for human rights and judicial reform in El Salvador."[5]

Over the next two years, Moakley's inquiry and its legislative outgrowth would have a major impact on American policy. William Walker, the U.S. ambassador to El Salvador, commented, "Moakley's activities and reports made us work even harder than we were in pushing the government to resolve the Jesuit case. They gave it a profile. I could invoke his name with President Cristiani."[6] "It is absolutely true," agreed the assistant secretary of state for inter-American affairs, Bernard Aronson, "that the Moakley task force helped focus pressure and attention, and forced the Executive and Cristiani to be more aggressive and vigilant in the processing of the case." Furthermore, Aronson continued, Moakley's and Senator Dodd's success in pushing legislation tying U.S. military aid to the government to *both sides'* performance in peace negotiations and human rights was "helpful and useful" because "the Executive could say to the government, 'If you do the right thing, Congress will aid you. If not, there is nothing we can do to save you'; it also sent a signal to extremists in the FMLN."[7] This is high retrospective praise from the official who led the administration's effort to minimize legislative restrictions. Several factors would contribute to the 1992 Salvadoran peace accord, including mutual exhaustion and recognition of a military stalemate, the democratic replacement of the leftist Sandinista regime in neighboring

Nicaragua and the waning of Communism, and the relatively moderate stances of presidents Cristiani and Bush.[8] But Ambassador Walker later observed, "The Moakley Task Force was a very important player. I think without them the war would have been wound down by now, but I think they shortened the process, made it come out better than it would have otherwise."[9]

Certainly changing international circumstances gave critics of U.S. policy toward El Salvador more political space than they had had in the early 1980s. Yet, as Aronson and Walker recognized, policy change was by no means automatic. In fact, the House's decision to appoint a special task force suggested a lack of confidence in "business as usual" even under new conditions.

Developing an Independent Perspective

The main reason the Moakley effort was so effective was that it adopted an activist style far different from Congress's previous approach to El Salvador policy. The break was in part a conscious one. The initial idea for the Jesuit investigation came from William Woodward, Representative Gerry Studds's (D.-Mass.) staff aide during the earlier controversy. Moved by news reports of the murders, Woodward quickly drew the lessons of his past experience with the Salvadoran cover-up of the churchwomen slayings and the failed Foreign Affairs Committee death squad inquiry. "Congress," he thought, "needed a focus where it could be a conduit of raw information quickly before the Salvadoran and U.S. governments reached the point of agreeing on the same script. And it needed to act at a high level."[10] Woodward's proposal was advanced by Representative Studds at a meeting of the Democratic Caucus's task force on Central America (an unusual party grouping in foreign policy that had been stimulated by the need to coordinate strategy for repeated votes concerning aid to contra insurgents in Nicaragua). "Everybody jumped" to embrace it, a participant recalled, "because it gave them something to tell their constituents."[11] Speaker Foley decided the new special committee would consist solely of Democrats, partly because of custom and partly, it seems, to avoid the "turf fights" and "paralysis" that had afflicted earlier committee decision making on El Salvador and Nicaragua. Republican members and staff did participate in a number of task force visits to El Salvador, however.[12]

The task force quickly mobilized the necessary human resources for its bold inquiry. Foremost among them was Representative Moakley, the chairman of the powerful House Rules Committee. Moakley was inexperienced in foreign policy though he had been a reliable vote against military aid to El Salvador, had known some of the slain priests from his efforts to assist Salvadoran immigrants, and was a strong Roman Catholic. But his very lack of initiation into the dominant congressional foreign policy culture left him with what his veteran staff aide Jim McGovern called "rough edges that were probably appropriate [to the task]." Beneath the "expert politician and consensus-builder," observed McGovern, was "a street-wise tough guy from South Boston."[13] Moakley in turn characterized McGovern as "an analytical mind who was also like a pit bull."[14] Enlisting Woodward for his ideas and experience, Moakley and McGovern also engaged a Salvadoran named Leónel Gomez who would become their principal man on the ground, investigator, and interpreter.[15]

Ambassador Walker considered Gomez "far and away the most unforgettable character I've ever met," and "the best informed, most plugged-in person in the country."[16] In describing his background, Gomez noted that he had descended from "conquistadores, priests, and pirates." His family owned coffee plantations, and the farm he grew up on "covered about 100 city blocks." At first, he led a comfortable "middle-class" life, ornamented by national and regional championships in marksmanship and motorcycling. But when political change came to El Salvador in the 1970s, he organized peasant unions and became chief adviser to the president of the Salvadoran land reform agency. When his boss was assassinated, along with two American labor advisers, after complaining about military and other corruption in the land reform program, Gomez fled to the United States. During the 1980s, Gomez testified at congressional hearings, appealing for support of political negotiations, and worked on Salvadoran and immigration issues.

Gomez returned to his country in 1989 with the help of Ambassador

Walker, with whom he had become friendly during an earlier assign-ment to El Salvador. In fact, he was already advising Walker and living rent-free in the embassy compound when he was recruited by Moak-ley. Gomez brought to the inquiry a rich knowledge of the local scene including diverse contacts developed during his own political evolu-tion. It was he who first introduced Walker to ARENA leader Roberto D'Aubuisson and Vice Minister of Defense Orlando Zepeda. Yet he was also well connected to parts of the FMLN (rebel leader Joaquím Villalobos was a "good friend") and of the Catholic Church. As Gomez later explained, he was not "formally" a member of the left, but "they knew I didn't scare and wouldn't mislead them." As for the right, "it had a love/hate relation with me. It was fragmented. There were people in the Right who deplored the Jesuit killings, thought it had lost the war, or thought corruption would lose the war." One thoughtful observer, Teresa Whitfield, has concluded that Gomez pos-sessed:

> a strange and complicated profile: while sectors of the political cen-ter and left believed he worked for the CIA, others on the right had him down as a member of the FMLN. Still others had appreciated—even as they admitted never being *quite* sure where he was coming from—that the role that Gomez filled as a back-channel bridge builder and conduit of information, was as useful to all concerned as it was unique.[17]

Armed with an ambitious mandate, unusually relevant expertise and experience, and the blessing of the House leadership, the Moakley task force went to work.[18] Beyond a few bipartisan trips to El Salvador, the heart of this unconventional operation lay in the staff work of Woodward, Gomez, and McGovern, supervised by an increasingly knowledgeable Moakley. The group dedicated itself to "knowing the [Jesuit] case" so well it would not end up "being deluged with details." This involved not only consultations with the American Embassy, which had set up its own monitoring team, but also first-hand examination of court documents, and discussions with the Sal-vadoran investigators, judges, and attorney general. It also included contacts with members of the military, other government officials, human rights groups, and witnesses—including some of the accused murderers. At one point, Moakley and McGovern met two junior officers who had been charged with the killings and tried to get them to implicate any higher-ups involved.

At critical moments, Moakley moved aggressively to cope with weak administration cooperation. Upset with the State Department's failure to respond for almost two months to the task force's initial questions about the case, Moakley threatened to exclude a department representative from the first members' trip to El Salvador. The answers soon arrived. At Moakley's insistence, an earlier State Department decision to withhold certain relevant embassy cables from the task force was reversed. When the Defense Department refused to allow the group to interview an American major who had important information concerning a high-level Salvadoran military cover-up, Moakley threatened to issue a Rules Committee subpoena. The Pentagon quickly proposed arrangements for access to the major "in lieu of proceedings before the Rules Committee in furtherance of a resolution to subpoena Major Buckland." Previously, while Moakley was visiting El Salvador, the administration had denied his request to see the major's affadavit. McGovern described (and Moakley confirmed) what followed:

> Moakley said to me, "Let's go." We got in a cab and went to see Lt. Col. [Manuel] Rivas at the Special Investigating Unit. Moakley said to him, "I'm sorry we chewed you out yesterday. Don't listen to what some of the congressmen said. You're doing a good job." Rivas started smiling. Then Moakley said, "You know that affadavit we discussed? I left it in the hotel room. I wanted to ask you some questions about it. Do you have a copy?" Rivas went and got the document. Then Moakley said, "Oh no, I don't have my reading glasses with me. Could you make me a Xerox?" When we returned to the embassy, Moakley went up to the ambassador with the affadavit, saying "Hey Bill, —— you."

The task force's public report of April 1990 discussed substantially the same unresolved questions about the murders that had occurred to the U.S. Embassy. Both agreed that, after a good start, the investigation

had failed to build a strong case against detained Colonel Alfredo
Benavides, whose subordinates had confessed to the murders, or to
address allegations that Benavides was part of a conspiracy that was
being covered up by the military. The congressional report also contained perspectives that did not appear in State Department cable traffic. Most important, it emphasized the possibility of high-level
involvement in the slayings. It did this mainly by reflecting upon the
importance of the crimes, what was known of Colonel Benavides's
character, the military's history of hostility toward the Jesuits, the overt-
ness of the murders, and the failure of individuals within the military to
come forward with information. It also gave credence to the American
major's testimony that a Salvadoran colonel told him that Benavides
had acknowledged his role and received protection from military superiors early in the investigation. The task force also stated, "The murders
of the Jesuits reflect problems within the Salvadoran armed forces that
go far beyond the actions of a particular unit on a particular night."
The institution itself was said to breed and protect human rights violations and to foster judicial paralysis. This cast doubt on the embassy's
expressed "hope" to "elicit a commitment [from the military] to work
together and pursue a vigorous investigation." Finally, the report
observed that the growing opportunity for a peaceful settlement [the
government had just agreed to U.N.-mediated talks with the FMLN]
could have "a profoundly positive effect on some of the problems discussed."[19]

By August, the State Department was at least internally prepared to
accept a follow-up Moakley press statement charging the Armed Forces
High Command with "engaging in a conspiracy to obstruct justice in the
Jesuits' case."[20] Then a private task force briefing provoked a dramatic
cable from Ambassador Walker revealing "what could be breakthrough
information." The task force's investigation had ineluctably progressed
from documenting the cover-up to penetrating it. As Gomez later
recalled,

> It was like going to Harlem to investigate crack. You needed to
> know the streets. I had to convince sources to tell the truth, to go to
> people who knew and ask: There was no way in El Salvador you

could say you don't know. This was a smaller country than Nazi Germany. Lots of people went to the same school, were related. . . . Think in terms of the ghetto. Seventy percent of the people were illiterate but the elites never changed.[21]

The essence of what Gomez discovered and told Ambassador Walker was strongly supported two years later by the finding of the Commission on the Truth that there was "substantial [that is, 'very solid'] evidence" that Armed Forces Chief of Staff Colonel René Ponce, in the presence of other members of the high command, gave Colonel Benavides "the order to kill Father Ignacio Ellacuría and to leave no witnesses," and that "all these officers and others, knowing what happened, took steps to conceal the truth."[22] As State Department documents indicated, Gomez had acquired his information from Colonel Carlos Rivas, "one of . . . the most senior and respected officers," who consulted "a multitude of subsources, the majority of whom are students at the command and general staff college" which Colonel Benavides headed at the time of the murders. Ambassador Walker was "not so certain" of the story due to reservations about "one or more" of the sources' possible political motivations, but allowed that "If [the] basic story is true, or if Congress believes it to be, our policy is at peril."[23]

From the beginning, the task force's recognized influence on U.S. and Salvadoran pursuit of the Jesuit investigation stemmed from its embodiment of a congressional threat to cut aid.[24] Now its information so heightened this danger that Walker, "to follow up on the allegations," proposed a quiet, temporary suspension of military assistance to coerce the military into "demonstrating that the institution is at last committed to surrendering the perpetrators of the crime to do justice." The State Department approved his suggested demarche, and Walker began his conversation with President Cristiani by referring to Moakley's critique of the military's "conspiracy to obstruct justice."[25]

Moakley did not go public with Gomez's finding until November 1991, when further corroboration had become available and the Salvadoran government had shown that it would search no higher than Colonel Benavides. Detailing the evidence provided by a few confidential sources, Moakley said it was "very possible" that "senior officers other than Colonel Benavides ordered the murders," adding, "I personally find this view of events more credible than the alternative which is that Colonel Benavides acted on his own, notwithstanding the chain of command, and took upon himself the awesome responsibility for these crimes."[26] The American Embassy, which had received a number of separate CIA and other reports of higher officers' complicity, reacted with customary caution, "We find Congressman Moakley's formulation of how the Jesuit murders were planned plausible but not proven."[27] Later, Ambassador Walker acknowledged, with refreshing candor, some of the restrictions on the embassy:

> We were trying to figure out what happened. Yet there were hurdles for the embassy to jump to push all out. . . . The U.S. ambassador can't stand up and say, "I think X did it" absent iron-clad certainty. [Also] there was a point where there was a conflict between the search for the culpable and [working with the government toward] a peace agreement. [Then] we were tied up with the military and wanted to look the other way. Well, not that, but there were times when I lent credence to what someone in the El Salvador government said, when I assumed the president wanted to get to the bottom of it. . . . Moakley didn't pay attention to the hurdles. He had more latitude.[28]

Making and Upholding the Law

In November 1990 Congress enacted legislation making military assistance to the government conditional on its "thorough and effective" investigation and prosecution of the Jesuit case, as well as both the government's *and* FMLN's respect for human rights and pursuit of peace. Half of the requested aid would be initially withheld, but it could be restored or cut off depending on both sides' performance. This imaginative attempt to use American aid to the government as leverage on both sides of the conflict was first proposed by Senator Dodd (D.-Conn.), but gained decisive impetus from early House approval.[29]

Moakley led the fight on the House floor, employing his task force's distinctive arguments that the Jesuit murders stemmed "from attitudes and actions that go to the very heart of the armed forces and other major institutions," and that a negotiated peace could bring about real military and judicial reform. He also helped mobilize church, liberal, and human rights groups behind his relatively moderate legislative approach to military aid. (The size of the broader Salvador "peace" constituency was unclear, although participants noted that it became larger and more Catholic following the Jesuit murders. Moakley observed that his position was still probably "not a political plus" in his own working-class Catholic district. Woodward pointed out, however, that the constituency, "though not high in numbers" relative to domestic issues, generated significant mail, was "relatively determined" and could convince many Democrats they would "pay a price" for straying on the issue.) Moakley's position as chairman of the committee that establishes the procedures for consideration of all legislation gave him unusual weight with his colleagues. "It wouldn't have happened," he said of his victory, "if I wasn't chairman of the Rules Committee."[30]

Another key figure "who proved critical in reaching members outside liberal circles" was Representative John Murtha (D.-Pa.).[31] Murtha was relatively conservative in foreign affairs, had visited El Salvador, and supported President Reagan's policy there. But his involvement in the task force carried him toward a new legislative role. "Joe Moakley will tell you," he informed the House, "I sat in his investigation and I said before it became public there was no question in my mind it was the military that perpetrated the killing. . . . We are trying to say to El Salvador, 'Reform your military; reform your judicial system.'"[32] Already, in early 1990, he was warning the Salvadoran military that "continued stonewalling on the case" would translate into cuts in military assistance.[33] According to Moakley, Woodward, and McGovern, Murtha's cooperation grew out of both the investigation and his personal relationship with Moakley. Murtha also had considerable clout as chairman of the important Defense Appropriations Subcommittee. McGovern was nearby when a member approached Murtha to impatiently inquire when the debate would close. "I close military bases," Murtha responded. "How are you on my amendment?"[34]

Moakley's assertiveness also did much to power an unusual congressional preoccupation with the implementation of the law. Soon after the "Moakley-Murtha Amendment" was enacted, the president determined he could restore the 50 percent of military aid initially withheld from the government because the FMLN had violated congressional conditions by receiving significant lethal equipment from abroad and directing violence at civilians.[35] "Throwing a bone" to its congressional critics, the White House delayed releasing the aid for another sixty days to further the peace negotiations. Moakley and Dodd promptly and publicly denounced what they considered a flouting of congressional intent:

> Moakley condemned the restoration of aid as "unbalanced" and "ill-timed" and said it was based on a "selective use of the facts" to punish the FMLN while the Salvadoran military stonewalled on the Jesuit case. Dodd decried the decision as "unwarranted and dangerous," sending the "wrong signal" about U.S. insistence on a negotiated solution and resolution of the Jesuit murders.[36]

Days before, Murtha had journeyed to El Salvador with the latest task force report to reinforce the legislation's message that the armed forces' "cooperation with the Jesuit investigation was of paramount importance."[37] As the sixty-day waiting period expired in March 1991, 116 representatives and 34 senators wrote President Bush requesting that aid continue to be withheld.[38] "In an effort to ensure the concurrence of Congress," Bush did not release any funds until late June.[39] So persistent congressional enforcement efforts delayed assistance for nearly six months, keeping the intended pressure on the government. In March, when the Salvadoran military invited the minister of justice to expand the Jesuit investigation, a U.S. Embassy cable commented, "It appears that worries about future military funding and pressure from domestic and international groups have had their effect."[40]

Even after aid was restored, Moakley and Dodd advanced the intent of the law. The former visited El Salvador in July, giving a speech at the University of Central America that lambasted the military's performance in the Jesuit case and put forth a plea for peace.[41] He also spoke to President Cristiani and, overcoming State Department objections, traveled with Walker to the town of Santa Marta in FMLN-controlled territory.[42] According to Cynthia Arnson, a key FMLN commander later told Moakley that his trip, and a subsequent official visit that included Senate Foreign Relations Committee staffer Richard McCall, were "turning points for the FMLN, signaling a new U.S. willingness to treat the rebels as legitimate participants in Salvadoran political life." Furthermore, "In a stroke of what may have been only dumb luck, the trips . . . did coincide with major progress in the peace talks."[43] When a Salvadoran jury convicted only Colonel Benavides and a lieutenant of the Jesuit murders, and acquitted seven other confessed killers, Moakley denounced the verdict and gave the world his evidence of high command involvement. Meanwhile, in the Senate, Dodd pursued legislation to guarantee a congressional role in the release of military aid for the following year. The administration was only able to stave him off by supporting a Senate filibuster—unlimited debate that can allow a determined minority to talk a bill to death.[44]

Mobilizing the Executive

It is easier for an assertive Congress to succeed if it can enlist some cooperation from at least part of the executive branch. This was particularly important for the more shadowy aspects of the Jesuit investigation. Fortunately for the congressional activists, key State Department officials considered the Jesuit case a crucial test of America's policy of seeking a democratic political solution. As Walker explained, "Despite the progress made, I felt personally and philosophically that until the justice system showed it could produce justice, we couldn't claim it was a working democracy. . . . For example, the opposition could be cheated in an election and pick up the gun."[45] In addition, Assistant Secretary Aronson had given early encouragement to political dialogue between the government and FMLN, indicating that the Bush administration would be less ideological than its predecessor.[46]

Perhaps the best illustration of the degree of cooperation that developed was Leónel Gomez's working for the Moakley Task Force and the State Department at the same time! The latter benefited from his broad political contacts, acquaintance with many of the official and church figures in the Jesuit case, and credibility with elements of the FMLN as negotiations got under way. On the other hand, the embassy greatly facilitated Gomez's work for the task force. Everyone concerned knew that Gomez's personal relationship to Ambassador Walker was critical to his personal safety. It also reassured his most sensitive sources that "someone in the embassy was acting in good faith" even if they distrusted the "embassy system" (particularly its intelligence components)—distrusted it enough to speak directly only to Gomez and his colleagues. The task force also felt that Walker "gave [them] leeway" for such bold Moakley initiatives as meeting with two of the confessed murderers at the police station after a family mass, and journeying to Santa Marta.[47]

At the same time there was tension in the legislative-executive relationship. It was mainly a matter of the "hurdles" Ambassador Walker discussed, the differences in official position and political perspective that still separated the two branches. For example, Walker cabled Washington in August 1990 concerning the Jesuit case, "I do not want the El Salvador Armed Forces to get away with this. . . . I do not want [it] to think it can trade this issue away or wait us out as it has in past cases."[48] But in November, the frustrated embassy resignedly began to explore a potential "bargain" with the military. Acknowledging two "possible" military cover-ups—that the high command either "ordered the murder" or "hindered the investigation"—the embassy now suggested that the United States "not . . . pursue the . . . allegations of cover-up" but "instead acknowledge the successful elements of the Jesuit investigation," mainly the evidence against Colonel Benavides and his lower-level "shooters." The rationale for the recommended switch was that the government and military "resent the Embassy insistence on a 'complete investigation'"[49] Although this suggestion was soon discarded, it indicated the continuing distance between the task force and even its most sympathetic State Department contacts.

Nevertheless, the uneasy partnership that did emerge helped the congressional critics make their case and push American policy further than the State Department would have wished. As partial recompense, the department could invoke congressional pressures in coping with the Pentagon's greater reluctance to press the Salvadoran military too hard. Moreover, as the peace negotiations advanced, Assistant Secretary Aronson found that the Moakley forces had developed enough trust to give him a few months' "running room" to achieve a peace accord before Congress again cut aid.[50]

PRESSURING THE PHILIPPINES

On Sunday, February 23, 1986, shortly after 9:00 A.M., the top U.S. officials concerned with the Philippines gathered at the home of Secretary of State Shultz. There they drew the implications for U.S. policy of a political drama that was mesmerizing the world. President Ferdinand Marcos, America's longtime authoritarian ally and guardian of its most important Asian military bases, had apparently been defeated by Corazon Aquino in an election marred by widely televised official fraud. And while Marcos was claiming victory, his defense minister and military chief were leading a mutiny that was attracting growing popular support. As the men in Shultz's living room moved toward their conclusion that "Marcos could no longer govern and the more quickly he left office the better," Secretary of Defense Caspar Weinberger had a caveat: "Our liberal establishment turned away from the Shah [of Iran] but did not consider the alternative. So the question is not how we get Marcos to live with Solarz, but what happens in the Philippines."[51] With this curious reference to the chairman of the House Subcommittee on Asian and Pacific Affairs, Weinberger highlighted something most of his colleagues already appreciated: the significant role Congress was playing in the unfolding of Philippines policy.

Congress's involvement had grown along with the political crisis in the country. The 1983 assassination of opposition leader Benigno Aquino (the husband of "Cory")—under military "escort" after returning from America—had galvanized urban political opposition and precipitated a sudden capital flight. Meanwhile, the Communist-dominated New People's Army (NPA, popularly dubbed "Nice People Around" in tribute to its sophisticated approach to the peasantry) had been gaining ground fast enough to "threaten the central government's stability" within three to five years.[52] Beneath these developments lay the deep corruption of the Marcos regime: its greed, its obsession with political loyalty, and its lack of accountability. A final complication was the dictator's failing health. "The political and economic life of the Philippines," observed the departing American ambassador, Michael Armacost, in April 1984, "is in a deep trough from which there appears no swift or easy escape."[53]

The administration's response was based on the assumption that "While President Marcos at this stage is part of the problem, he is also necessarily part of the solution." The U.S. set about working with "the Philippine Government and moderate elements of Philippine society" to forward a three-part reform agenda:

1. "revitalization of democratic institutions in order to assure . . . a smooth transition when President Marcos does pass from the scene;"
2. "exposing the economy . . . to the interplay of free market forces;" and
3. "restoring professional, apolitical leadership to the Philippine military."

The basic strategy was to employ public and private "dialogue" in conjunction with the "incentives" of increased military and economic assistance. Although most U.S. policymakers gradually realized that Marcos would not cooperate, the administration never formally contemplated stiff sanctions. At most, they considered chastising Marcos through delays in projected "new assistance." No one wanted to fool with the existing five-year package of $900 million in military and economic "security assistance." That was "rent" for U.S. bases.[54]

It was Congress that supplied the "sticks" that strengthened the credibility of the administration's reformist stance. These included reductions in the military proportion of American aid, threats of further cuts, and high-profile criticism of Marcos's political behavior. As in El Salvador, congressional activists forged a relationship with key officials who, though disagreeing with certain tactics, were prepared to at least threaten the Philippine regime. In fact, there was enough analytical consensus between legislators and friendly officials for the administration to put aside some of its usual guardedness. "It is no secret," Under Secretary of State Michael Armacost awkwardly noted as the crisis reached its denouement, that "we have testified with some candor on the Hill now for over one year. We have not tried to conceal the assumptions of policy."[55]

Congress's impact on U.S. diplomacy was subsequently hailed by President Aquino, who told a joint session of the House and Senate, "Many of you here today played a part in changing the policy of your country toward us. We Filipinos thank you for what you did."[56] "There was quite a bit of congressional influence," recalls Gaston Sigur, a member of the National Security Council staff who followed the Philippines for the White House.[57] "Congress was important," agrees Richard Armitage, assistant secretary of defense for international affairs. "I think it's one thing for Congress to raise hell and another for the administration to do it. We used the Congress."[58] His close colleague Paul Wolfowitz, assistant secretary of state for East Asian affairs, elaborated, "It was frequently part of a good cop, bad cop act, making our position more credible to Marcos by threatening him 'If you don't do this, Congress will do that.'"[59] Furthermore, congressional interest and pressure reinforced the position of the "good cops" within the administration. President Reagan, Secretary Weinberger, and others were reluctant to pressure Marcos because he "had been an ally for many years."[60] Stephen Bosworth, the American ambassador to the Philippines, thinks that "it might have been more difficult to open up distance from Marcos under President Reagan if Congress was not involved."[61] Similarly, Armitage believes that without Congress "the administration would have taken a longer time to arrive at its ultimate position."[62] As in El Salvador, many U.S. officials credit Congress for assisting a relatively peaceful democratic transition that also reduced the Communist military threat. "If there were no congressional involvement," says Armitage, "it would have been bloodier, the change less quick."[63]

Developing an Independent Perspective

In contrast with the ad hoc Moakley initiative, unusual attention from key bipartisan leaders of the House Foreign Affairs and Senate Foreign Relations Committees largely accounted for this congressional success. Representative Stephen Solarz (D.-N.Y.) and his subcommittee had the most sustained involvement. As a new member of the Foreign Affairs panel, Solarz visited the Philippines in 1975, returning twice before assuming the chairmanship of the Asian Subcommittee in 1981. American ambassadors who hosted these and subsequent visits rhapsodized over their "energy and seriousness of purpose."[64] During his trips, Solarz broadened his knowledge by meeting with a variety of government as well as opposition, independent, and international figures, and by traveling to outlying areas. His main technique, familiar to me from his previous stint as chairman of the Africa Subcommittee, was to patiently pursue, in depth, a few key questions and to try out prospective U.S. policies on his interlocutors. Solarz also dispatched his capable staff director, Stanley Roth, to the islands about twice a year during the crisis. At home, Solarz held hearings every year on the Philippines, summoning not only administration officials but former U.S. policymakers, academic experts, and members of the Filipino opposition as well. Informally, he hosted meetings with representatives of the U.S. intelligence community and with traveling Filipinos. And he wrote op-ed and other pieces to publicize his views.[65]

A strong human rights liberal, Solarz began his long-running seminar with the belief that the United States "ought to make it clear that it was unhappy with the continuation of martial law and the desecration of democracy" lest it "pay a very heavy long-term price . . . in our relationship with the Filipino people." Discovering, however, that there was "possibly some justification" for martial law in the "anarchic conditions" of the country, and encountering a "weak and divided" opposition, Solarz at first wondered whether "we actually had the ability . . . to facilitate . . . the re-establishment of democracy." But he gradually became convinced that Marcos "had lost the confidence of the people," and that his justifications for authoritarianism were "puerile rationalizations."[66] With the rise of democratic and Communist-led opposition movements, and their potential threat to American base rights, Solarz persuaded fellow Democrats and moderate Republicans on the Foreign Affairs Committee to "signal" Marcos and the Filipino people that the United States desired fundamental reforms. Hence, in 1984 and 1985 the House voted to reduce the proportion of military assistance in the annual aid package (to go further and reduce *total* aid was politically unfeasible because it seemed to violate the understanding in the base agreement).[67]

In 1984, the Senate Foreign Relations Committee endorsed a more moderate proportional cut, but its foreign aid bill died in committee. Meanwhile, Fred Brown, a former Foreign Service officer with extensive experience concerning Southeast Asia, rural revolution, and Communist affairs, had joined the committee's Republican staff and had begun "looking for an issue." After chatting with colleagues, he and a Democratic aide (Carl Ford, an ex–CIA analyst) decided to visit the Philippines. They spent about three weeks there in May and June, writing a report that Ambassador Bosworth later described as a "time bomb in the Senate." According to Brown, their first meeting with the U.S. Embassy staff was "a totally whitewash briefing: There's no problem here. The NPA is weak, the opposition fractured. Marcos is in control." With some help from more critical members of the embassy, Brown and Ford conducted an extensive investigation and arrived at very different conclusions.[68] Their itinerary is worth quoting as an illustration of the kind of effort required for meaningful congressional participation in foreign policy:

> We traveled to 18 of the country's 73 provinces, spending 10 days outside Metropolitan Manila. Cebu and Devao, the second and third largest cities, were also visited.
>
> Over a 19-day period, we talked with cabinet and subcabinet-level officers, provincial governors and service chiefs, mayors, *barangay* (village) personnel, and officials in the ministries of the central government. We were briefed by military officers in 5 of the country's 12 Regional Unified Commands (RUC) as well as individual field commanders at the batallion and brigade level. We had meetings with the Commission on Elections (COMELEC), the National Citizens Movement for Free Elections (NAMFREL) and

politicians of both the government party and the opposition, including a dozen national assemblymen. . . .

We met with a number of Catholic priests and educators in Manila and elsewhere, and [with] Jaime Cardinal Sin, the senior Catholic Church figure in the Philippines. We also talked with several Protestant missionaries working in the *barangays*. Finally we had the chance to meet with a broad range of private citizens—political figures, businessmen, university professors and students, lawyers, think-tank staffers, and journalists.[69]

The Brown-Ford report was a wake-up call for American policy, filled with such troubling statements as these:

The country's leadership is virtually bankrupt in terms of public confidence. . . . There is a general perception that the leadership, their families and business associates have made billions of dollars out of the Philippine economy, sent much of it permanently outside the country, and ruined the economy in the process through mismanagement. . . . A disciplined, purposeful Communist insurgency . . . has become a major threat to Philippine democracy.[70]

By the time the report appeared, the administration was also increasingly concerned with the situation. Embassy officials even commented on the authors' drafts.[71] But the most important consequence of the Brown-Ford mission was to draw the incoming chairman of the Foreign Relations Committee, Senator Richard Lugar (D.-Ind.), deeply into American policy making. Frustrated by a lack of interest on the part of the head of the Senate Asian Subcommittee, Brown helped persuade Lugar to take on the Philippines as a "chairman's issue." Lugar subsequently characterized Brown's contribution to the committee's work on the Philippines as "enormous."[72]

The new chairman, described by former staff members as "smart" and "a voracious acquirer of knowledge,"[73] wanted to reorient the panel into "an activist committee that is going to be the focal point of foreign policy considerations in the Senate."[74] But unlike Solarz, Lugar was a a conservative Republican who also looked forward to working with the administration because "I share the basic assumptions of the President and Secretary of State in regards to foreign policy."[75] Lugar at first avoided a potential conflict between what he was finding out about the situation in the Philippines and what the administration was doing there when key "good cops" in the State and Defense departments used the committee as a theater to toughen up official policy. In public testimony, assistant secretaries Wolfowitz and Armitage outlined the need for reforms, praised the Brown-Ford staff report, and used the unwanted House military aid cuts as an excuse to threaten, "We are not prepared to simply go forward with this [aid] in the absence of a continuation of military reform."[76] Assuring his committee that the administration had "on balance" been "remarkably adept" at furthering democratic institutions, Lugar initially got the Senate to sustain military aid to "encourage the reform elements in the armed forces."[77]

But as 1985 wore on, it was increasingly apparent that the administration's policy was not working. After spending two additional weeks in the Philippines in August, Brown carried back the "overall impression . . . that the political and insurgency situation has deteriorated further. The prospects for the near term (two years) are not good." Marcos "has not gotten the U.S. message about the urgent need for reform."[78] During an October committee hearing, Wolfowitz worried that "time is of the essence . . . and time is not being used very well."[79] Lugar, who was also hearing from American businessmen about Marcos's health problems, preoccupation with "personal business deals," and "crony capitalism,"[80] became impatient with the administration. "I gather," he sniffed, "our current policy is one of sort of keeping things afloat, hoping that maybe some fortuitious circumstances may intervene to sort of save us from what apparently is a long-range trend." "Where are the leverages in the situation?" he wondered, warning Wolfowitz that if Marcos remained obtuse, "the sort of debate we will be having next year on economic or military assistance would be a very different one." Other members of the committee, especially Senator John Kerry (D.-Mass.), expressed similar concerns.[81]

By this time, Manila had ample evidence that the congressional "bad cop" was actually moving U.S. policy. In its 1984 appropriations, Congress cut nearly half of the administration's military aid request, transferring the funds to economic assistance. In 1985 the administration fought harder for the money,[82] but a House-Senate compromise provided only $70 million of the requested $100 million.[83] And now Lugar was publicly querying Wolfowitz, "What argument [for increased aid] do I use next year?"[84] Although total security assistance to the Philippines had not yet changed, the slashes in aid to the repressive apparatus were, in Ambassador Bosworth's words, "symbolically important." A struggling Marcos "wanted the blessing of the U.S."[85] His anxiety had undoubtedly been intensified by other congressional actions that encouraged his opposition: Solarz's flying in from Thailand to offer the Aquino family his condolences after the assassination,[86] the issuance of critical staff reports that were well publicized in the Philippines, and negative judgments at public hearings. Washington's views had a strong psychological and political resonance in America's only former colony.[87] A good illustration of the importance Filipino politicians attached to congressional opinion was Marcos's and his wife's willingness to spend time with Brown during his 1985 visit. "It boggles my mind," he remarked, "that they'd give seven hours to a lowly staffer."[88]

In mid-October, the administration dispatched Senator Paul Laxalt (R.-Nev.), a friend of the president, to convince Marcos that Reagan fully backed reform. It is widely believed that the Laxalt mission ratcheted up reform pressures on Marcos, which he tried to "deflect" in November by announcing an early presidential election on American TV. Marcos hoped to catch the opposition off guard and arm himself with a new legitimacy. It also appears that Laxalt, acting on his own, encouraged the "snap" election, quite possibly at the suggestion of CIA director Casey.[89] The election, however, was to result in Marcos's downfall.

Significantly, the specter of a congressional sword of Damocles hanging over the Philippines was a prominent feature of the Laxalt-Marcos discussions. This "good cop–bad cop" ploy was hardly surprising given President Reagan's reluctance to threaten traditional U.S. allies. A State Department draft of "Themes for Meeting of President's Envoy with President Marcos" had stressed that the administration's "deep concern" was "shared as well by the Congress in broad bipartisan fashion." In fact, considerable emphasis was placed on the administration's difficulty in obtaining sufficient military aid:

Congressional agreement to authorize the military assistance . . . for FY 1986 was achieved only by an all out Administration effort. . . . Absent . . . demonstrable progress on military reform, we are convinced that even that level of effort will not again be successful.[90]

Ambassador Bosworth, who accompanied Laxalt to his two meetings with Marcos, recalls, "His prime message was that if there was not some progress in these areas, my president would lose control of the relationship. He pointed to what had happened with South Africa due to Congress and public opinion."[91] At the time, Laxalt said he told Marcos that reinstatement of suspected Aquino assassination plotter General Fabian Ver as armed forces chief "would cause the Congress to react and react violently."[92] Reviewing his meetings and subsequent phone conversations with Marcos, Laxalt says,

I told President Marcos on more than one occasion that U.S. financial aid for the Philippines was in jeopardy unless appropriate reforms were undertaken. This was not intended as a threat, but rather a statement of political reality based on discussions with several of my colleagues on Capitol Hill.[93]

Marcos, he noted, understood "how Congress fits into the equation," and "the limitations of our Presidency."[94]

Assessing the impact of the Laxalt mission, the American Embassy concluded that, facing a "perilous" economy and a "decaying" political and military situation, Marcos "knows that he must more than ever depend on his relationship with us for critical economic and military assistance and political support." After two years of holding American reformers "at bay," he had "no trouble discerning the impact of Laxalt's visit." "Consummate political manipulator that [Marcos] is," he undertook a "pre-emptive strike on U.S. policy" to confront the United States with the "'fact' of a fresh popular mandate."[95]

Making and Upholding the Law

Congress's impact on U.S. policy and the Philippines flowed in part from its determination to legislate. As usual, there was no foreign aid authorization bill in 1984, but Solarz had used his informal influence with the House Foreign Operations Subcommittee to achieve a major reduction in military aid in the foreign aid appropriation.[96] There *was* a foreign aid authorization in 1985, largely due to Lugar's drive to build sufficient consensus to revive his flagging committee.[97] This permitted Congress to methodically determine aid levels and relate them to overall policies.

Even more surprising was Congress's atypical willingness to follow through and uphold the intent and spirit of the law. The aid bill included a provision originated by Senator Kerry linking future U.S. aid to "the revitalization of democracy." Emphasis was placed on the government's guaranteeing "free, fair and honest elections."[98] Just days after the announcement of the "snap election," Congress passed a resolution reiterating the link between democracy and aid and setting forth specific criteria for an honest election, including an independent Elections Commission and a citizens' election monitoring organization, opposition access to the media, and a neutral military. The resolution (and a subsequent letter to Marcos drafted by Solarz and Lugar)[99] reinforced like-minded State Department initiatives. "If Marcos [went] ahead with election fraud," Wolfowitz feared, the United States "would be facing a disaster"—"a real collapse of political confidence," further economic decline, and the growth of Communist-led insurgency.[100]

Congress also took the lead in the official U.S. mission to observe the elections. The notion of congressional election observers had figured in Laxalt's discussions with Marcos.[101] It appealed to the State Department as another means of keeping Marcos honest.[102] But Lugar, along with other key members, was apprehensive about "associating ourselves with a spurious election."[103] So, with Democratic support, he took an intermediate step. The Committee commissioned the Washington-based Center for Democracy to take a bipartisan group of U.S. elections experts to the Philippines and report on preparations for a free vote.[104] Following two committee hearings on the subject and a last-minute negotiation with the visiting Philippine foreign minister, Lugar concluded that, despite "serious reservations," he should observe the election. After all, "the Senate had already gone far down the road in support of the democratic process," and it was important to "show our interest and kinship with the Filipino people."[105]

Shortly, President Reagan appointed Lugar and Representative Murtha to co-chair the official U.S. public and private observer delegation. Of the nine members of Congress who went, seven were relatively conservative in foreign policy, though Lugar's liberal colleague, Kerry, was also aboard.[106] Solarz declined to participate, fearing Congress might legitimate a flawed process or that his history of opposition to Marcos would diminish the credibility of any criticisms. But he gave Murtha a long predeparture briefing, cautioning him not to come to a judgment too quickly.[107]

Lugar and his staff took special precautions against the possible attenuation of their effort by a White House reluctant to confront Marcos. The senator preempted his president by publicly declaring his willingness to go to the Philippines even before Reagan accepted the official invitation to send observers. This helped ensure Lugar's leading role. Upon accepting the co-chairmanship of the mission, Lugar used his careful preparatory work to send Reagan a letter to "pin down the framework" for a free election, including a "quick count" by citizen monitors to forestall delays to manipulate the tabulation, and free access by the observers and media to polling areas, tabulation centers, and election headquarters. As the trip got under way, Lugar succeeded in diluting a proposal by White House counsel Fred Fielding, a delegation member, to cut short the planned observations and possibly leave a day or so early for security reasons. (Had the group departed, it would have missed the dramatic walkout of official election workers, who abandoned their computers charging the government with manipulating the results. This turned out to be the smoking gun of Marcos's attempted fraud).[108]

The observers' interim conclusions would help speed America's disengagement from the Marcos regime. Initial White House statements about the election results seemed to suggest that Aquino should find a peaceful way to work with Marcos, who was claiming victory. There was little mention of fraud and of those who might be responsible.[109] Pressed by a very concerned secretary of state, Lugar quickly returned to explain personally to President Reagan that Marcos was "cooking the results."[110] Similar information had arrived from the American Embassy,[111] but Reagan was resistant, preferring to believe, as he told a press conference, that "fraud could be occurring on both sides."[112] Still, the White House desisted from further homilies about the triumph of the two-party system in the Philippines and agreed to Shultz's recommendation to send presidential troubleshooter Philip Habib to Manila to assess the situation.[113] Soon the president, referring to the observer delegation, admitted, "The elections were marred by widespread fraud and violence perpetrated by the ruling party."[114] Key State Department officials attribute the turnaround to their provision of "nuggets of raw intelligence," including "direct evidence of Marcos' personal involvement in manipulating the elections."[115] It is likely, however, that Lugar's report and subsequent public statements also had a strong impact. NSC staffer Sigur, who attended Lugar's briefing of the president and consulted with the latter on his turn-around statement, says, "Congressional attitudes did affect him. It was not just intelligence. He had a lot of respect for Dick Lugar."[116] Philip Habib thought Lugar's report was one of the "decisive factors" influencing the president.[117] Lugar himself believes that if there had been no congressional observer report, "the President would have had no reason whatever to send Habib, think about another statement, and repudiate Marcos."[118]

More fundamentally, the observer mission helped alter the whole political context underpinning U.S.-Philippine relations. Through an unprecedented 180 minutes of network television news coverage over four weeks, Americans had been directly exposed to official fraud and violence, an obviously lying Marcos, and a saintly-seeming Cory Aquino. It was, as Stanley Karnow later commented, "a morality play in an Americanized setting with the principal characters speaking English."[119] A congressional foreign policy issue that had previously been an "inside-the-Beltway affair" generating only about a hundred letters a year to Solarz's office suddenly produced a relative flood of mail and public interest.[120] One should not exaggerate the size or solidity of this unorganized and transitory constituency. Lugar recalls "getting quite a reality dose" when he returned to Indiana to find most of his constituents "hard pressed to see why I'd gone to the Philippines and done what I was doing." Nevertheless, for both their congressional colleagues and an emerging broad-based constituency, the observers' report gave a middle American stamp of credibility to the images on the tube. (Laxalt remarked, "Dick [Lugar] has a great deal of credibility and when he said that fraud was present . . . Marcos's assertions that he had won fair and square fell on deaf ears in the United States.")[121]

Just as important, Lugar's media blitz, including weekly appearances on nearly all the Sunday public affairs programs, defined an appealing political agenda: Marcos's resignation, to be encouraged by withdrawal of U.S. security assistance.[122] On February 19, the Senate rejected the election as fraudulent. The next day, after supportive testimony from Lugar and Murtha, Solarz's subcommittee unanimously decided—over objections from the administration—to place U.S. security aid "in escrow" pending the establishment of a "legitimate government."[123] Thus, even before Marcos's generals finally revolted, precipitating President Reagan's fateful decision to "facilitate a peaceful transition [from Marcos]," Congress was hemming in the president's options.[124]

Withdrawing Executive Leeway

Certainly the new and urgent situation in the Philippines in the third week of February was the kind in which the executive branch has almost always been able to obtain "the benefit of the doubt" from Congress. In the Philippines, two individuals were claiming to be president; the military was reportedly restive; society was rapidly polarizing; and a special presidential envoy had not yet returned. There was a Communist-led insurgency and American bases were at stake. Yet, as a result of their intense involvement, the key congressional actors felt confident enough to reject the administration's plea that they not move to cut off aid. As Solarz related,

> I remember Wolfowitz and Armitage came to see me. They had heard I was going to take this step. They pleaded with me not to do it, basically arguing that the Communists could be at the gates of Manila if we cut military aid off. Morale would collapse. There would be shortages. My response was that Marcos was the number one recruiting agent

for the NPA, especially after stealing the election, and the only hope was to get him out. By acting we could facilitate his departure.[125]

Resisting "Special Interests"

When leading members of Congress are well-informed and active, and broader-based constituencies begin to develop, narrow-based interests lose much of their clout. During his occasional freelance discussions with Marcos, Laxalt had urged him "to get his message across to the American people through an effective public relations effort."[126] Shortly after this, the Chamber of Philippine Manufacturers, Exporters, and Tourism Associations signed a $950,000 one-year contract with Black, Manafort, Stone and Kelly. Manafort described the Chamber as including "a number of businessmen close to Marcos." BMSK quickly became preoccupied with "making sure there were no problems for business in the political atmosphere." This meant counseling "members of the Marcos Administration with respect to press and media strategies," and assisting them to "make contacts with the press and media, the U.S. Congress and the Executive Branch, with respect to the upcoming presidential election." It also meant monitoring Solarz's aggressive investigation (including subpoenas and contempt citations) into credible press reports of the Marcos's hidden wealth in Manhattan real estate, an investigation that contributed to the further delegitimation of Marcos in his own country. To help Marcos prepare a "credible election," BMSK encouraged the Center for Democracy to get involved in elaborating the necessary conditions (Manafort was a member of the board and Kelly was chairman).[127] Ironically, the center's more significant relationship with the Senate Foreign Relations Committee wound up contributing to the discrediting of BMSK's client!

In this case, BMSK was marketing a product whose image had been tarnished over the years, partly by bipartisan congressional actions. Moreover, although Marcos obtained excellent access to American media, his assertions were directly contradicted by their coverage of the elections and their reports of congressional reaction. Marcos's appeals did not exactly fall on deaf ears; they fell on great numbers of eyes and ears that were seeing and hearing more credible testimony.

SANCTIONS ON SOUTH AFRICA

In both 1985 and 1986, Congress overcame administration resistance and forced the adoption of limited U.S. economic sanctions against the apartheid regime of racial domination in South Africa. In the first instance, it pushed the president into issuing an executive order accepting most of the sanctions it was about to enact. In the second, it passed an even stronger bill and amassed the necessary two-thirds majorities to override the president's veto—something Congress had not done in foreign policy since 1973.

Alongside other forces, these extraordinary legislative actions contributed to an unexpectedly swift and positive political evolution in South Africa. Barely three years after passage of the Comprehensive Anti-Apartheid Act of 1986 (CAAA), President F. W. De Klerk began taking the bold political steps that allowed President Bush to lift sanctions in July 1991. African National Congress leader Nelson Mandela was released from prison after twenty-seven years to take his first, firm steps on a political journey that would lead to his 1994 election as president of South Africa. The state of emergency was ended; political parties were "unbanned"; the government agreed to negotiate a new political order with representatives of the black majority.

Eventually, South African leaders indicated that congressional sanctions were prominent among the internal and external pressures to which De Klerk was responding. On the day President Bush determined that the government had made sufficient progress under the law to lift sanctions, Foreign Minister Pik Botha exclaimed, "This is a great day for us. We can now look forward to South Africa achieving greater economic growth." He expressed confidence that "this momentous decision will lead all over the world to the termination of sanctions, particularly by those governments who indicated that they were waiting for the lead of the United States."[128] Soon afterwards, Justice Minister Koebie Coetsee, a key participant in De Klerk's moves, informed the ruling National Party Congress, "We worked to have that law lifted. . . . We were absolutely convinced that this act had to fall."[129] In parliament, Botha discreetly suggested a linkage between De Klerk's political moves and American sanctions:

I had the privilege of standing next to the hon. the State President on the lawns of the White House during the historic visit to the USA in September 1990. While we stood there, the hon. the State President took the historic initial steps which led to the lifting of sanctions against this country by President Bush. . . . I think the whole of South Africa is pleased that we are back in the international arena.[130]

From another perspective, the "central theme" of the newly released Mandela's meeting with a congressional delegation had been "the need to maintain sanctions . . . the only way to insure that the . . . Government will meet the preconditions . . . to create a climate for negotiations."[131]

Even American officials who had been skeptical of sanctions tended to agree they had had a beneficial impact. An October 1990 report by President Bush stated, "Existing pressures, including market forces and other sanctions, played a role in helping convince the South African government and the minority white community that it had to move beyond the failed policies of the past."[132] President Reagan's ambassador to South Africa, Edward Perkins, had publicly welcomed the immediate political benefits: "As a statement of abhorrence by the American people," he said, the CAAA "was an unmitigated success. There is no question about where the American people stand with respect to South Africa and its government at this time."[133] After the sanctions were lifted, Senator Lugar, who had embraced them reluctantly, "debriefed" South African leaders. He found that "sanctions did have an impact through our political relationship. . . . The ground shifted. There was a sinking feeling that life would never be the same again."[134]

As Lugar's remark suggested, the effects of the CAAA went far beyond the relatively modest short-term costs of specific American or American-encouraged sanctions. Indeed, many sanctions, like the bans on new loans and investments, were already largely operating through market responses to political instability by the time the legislation finally passed. The effects of other official sanctions, such as bans on the importation of South African products, could often be evaded, though at a cost.[135] The CAAA, however, with its legal sanctions, listing of political conditions for their termination, and threat of further restrictions, conveyed a series of powerful messages to South Africa's white elites about their political and economic future. It said that the leader of the West considered their situation hopeless without fundamental political change, a judgment of political, psychological, and economic importance. It warned that even if the government gained some temporary stability through repression, U.S. law would stand in the way of a positive international market response. It said help was unlikely to be forthcoming in the event of new external and internal challenges and that, in the absence of change, sanctions would intensify.[136]

How was Congress able to inflict such major defeats on a president as popular as Ronald Reagan, and do so without the cooperation from the administration that characterized the cases of El Salvador and the Philippines? Two factors were central. First, the South African issue generated a significant though largely unorganized constituency for some kind of stronger American action against apartheid. And this constituency was increasingly alienated by Reagan's apparent insensitivity to the plight of black South Africans. Second, in a particularly sustained drive, a cadre of determined legislators did what it took to develop an independent outlook and build the supermajorities necessary to make a legislative imprint. As a participant, I had a privileged vantage point from which to observe many of these developments.

THE CONSTITUENCY

Before the fall of 1984, there was no major political constituency in the United States on South Africa. There were, to be sure, a number of small but effective grass-roots efforts primarily directed toward pressuring American businesses to leave South Africa. In addition, several important labor, church, and civil rights organizations had officially endorsed legislative or other proposals to penalize apartheid. On the other side, South African government and business lobbies carried out propaganda and other activities. But there was no sense on Capitol Hill that more than a relatively few Americans were deeply concerned with events there or were pushing hard for a new policy.

Under the Reagan administration, the American approach to South Africa was called "constructive engagement." Its guru, Assistant Secretary of State for African Affairs Chester Crocker, believed the P. W. Botha government had become a "modernizing autocracy" with an "explicit commitment" to "domestic change."[137] Crocker further thought the United States could cooperate with a reform agenda that stressed economic and social rather than immediate political change. Thus a State Department colleague could assure the Senate Foreign Relations Committee in 1985, during a state of emergency, "More progress towards justice in that society has been made in the last few years than in the preceding three decades."[138] Crocker's patience—and nonpunitive policy—depended heavily on his assumption that "the essential precondition for progress is change in the hearts and minds of white South Africans."[139] Less delicately, the American ambassador to South Africa, Herman Nickel, assured me and other congressional staff in 1984 that "whites will dictate the pace of change till at least 2000. It's important to keep influence with the whites who run the place."[140]

Beginning in September 1984, more than a year of television coverage of the burgeoning black revolt in South Africa's townships tore away the emotional acceptability and intellectual credibility of constructive engagement. The recurring images were those "of the padded, faceless policeman, club raised [and] of a black youth with fear covering every inch of his face as he throws a brick."[141] In the view of House Africa Subcommittee chairman Howard Wolpe (D.-Mich.), "Probably the single most significant factor creating a political capacity to pass sanctions legislation was the televised coverage of some of the killings that occurred. . . . People were back in the civil rights movement with these pictures. It humanized the struggle, made it real and concrete."[142] The October 1984 award of the Nobel Peace Prize to South African Bishop Desmond Tutu gave the struggle a compelling international spokesman.

In addition, an innovative campaign of civil disobedience at the South African Embassy and consulates "kept the issue in front of the public for an extended period of time."[143] The Free South Africa Movement was spearheaded by Randall Robinson, executive director of TransAfrica, then "a fairly low profile black foreign policy organization." Attracting several thousand activists, including eighteen members of Congress, representatives of church, labor, civil rights, and other groups, and celebrities, the movement gave on-going anti-apartheid efforts a shot in the arm and fostered the idea that Americans could do something about injustice in South Africa.[144]

By the fall of 1985, polls reported a plurality of Americans favored additional U.S. pressure against apartheid, including economic pressure—a significant change from the past.[145] In Congress, the rising tide of public concern and organizational activity had various effects. It helped "energize" liberals, mainly Democrats, whose African-American and other supporters were the most concerned, as well as conservative white Southern Democrats trying to "get right" with their black constituents.[146] Suddenly Representative William Gray (D.-Pa.) noticed "more and more people in the House coming to me and asking about my sanctions bill."[147] In addition, antiapartheid sentiment became grist for various partisan agendas. Democratic leaders grasped at a means of distinguishing their party's foreign policy concerns that did not leave them open to charges of being "soft on Communism."[148] And a new breed of conservative Republicans, some of them ex–civil rights demonstrators, wrote the South African ambassador threatening to support sanctions in an effort to reposition their party within the "national consensus favoring racial justice" and "human rights."[149] In these circumstances, less attention seemed to be paid to South Africa's $2 million to $3 million a year lobbying effort and the antisanctions expressions of American businessmen.[150]

However necessary it was to the final outcome, a changing public opinion alone would not have produced such rapid and significant congressional action. Leading congressional actors emphasized the critical impact of President Reagan's failure to "light a symbolic candle for apartheid's victims."[151] As Crocker himself wrote, "The President tended to discredit his case by sounding so much like the government from which he was so reluctant to distance himself."[152] Also, despite the opinion polls and organizational expressions, congressional mail on South Africa legislation was relatively light.[153] An April 1985 National Citizens Lobby Day sponsored by the church-supported Washington Office on Africa at the height of the protests drew only

350 "people from grassroots America" who visited just forty congressional offices. TransAfrica, which had only about 1,500 members in the late 1980s, was more of an inspirational and media force than a grassroots lobby.[154] While sensing the increased popular acceptability of sanctions, the key congressional leaders who would push through sanctions legislation did not themselves experience compelling con-stituency pressure. Wolpe recalled that South Africa "never became a very salient issue for my personal constituency." Solarz could not think of a lobby to whom he was responding. Lugar thought the sanctions lobby in his state "not very vocal" and guessed that "a slight plurality" of his constituents would have thought his actions too bold.[155]

In sum, although it had grown rapidly and picked up organizational strength, the antiapartheid constituency was largely unorganized. Since it was, however, a potential political force, most members of Congress were probably disposed to do something to please it. But what precisely that was remained unclear. Considering too Congress's individualistic tendencies and the administration's steadfast defense of constructive engagement, there was no guarantee of timely, thoughtful, and significant action by the requisite two-thirds majorities.

A CONGRESSIONAL CADRE

This is where congressional leadership came in. An important marker was 1980, the last year of the Carter administration, when three members of the House Africa Subcommittee—Chairman Solarz and freshmen congressmen Gray and Wolpe—began to collaborate on sanctions legislation. By 1983, over a year before the South African issue exploded into public consciousness, they had persuaded the House to adopt some of the leading sanctions eventually imposed: bans on new investment and loans, and on sales of gold Krugerrand coins. While they made only modest progress in a committee conference with the Republican-controlled Senate, they had succeeded in marshaling a broad congressional base for a credible alternative policy. This would greatly facilitate future action.

Behind this early victory, and instrumental in the larger ones to come, was an extraordinary effort to master and publicize the issue and develop viable legislation. Debating the 1983 bill, Solarz referred to "close to a dozen [public] hearings on the situation in South Africa" held by him and Wolpe (his successor as chairman) over the previous three years.[156] That pace would continue throughout the early 1980s. Also important was the assistance of a highly specialized and politically experienced Africa Subcommittee staff. Moreover, Solarz, Wolpe, Gray, and the staff traveled periodically to South Africa, getting to know the situation better and exploring various legislative approaches. The latter were ultimately tested for political and legislative feasibility in committee, with the Congressional Black Caucus (of which Gray was a prominent member), and in consultations with TransAfrica, the Washington Office on Africa, and other organized interest groups. Faced with administration and business criticisms of their proposals, the House activists found they had to retail them member-to-member to build the necessary supermajority. For example, in 1983 Gray talked privately to "literally dozens and dozens of members" to muster support.[157] His recollections convey some of the flavor of this intense, unobserved process:

> I'd argue we had sanctions against eighteen countries, including five total embargoes. I said, "If sanctions don't work, why don't we lift them against North Korea?" They'd say, "Well, that's not what America is about." I'd say, "It's the same thing about apartheid." When they'd argue that sanctions could end "dialogue," I'd ask, "What have they [the South African government] done in thirty years? In the last two years, what new rights and liberties have they provided? No, they have gotten worse." Then I'd argue about sanctions hurting blacks, "Sanctions may hurt, but apartheid kills." I'd also argue that, unlike Communist countries, South Africa saw itself as a "Western, industrialized country" and cared about Western democratic opinion. So moves to ostracize it would have a more significant impact. I got moderates and conservatives to change their position. I got [Robert] Livingston [R.-La.], [Ike] Skelton [D.-Mo.], [Jack] Kemp [R.-N.Y.].[158]

Wolpe, who managed the 1985 and 1986 bills on the House floor, remembers that

People were very torn because you had moderate to liberal Republicans and Democrats who bought into the idea that sanctions hurt the people you most wanted to help. A lot, especially Republicans, needed to be talked to and felt less than confident about what they had to do.[159]

Beyond their leading role in the House (amplified by accumulating seniority and Gray's ascent to the chairmanship of the powerful Budget Committee), the antiapartheid triumvirate forged an unusually close alliance with sanctions advocates in the Senate. Legislation was drafted by the House leaders, then co-sponsored by such Senate leaders as Edward Kennedy (D.-Mass.), Lowell Weicker (R.-Conn.) and Alan Cranston (D.-Calif.). There were regular meetings of members and staff to share information and plot strategy, and joint press conferences. Given the plethora of proposals to do something about South Africa (in 1985 over 20 bills were introduced in the House alone), and the widely recognized relationship between timely House action and pressure on the more recalcitrant Senate to consider the issue, interchamber collaboration was critical for swift and unified action.[160] It also provided a clear focus for an emerging political constituency.

In 1985 the House voted 295 to 127 (just five more than the two-thirds necessary to override a presidential veto) for a bill that expanded on earlier sanctions proposals, spelled out political conditions for lifting sanctions, and threatened further action. Here were the structural outline and many of the specific details of the eventual CAAA. The next year, an even stronger bill was on the verge of passing overwhelmingly when a last-minute Republican maneuver enabled Representative Ronald Dellums's (D.-Calif.) amendment for a total economic embargo to prevail by an anonymous voice vote (observers believed it would have attracted no more than 120 recorded votes).[161] Guiding the House Republicans was Representative Walker (R.-Pa.), the main author of the 1984 new breed conservative letter threatening sanctions, who now had a different slant. "The administration," he explained, "was going to be put in a pretty difficult position if the more moderate bill passed. If the more radical approach passed, it was pretty clear it couldn't have been sustained."[162] The ranking Republican on the Africa Sub-committee, Mark Siljander (R.-Mich.), went along, partly "as a way of expressing frustration with the administration and House Republican leadership who were leaving all the opposition to me. I didn't feel like trying to be an apologist [for apartheid]."[163] The Republicans had hoped to tar the sanctions movement as extremist, but there was "consternation later," Walker admitted, "when we saw the House negotiating position with the Senate would be the Dellums approach. Then it was clear we couldn't prevail."[164]

Given the threat of a veto, it is almost impossible to imagine that sanctions could have been imposed without the support of two-thirds of the Republican-controlled Senate. (Sometimes Congress performs implausible feats, as when it tacks a controversial measure onto a last-minute appropriations bill and the president swallows the offending provision rather than risk closing down part of the government. These are rare occurrences, not to be counted upon.) As events developed, the key to final Senate support was Senator Lugar's exceptional determination that Congress shape and enact policy.

He had been concerned with the situation in South Africa for some time. A major influence, he remembered, was the 1981 report of the blue-ribbon Study Commission on U.S. Foreign Policy toward South Africa, chaired by Franklin Thomas, president of the Ford Foundation—especially its conclusion that blacks would eventually alter the status quo through either "a slow, uneven, sporadically violent evolutionary process" or "a slow but much more violent descent into civil war." Lugar had discussed the report in depth with a member of the commission, J. Irwin Miller, chairman of the Cummins Engine company in his home state. When the issue got hot in 1984, Lugar joined Senator Nancy Kassebaum (R.-Kan.), who chaired the Africa Subcommittee, in a private letter to President Reagan urging "a major review of the South Africa policy in part because of its implications for the country and for the Republican party." South Africa's racial conflict had a special resonance for Lugar, a former mayor of Indianapolis who had been active in local voluntary school desegregation efforts and had worked successfully with black leaders to avoid rioting in the aftermath of the 1968 Martin Luther King, Jr., assassination.[165] His Foreign Relations aides considered him "a genuine nonracist" who "viewed South Africa as a civil rights as well as a foreign policy issue."[166]

On the other hand, the senator was a conservative with serious reservations about disengagement from the South African economy and a strong inclination to work with his party's administration.[167] His first attempt to blend these ingredients was his April 1985 legislative proposal. It condemned apartheid, offered support to black students and entrepreneurs, and encouraged all American companies to observe the widely endorsed Sullivan Principles of fair employment. But it only *threatened* to adopt sanctions in two years if there weren't significant progress against apartheid.[168] Even his stronger July 1986 proposal, influenced by a new state of emergency and lobbying by the British Commonwealth Eminent Persons Group, added only one significant economic sanction to the measures already in place.[169]

Yet, as chairman of the Foreign Relations Committee, Lugar was willing to accept and advance proposals for somewhat stronger sanctions. He did this out of "a desire to have virtual consensus if that was possible. Without a consensus from the Committee, the odds that [a bill] could survive in that shape and be considered by the [Republican] leadership, be allocated time, and have some momentum through the House were low."[170] In other words, instead of allowing himself to be narrowly outvoted in his own committee, Lugar chose to pitch in and help shape a broad bipartisan consensus to give Congress a chance to make law. On the Senate floor, he worked to preserve and expand that consensus. In 1985, for example, Senator Helms (R.-N.C.) threatened to kill the committee bill by leading a minority filibuster that would indefinitely delay its consideration. On the other side, Senators Kennedy and Cranston wanted to strengthen the legislation by adding a Krugerrand ban and other provisions, even though they appeared to lack more than a slim majority for their changes. Lugar enlisted Republican leader Robert Dole (Kan.) in a successful strategy, telling both sides they would assemble the sixty votes needed to curb a Helms filibuster if the liberals gave up trying to amend the committee's bill. The final product was then approved 80 to 12.[171] During a subsequent House-Senate conference, Lugar very reluctantly yielded to the prevailing desire to accept the House's Krugerrand ban, then publicly defended it as part of "a carefully crafted bill developed by a bipartisan consensus of both houses of Congress that has not been displayed since Vietnam."[172] In 1986 he pursued a different floor strategy of giving both conservatives and liberals opportunities to add amendments to the committee bill. The CAAA passed 84 to 14.[173]

While assembling veto-proof majorities on the Senate floor, Lugar still hoped to engage the president so the nation could speak with "one voice."[174] Thus when Reagan, to avoid an embarrassing veto override in 1985, issued an executive order accepting most of the congressional sanctions, Lugar was willing to take the extreme step of purloining the House-Senate conference papers to derail a Senate vote on the full sanctions package.[175] Still, his Democratic colleagues seemed to forgive and forget fairly quickly. They appeared to realize how indispensable he was. They knew, for example, that they had lacked the sixty votes to shut down Helms's threatened filibuster against the Krugerrand ban,[176] but that as a result of Lugar's consensus-building, it had eventually become part of the president's executive order.

Confronting another likely veto override in 1986, the administration again approached Lugar, offering to issue an executive order encompassing the sanctions in the committee bill, but not the additional ones he had accepted during floor debate. This time the senator wouldn't play. His passion for legislative consensus-building had taken him too far. He had made new commitments not only to his Senate colleagues but also to House antiapartheid leaders and the Congressional Black Caucus. The latter had agreed to abandon the Dellums bill in favor of the CAAA since there was no time for a House-Senate conference before the congressional session ended. In return for their cooperation, Lugar had agreed to lead the anticipated override effort. As he later wrote, "It would not work a second time. I had worked hard to gain the trust of people in both houses and on both sides of the aisle."[177]

In the end, the Senate overrode Reagan's veto with eleven votes to spare. It seems extremely unlikely that the CAAA or anything much like it would have emerged without Lugar's persistent consensus-building. Conversely, had he chosen to collaborate with the administration's sporadic strategy of resistance, delay, and issuance of a moderate exec-utive order, it is difficult to envision Congress moving as quickly and significantly as it did.

With its performance on South Africa, Congress showed how an unusually knowledgeable and determined group of bipartisan leaders, drawing strength from and educating a broad political constituency, could make a major contribution to American foreign policy.

Contemplating these rare examples of congressional counterculture in foreign policy, it is tempting to focus on the personalities involved. One thinks of Moakley's "rough edges" and his personal relationship with some of the slain Jesuits, Solarz's "almost limitless supply of energy and his intellectual curiosity,"[178] Wolpe's long involvement in civil rights and his background as a scholar and professor of African politics, Gray's own civil rights commitment and zest for inside poli-tics, Lugar's intellectual depth and dogged persistence. Yet the reason that personalities loom so large in these three cases is that the domi-nant culture of deference does not normally produce such activism in foreign policy. Exceptional personalities may have given members of Congress the strength to challenge the predominant culture and develop alternative ways of learning and legislating.

Members and their staffs were usually aware of their trespasses against the prevailing style. Moakley put it baldly when he told a reporter,

> You know what bothers me? If some Speaker had organized a task force when Archbishop Romero was killed to challenge the Admin-istration, the aid could have been cut a long time ago.[179]

Lugar saw a sharp contrast between the Foreign Relations Commit-tee's performance during his brief chairmanship (1985–86) and its subsequent development:

> The Senate Foreign Relations Committee barely gets into discus-sions at all. There's no disposition to be involved legislatively. We have the Secretary of State in occasionally, and quiz him about what he's doing and why he's doing it badly. . . . Consensus building—to

get fifteen people together behind a point of view that will be taken seriously by the rest of Congress—doesn't happen.[180]

As one might expect, cultural outlaws often paid a price. Lugar is widely believed to have failed in his effort to move ahead of the more senior Helms as ranking Republican on the Foreign Relations Committee partly because of lingering resentments of his forward role on South Africa and the Philippines. According to Lugar, Republican leader Dole thought he was "far too out front . . . maybe he didn't feel sufficiently consulted."[181] And sitting in the House Foreign Affairs Committee's markups, one had only to watch Chairman Zablocki calling on Solarz as "Mr. Amendment" to sense the cultural tax on his legislative effervescence.

Beyond their common thrust toward participation, each example of congressional initiative contained some unique emphases. In particular, El Salvador showed that Congress had the tools to ferret out the most sensitive, policy-relevant information, with and without the cooperation of the administration. The Philippines demonstrated what Congress could accomplish even before there was any substantial public involvement, and highlighted the importance of following up on the spirit and intent of the law. South Africa displayed the democratic promise of a marriage between a Congress that is willing to lead and an emergent, broad-based constituency.

6

Toward Congressional Revival

This book has argued that Congress, as an institution, possesses a distinct way of learning and a special quality of action when it comes to foreign policy. This gives rise to a predominant culture that can be described as deferential because it engenders respect for and yielding to the executive branch as well as to narrow-based interests.

As we have seen, that does not mean that exceptional individuals in Congress, often interacting with broader-based constituencies, do not sometimes perform feats of policy making. Nor does it signify that Congress has totally abandoned its constitutional responsibilities. After all, deference is more than slavery; it implies a relationship, however unequal, between independent parties. So Congress still debates and votes on a number of important foreign policy issues. Its appropriations committees continue to make incremental adjustments in the administration's financial requests (partly with an eye to competing domestic priorities). Congress also continues to reflect broad constraints in public opinion, as in its reluctance to commit American troops to combat without a compelling demonstration of national interest. On occasion, a rush of public concern will provoke a legislative reaction, though, as we have seen in Somalia and Bosnia, it may be an ill-considered one. And if Congress is directly confronted with an undeniable assault on its integrity—as in the contra affairs—it will respond with at least temporary outrage.

Nevertheless, the perceptions of Congress's own inhabitants and specific analyses of congressional behavior reveal that there is a power-ful bipartisan culture of deference in foreign affairs, one that poses a major challenge to sound and democratic policy making. From time to time partisan interests may loosen individual members' adherence to aspects of this culture—as in El Salvador during the early 1980s and, more recently, Haiti—but never enough to override the collective attachment.

Notwithstanding recurrent complaints of congressional "micro-management," recent academic research largely confirms that "the president (and by extension his advisers and the foreign policy bureaucracy) remain the dominant actors on foreign policy," and Con-gress "functions as a secondary actor."[1] A new study by a leading scholar of Congress bears the arresting title, *Less than Meets the Eye: Foreign Policy Making and the Myth of the Assertive Congress*. Examin-ing a broad range of behavior over the past three decades, Barbara Hinckley finds "little evidence for an increase in congressional activ-ity." Beyond the fact that "Congress has consistently supported the executive [on the use of force], with few exceptions over the years," Hinckley points to *decreasing* congressional activity since the 1970s regarding arms sales, foreign assistance, intelligence, and the annual "working agenda" of recorded floor votes. She contends that much of the bustle in Congress on foreign affairs—the growing number of sym-bolic resolutions, hearings, and requests for presidential reports, the "one or two very visible struggles each year"—amounts to no more than "symbolic action: the highly stylized substitute for the thing it seeks to represent . . . Congress's special effects."[2]

Hinckley's work suggests that Congress's overall influence is even less than might appear from the cases highlighted in this volume. For beyond the activity that "meets the eye," she discerns "less opposition and struggle, too, below the visible surface. Indeed it is striking how small and selective the legislative agenda is."[3] Thus to fully plumb the impact of congressional culture one must also consider the many important issues Congress ignores. Two poignant examples from my own experience concern the weakness of legal controls over the prolif-eration of U.S. weaponry abroad and the uncertain impact of billions of dollars of U.S. foreign aid for economic development.

INVISIBLE ISSUES

During the late 1970s, the Space Research Corporation of Vermont, headed by a Canadian-born, naturalized American physicist named Gerald Bull, illegally shipped South Africa approximately 60,000 155 mm. extended-range artillery shells, at least four 155 mm. guns, and the technology to establish its own gun and ammunition manufacturing and testing facilities. As a result, the apartheid regime acquired superior long-range artillery, strengthening its military position in Angola and reaping substantial foreign exchange revenues from weapons sales to Iraq, Iran, and other countries.

A 1982 House Africa Subcommittee staff investigation concluded that this was no accidental occurrence, but rather the product of "structural" weaknesses in U.S. arms export restrictions worldwide. The Space Research case had unearthed a "nonsystem" of governmental enforcement verging on farce. The State Department's Office of Munitions Control, which licensed arms exports, misapplied its own regulations. What is more, it accepted without evidence Space Research's claim that its technology, developed on a U.S. corporate compound straddling the Vermont-Canada border, was not of U.S. origin. Acting under loose procedures, the U.S. Army approved the use of a government-owned plant to manufacture the artillery shells, and the CIA failed to supervise one of its agents who helped bring the company and the South Africans together. Moreover, the U.S. government had no clear scheme of organizational responsibility for obtaining, sharing, and acting upon information concerning illegal arms exports. Hence, when a Space Research container burst open as it was loaded onto a South African ship in Antigua, and dockworkers alleged it contained illegal weapons exports, U.S. agencies were slow to react. Even after U.S. Customs launched the official inquiry that ultimately put Bull and a colleague in jail, Space Research managed, over a period of months, to ship 32,000 additional artillery shells to South Africa.[4]

Although the staff report included a series of policy recommendations, formed the basis for a public hearing by the Africa Subcommittee, and received recurrent press attention over the years, there was no

visible follow-up by the congressional committees with principal jurisdiction over the arms export nonsystem. This was one of those issues
that was essentially off the congressional screen.

A decade later, in January 1991, the United States was contemplating a ground conflict in Iraq that might cost thousands of American
lives. Among Iraq's estimated 3,700 artillery systems, the most threatening were 520 155 mm. weapons with ranges greater than the best
U.S. artillery and the capacity to deliver chemical warheads. They had
been designed by Gerald Bull and imported from his clients in South
Africa, Austria, and China. Bull and his associates had also helped Iraq
modernize its Soviet cannons and develop new weapons, including a
"supergun" capable of delivering nuclear, biological, and chemical
weapons.[5] *Furthermore, the military technology behind all of this was
partly American and had been illegally exported and reexported
throughout the 1980s.* This was the overwhelming evidence of Customs Service documentation that had been provided to, and accepted
by, the Office of Munitions Control since the late 1970s.[6] In fact, the
technology had been largely developed by U.S. citizens working in
Bull's U.S. corporate compound on the exposed South African project. Yet Bull and his foreign customers had somehow continued to
illegally export this technology to other banned recipients, including
China, Iran, and Iraq, with total impunity.

The nonsystem seemed to have prevailed again. No U.S. agency
had assumed the responsibility of formally declaring Space Research's
escaping technology "American," so no real attention was given to its
illegal foreign marketing. In fact, when the State Department became
concerned in 1986 that Austria was shipping Bull-designed weapons
to Iran, it mistakenly pleaded with Austria to apply its own restrictions
rather than U.S. ones, and referred to Bull's former company as
"Canadian."[7] After emerging from four months of imprisonment unre-
pentant and bitter,[8] Bull set up new Space Research offices in Europe,
and recruited former U.S. employees to supply illegal technology to
China.[9] He also continued to try to cover his operations by telling the
Office of Munitions Control that he was sending "non-U.S." technology to China and probably making a similar claim about Iraq.[10] Yet no
U.S. intelligence agency appears to have monitored his activities until

almost the eve of Iraq's invasion of Kuwait.[11] While there is significant evidence that U.S. officials secretly countenanced and encouraged other countries' sales of banned arms and military technology to Iraq, at least during the 1980–88 Iran-Iraq war, these apparently did not include such large, visible, and internationally threatening items as long-range artillery and superguns. Moreover, any American complicity in such sales would certainly have been complicated by the existence of an effective arms export control system.[12]

Bull's enemies assassinated him in Brussels in March 1990. But Congress has continued to ignore the glaring lapses in U.S. arms export controls. Despite its importance this issue has not aroused the interest of members or constituents.

Intimations of ineffectiveness also haunt America's programs to assist economic development in poor and struggling countries—programs that cost $4 billion to $5 billion yearly. Certainly a convincing case for their success has not been made to Congress. The 1989 Hamilton-Gilman House Foreign Affairs Committee Task Force on Foreign Assistance concluded,

> Accountability of U.S. foreign assistance is extensive but ineffective. Accountability is focused on anticipating how assistance will be used, rather than on how effective it is and has been used. . . . In spite of 1,300 pages of Congressional presentation, over 700 Congressional notifications annually, and innumerable reports, Congress does not know what actual progress is being made towards the solution of serious global problems.[13]

During my twelve years with the House Africa Subcommittee staff, I was well placed to witness the poverty of official evaluation of U.S. development assistance to the poorest continent. The State Department's Agency for International Development (AID) and the Treasury Department (which oversaw U.S. contributions to international development banks) were mainly interested in the immediate *outputs* of programs—the numbers of agricultural tools or condoms distributed or economic policy reforms accepted—not their long-range *outcomes* for broad-based, environmentally sustainable economic growth. Thus neither the Carter administration, with its commitment to "basic human needs," nor the Reagan and Bush administrations, with their faith in the liberation of the "private sector," had the facts to persuasively argue that their approaches were succeeding. In fact, there were recurrent glimpses of failure. A special AID evaluation of a rural road-building project in Liberia revealed that the main beneficiaries were absentee landlords, not local small farmers. Congressionally encouraged reexaminations of a rural development project in Zaire disclosed that AID had plunged ahead without scientific soil surveys and information about previous production, and that the project was significantly hampered by exploitative local merchants and an indifferent Zairian government. A 1989 House Foreign Affairs Committee staff study of U.S.-supported "structural adjustment" economic policy reforms in Ghana and Senegal found that they had produced "little enduring poverty alleviation." In some instances, such as the imposition of health fees in Ghana and draconian health budget cuts in Senegal, they actually appeared to have hurt the poor and discouraged the development of a healthy, productive labor force.[14]

Here again Congress hardly intervened. Economic development was a particularly complex issue. In addition, as George Ingram, the senior foreign aid staffer on the House Foreign Affairs Committee, explained, "What's on the front page of the *New York Times* and *Washington Post* and on TV is of much greater interest to members and staff. Members hear from constituents on jobs, Bosnia and Somalia, not on how population programs in Rwanda are being carried out."[15] Former committee chairman Dante Fascell (D.-Fla.), who cared about development programs more than most, lamented, "It's a boring issue."[16] It would be surprising to learn that any congressperson or senator had ever studied in depth a single foreign aid development project. In the aftermath of the devastating Ethiopian and African famine of 1984–85, the Africa Subcommittee sponsored a series of workshops with experts on development problems. Virtually no members of the subcommittee showed up except for the chairman. Nor was there a rush of interest on the part of invited staff.

The Hamilton-Gilman task force did recommend the establishment of a Foreign Assistance Oversight Subcommittee or an ad hoc group with a strong staff to oversee foreign aid.[17] But five years later nothing had been done. With only one Ph.D. economist between them, and that one effectively part-time, the House Foreign Affairs and Foreign Operations Committees continued to indifferently patrol their largest legislative jurisdiction.[18]

Given this reluctance to monitor the effects of development assistance, how does one account for Congress's persistent, if largely futile, efforts to "micromanage" foreign aid via extensive requirements for executive reports and pages of committee recommendations for improved approaches? One possible explanation is that Congress instinctively believes that it *should* really be responsible for these programs outside the conventional parameters of "national security," even as the predominant foreign policy culture of Congress denies it the tools (adequate staff, a zest for making binding law) to effectively carry out its obligation. Obsessive "micromanagement" thus appears not as a counterpoint to the culture of deference but rather as its ironic and perverse fulfillment.

REFORMS

America has important economic, political, moral, and security interests in an increasingly interdependent world. Today, as throughout their history, Americans have divergent (and potentially divergent) opinions and interests regarding the appropriate priorities and approaches for U.S. foreign policy. Even the unifying force of the Cold War could not produce a single public compass for American diplomacy. According to the American system of democratic and representative government, these differences are best debated and resolved by Congress and the president, interacting with concerned constituencies. In fact, when Congress begins to fall out of this equation—as it did in El Salvador, Angola, Nicaragua, Somalia, Bosnia, Iraq, and elsewhere—American interests may well suffer. Yet when Congress rises to its constitutional responsibilities—as it did in South Africa, the Philippines, and the recent phase in El Salvador—American interests may well be enhanced, and broader-based constituencies empowered.

In a finely balanced and comprehensive new study, Professor James Lindsay discusses the "costs" of Congressional participation in foreign policy making, including occasional micromanagement of details, sometimes abusive treatment of ambassadorial nominees, and periodic policy errors. However, he concludes that "instances in which congressional activism clearly hurts the national interest or the cause of good policy are in short supply." Furthermore,

> Complaints about the vices of congressional activism overlook its virtues. . . . Members of Congress frequently strengthen the president's hand in international negotiations. Members also bring values and perspectives to bear on policy debates, views that provide a useful political scrub for administration proposals. Last . . . active participation of members in decision making helps to legitimize U.S. foreign policy both at home and abroad. Precisely because the United States is a democracy it is important that policy decisions be made democratically.[19]

With the disappearance of the traditional Cold War basis for the culture of deference, there would seem to be at least the potential for a revival of congressional influence. There has been little serious discussion thus far, however, of how meaningful and constructive change might occur. Perhaps the most frequent suggestion has been to designate a small group of congressional leaders (including some junior members) to consult with the president on the use of force and broader issues of "national security."[20] Certainly a requirement for authentic prior presidential consultation with a prestigious congressional group would represent an important advance over the inoperative War Powers Resolution that was supposed to involve Congress in decisions to use force. Yet there are good reasons to question the overall adequacy of this approach to congressional participation in policy making. In the first place, bringing a small group of congressional representatives into confidential meetings with the administration is more often a recipe for co-optation than it is for authentic participation. We have only to remember how the intelligence committees monitored the Boland and Clark Amendments or how the House Intelligence Committee decided on policy toward Angola. More fundamentally, consultation per se does not address the attitudes, beliefs, and practices that make up the culture of deference. The Senate Foreign Relations

Committee and House Foreign Affairs Committee were more than consulted regarding the situations in El Salvador, Somalia, and Bosnia. They had the opportunity to make and uphold binding law. Yet their performance was hampered by a series of self-imposed shackles.

Some of the general reforms of Congress undertaken after the 1994 elections, or under continuing consideration, hold a modest promise for weakening the culture of deference.[21] For example, the House's reduction in the number of committees and committee assignments of frazzled members could encourage more concentrated attention to foreign as well as domestic issues. Possible future curbs on the Senate's increasing utilization of minority filibusters and individual holds on legislative action would ease the path of all legislation. So might the achievement of better interparty relations in the House through the new House leadership's promise of a fairer allocation of staff and opportunities for floor debate to the minority. Finally, the enactment of even partial limits on private campaign contributions and gifts would go some way toward reducing the advantages of narrow-based lobbying interests. Still, the special character of foreign policy—its hidden nature, its dearth of constituencies, and its susceptibility to executive branch–led deception—requires a more tailored approach to reform.

Although foreign affairs issues cannot generally sustain the levels of political interest of more immediately felt domestic ones, a new congressional culture of participation and partnership with the executive is no utopia. We have seen its major elements embodied in several outstanding examples of congressional initiative. Its *institutionalization*, however, would require a major reexamination and revision of congressional custom, particularly by members of foreign policy committees and their party chiefs. Outside efforts to encourage the development of sustained, broader-based political constituencies would also be essential.

Drawing upon the lessons of past experience, it is not difficult to discern the basic elements of such an alternative culture, including many of the specific changes in congressional attitudes and practice that would be necessary. Of course, there is no single road map to cultural renovation. And should change occur, it is likely that delicate areas where the president appears to incarnate the nation itself, such as the use of force, would be affected later and less completely.

Imagine, then, the cultural anatomy of another possible foreign policy Congress, one that could emerge out of a future revival of democratic leadership:

Congress would limit the president's leeway to unilaterally take new and urgent initiatives that imply a future commitment of legislative support.

The president would continue to act alone in situations of true emergency or those requiring nearly absolute secrecy, but only after consulting with a small, diverse core group of party leaders and representatives of foreign policy committees. Such occasions would be exceedingly rare. In other cases involving the use of force, Congress would also be consulted and, except for minor and noncontroversial matters, would conduct open hearings, debates, and votes. Thus it would be involved in precisely the sorts of decisions it previously declined (despite the War Powers Resolution) in places such as Lebanon and Somalia. After all, if Congress could, however belatedly, debate and vote on the Persian Gulf war—the most sensitive and dangerous commitment of U.S. military forces since Vietnam—why should it be handcuffed in the less intimidating circumstances of a Haiti, Bosnia, or Somalia?[22] Covert actions would also normally be approved in advance by the relevant committees. Members would feel a greater responsibility to supervise ventures they themselves helped launch.[23]

Where major political developments appeared to require in-course corrections in annual foreign aid allocations or similar policies, the revisions would be carefully considered by the Foreign Affairs and Relations Committees as well as the traditional appropriations watchdogs. The former's mandates and staff complements make them generally best qualified to evaluate broad policy issues. In these new congressional deliberations, the president would no longer receive the benefit of the doubt as before. Congress would be justly wary of short-range fixes that might usher in dubious long-term commitments.

Congress would wield its weapons against executive deception.

When members of the executive branch testified before Congress, especially on potentially controversial issues, they would be subject to the solemnization of an oath of truthfulness. In addition, foreign policy committees would insist that the administration provide them with information of major relevance to the decisions they take (Congress and the executive would together elaborate precautions to protect the intellectual independence of officials and preserve necessary secrecy). When the committees requested information from the administration, they would have the support of each other and of the party leadership. If there were resistance, they would have recourse to the subpoena. In the past, administrations have often been willing and even eager to furnish their "friends" in Congress from both parties with voluminous cable traffic and special briefings. Now Congress would require they treat members equally in the interest of fully informed debate. Finally, the committees would establish and utilize procedures for rapidly declassifying information essential to broad public understanding while continuing to safeguard sources and methods of intelligence.

Congress would deploy its resources to ensure that it develops an independent perspective.

Congress would recognize the major consequences of its responsibility to provide democratic leadership in the special sphere of foreign affairs. Congressional party leaders would promote serious participation by members of foreign policy committees. They would act on the principle, suggested by former House Foreign Affairs chairman Fascell, that "By God, we are going to put our prestige behind this, lend our name, spend time, build up the perception that this kind of assignment is important and unique."[24] The models of learning provided by the Solarzes and Lugars would be followed and developed. While the total number of committee staff would not significantly increase over 1994 levels, its quality would be dramatically upgraded. It would possess the educational background, practical experience, investigative tradition, and political skills suitable to a larger and more constructive congressional role. (Congress's central policy support staff could also be rebalanced. The General Accounting Office could complement its traditional accounting orientation with new capacities in broad policy analysis. Similarly, the Library of Congress's Congressional Research Service could go beyond its tradition of neutral fact-finding to incorporate an additional capacity to provide independent policy analysis from diverse perspectives.)

Aware that Congress's foreign policy agenda will inevitably be more limited than its domestic one, committee leaders would make special efforts to establish priorities, including some formerly invisible issues like evaluating development assistance and controlling arms exports. Public hearings would become real vehicles for examining conflicting perspectives on foreign policy problems. At times, members of the administration or Congress could even be persuaded to sit on panels with each other and with private witnesses in order to directly discuss each other's assumptions. Where this was not feasible, nongovernmental witnesses could be invited to testify first so that members would have their views in mind as they questioned the more august officials. There would be a general damping down of member behavior without a legislative focus, such as long, "expressive" personal statements of beliefs. Questioning of witnesses by members would sometimes be organized so that committees could make the best use of limited time. And attendance at important meetings would be promoted by a decrease in such time-consuming diversions as the largely ritualistic committee breakfasts and teas for visiting foreign dignitaries.

The committees and other members would also learn by tapping into modern satellite communications to directly interview foreign actors and observe remote events. Travel would generally focus on more sustained exploration of major issues. Brief tours of countries and their political leadership would no longer be in vogue.

Congress would have a strong commitment to making and upholding clear and binding law.

Congress would continue to affect U.S. policy through public pronouncements and threatened actions. But its major source of direct influence and overall political credibility would be, as always, its laws. Committee and party leaders would therefore work closely together to build as broad a consensus as possible for the enactment of legislation, including the important foreign aid authorization which speaks to U.S. policy concerns worldwide. As legislation was drafted, every effort would be made to take the time necessary to clarify its meaning and impact. Congress has long had sufficient legal drafting skills; problems have mainly stemmed from the atmosphere of casualness and political expediency that has discouraged their proper use.[25]

Once a law was enacted, Congress would monitor, and insist upon, its implementation in letter and spirit. While avoiding an unsuitable and distracting involvement in day-to-day implementation, it would sometimes act diplomatically (in consultation with the administration) to further the clear intent of the law—as Moakley and Murtha did in El Salvador.

Congress would increasingly mobilize, and reflect, broader-based interests.

The recently interrupted trend of campaign financing and lobbying reforms would resume and eventually trim the sails of narrow-based interests. But the latter would remain important in a society where the resources for communicating political preferences remain unequally distributed, and the well endowed are likely to have the best political and personal connections. The Constitution's provision for freedom of speech restricts any effort to level the playing field by clamping down on the advantaged.

Nevertheless, a certain more democratic counterweight would emerge naturally as a result of Congress's newfound leadership in foreign policy. By giving form and direction to broadly felt, but complex, international concerns, Congress would help translate troubling information into constructive, well-thought-out public responses. By doing so, it would promote greater constituency involvement in foreign policy, as it did in the Philippines and South Africa.

Still, the task of developing more broad-based constituencies for foreign policy would surpass the resources of even a reformed Congress. Here the contribution of outside forces would be critical. Americans will sporadically continue to throw up such ideologically diverse grassroots movements as the opposition to the Panama Canal treaties of the 1970s and the nuclear freeze campaign of the 1980s. More important, though, would be decisions by organized interest groups, churches, and philanthropies to support the growth of broader, more sustained foreign policy constituencies.

As we have seen, there is a long history of interest-based public participation in American foreign policy making. Even during the confining Cold War era, broad-based national interest groups helped lead influential public campaigns to promote superpower negotiations on nuclear weapons controls, encourage various resolutions to conflicts in Central America, and foster an end to apartheid in South Africa. Today's interest groups dwell in a less familiar world where the quietism of American policy also makes it harder for them to seize the high moral ground. However, there is political space for a range of new concerns and increased "real time" awareness of international developments. Americans, say the public opinion analysts, continue to generally favor active U.S. involvement in the world, but lack leadership to help them draw connections between what is going on abroad and the national interest.[26]

Considering Americans' rapidly growing participation in non-materially-based "cause" and "public interest" groups, there appears to be no inherent barrier to mobilizing them around many major foreign policy concerns. For example, if hundreds of thousands of people are willing to join groups lobbying for animal rights and government ethics, why could tens of thousands not be organized against genocide and other major human rights violations in places like Rwanda and Bosnia, or in favor of more effective humanitarian and development aid to the poorest countries? (As one who has long worked on Africa policy, I am convinced that there is a large latent constituency for African issues among church groups, Peace Corps returnees, African-American and civil rights groups, students, and others with significant ties to the continent.) The increasing preoccupation of the major environmental organizations with international issues also suggests there is a larger potential constituency for foreign policy issues than many had thought. Greater attention to effectively organizing this constituency would help rectify the notable imbalance in Washington between the number of well-supported "think tanks" with good ideas about foreign policy and the amount of political force available to guarantee their consideration.[27] According to many interest group representatives and informed observers, an effective contemporary approach would encompass broad dialogue among groups concerning the principles of United States foreign policy in the post–Cold War era, strengthened collaboration among groups working on similar issues, and increased emphasis upon outreach to, and mobilization of, potential constituents.

Congress would consider relatively few major executive policies in secret.

The intelligence committees would no longer deal with covert actions of a scale likely to bring them to public attention. Hence the so-called overt-covert action that escapes adequate congressional review—the Angolas and Afghanistans—would become extinct. Also, while the intelligence panels would continue to supervise lesser operations, they might try to monitor them better by carefully involving other committees. For instance, they could interpret longstanding legislation and rules obliging them to bring "relevant information" to the attention of other foreign policy panels as permitting informal consultation with small groups on particular operations.[28]

It is remarkable how few laws or formal rules would have to be changed for Congress to recover much of its former stature in foreign policy. Still, a major reform of the way Congress handles foreign policy is not yet on the nation's political agenda. The advent in January 1995 of the first Republican-majority Congress to confront a Democratic president in half a century does not by itself herald significant change any more than past juxtapositions of Democratic-majority congresses and Republican presidents have. Certainly President Clinton can anticipate increased difficulties in Congress, especially over the few issues uniting Republicans (like cutting foreign aid and legally restricting foreign command of military operations involving American troops) and the occasional political appointment or treaty, where he lacks recourse to the veto. Still, many of the new legislative leaders in foreign policy are veterans of the traditional culture, and there are no early signs of a

major challenge to its postulates.[29] Indeed, the Republicans were neither bold nor effective in earlier confrontations with the Clinton
administration on issues like Bosnia and Haiti, where they held the
political upper hand despite formal Democratic control. Moreover,
their recent political history has turned them into even more of a presidential party than the Democrats. Will they attempt to seriously
weaken executive branch prerogatives they hope to recapture in the
1996 presidential election? Finally, some of the changes sponsored by
the new House leadership are likely to have the unintended consequence of *reducing* congressional influence over foreign policy. Giving
the president a line-item veto over appropriations bills could have a
particularly large impact on foreign policy, since Congress has all but
ceased formulating policies through normal authorization bills. And a
one-third cut in committee staffing could, in the absence of other measures to improve staff quality, weaken Congress's ability to cope with
the special hurdles in foreign affairs.

As the Republicans prepared to take control of Congress, the politically flamboyant chairman-to-be of the Senate Foreign Relations
Committee, Jesse Helms (R.-N.C.), garnered considerable press coverage. In many ways, Helms departs from the usual mold. He has strong
ideological commitments, in the pursuit of which he is often willing to
defy certain norms. Yet he seems ill-suited to lead Congress toward an
alternative culture. He has shown great skill in using legislative procedures to obstruct and delay unwanted foreign policy initiatives. But his
views have been too narrow and inflexible to enable him to produce
much positive political consensus or enduring law. He challenges
undue executive branch secrecy, but sometimes through apparently
unilateral and indiscriminate disclosures that his colleagues condemn.
He does not shrink from attempting to organize public opinion
against the president's policies, but has lately used words that many
interpreted as menacing the president's person.[30]

The new chairman of the House International Relations Committee
(renamed from Foreign Affairs), Benjamin Gilman (R.-N.Y.), is a more
representative Republican leader. The outgoing chair, a longtime colleague, characterizeed him as being "in the broad mainstream of
American foreign policy." From my own observations, this is true for

process as well as substance. Significantly, in his debut press conference, Chairman Gilman paid special tribute to the reigning myth surrounding the culture of deference: the need for firm and forceful presidential leadership in foreign affairs. Criticizing the "inconsistency and . . . vacillation" of the Clinton administration, he emphasized the need for "a strong steady signal on foreign policy coming from Washington." "In our committee," he promised, "we intend to do all that we can to help the administration re-establish and present a consistent and coherent voice in foreign policy that the American people and the world community need and expect."[31]

Perhaps congressional and public interest in reform will grow with increasing consciousness of the plethora of post–Cold War problems and the inadequacy of solutions put forth by isolated administrations and determined "special interests." Perhaps a combination of international events and citizen leadership will begin to expand the constituency for foreign policy, energizing the elected representatives. One thing is certain, however. Change will not begin to occur until members of Congress, and other Americans, become more critically aware of the quiet accumulation of mores that has caused a distinguished political institution to relinquish what Senator Byrd has aptly called its "will to lead."

Epilogue:
The New Republican Congress and Bosnia

[With regard to Bosnia] Congress has chosen not to claim the power of deciding when to deploy American forces when our Nation is not under attack and when our vital national interests are not immediately at stake. So we are where we are because we were not willing to risk the consequence of action. We have deferred, we have debated, we have waited, we have talked, and we have let the President take us to where we are today.
— *Senator William Cohen (R.-Maine)*[1]

We have been presented a fait accompli, a done deal . . . [but] it is not really just the President's fault. It is Congress's failure to insist on a procedure whereby there is a true organized debate, involving public participation, and culminating in a vote that the public will understand to mean that if we say it is a good thing to do, it will happen, and if we say it is not a good thing to do, at least there will be serious consideration on the part of the Executive that it should not go forward. — *Senator Russell Feingold (D.-Wisc.)*[2]

The biggest foreign policy issue of 1995 was the conflict in Bosnia. Majorities in the new Republican-controlled Congress took their distance from the Democratic President's positions. Toward the end of September, Republican Senate majority leader Bob Dole warned,

It cannot escape the administration that the Congress has repudiated its approach towards Bosnia for the past two years. An overwhelming majority has opposed the arms embargo, and Congress has voiced concerns with respect to peace plans that would destroy the sovereignty and territorial integrity of Bosnia and Herzegovina. So, to operate under the assumption that Congress will approve administration plans to send thousands of Americans in harm's way to enforce a settlement is a major error. The fact is that the Clinton administration may be making promises it cannot or should not keep.[3]

Yet, as the above statements by Senators Cohen and Feingold indicated, the Republican Congress ended up yielding to the President's plan for Bosnia just as its Democratic predecessors had given way on Somalia. By November, Dole was sending a very different message:

> It is time for a reality check in the Congress. The fact is that President Clinton has decided to send U.S. forces to Bosnia. . . . The Congress cannot stop this deployment from happening. . . . We should find a way, if possible, to support the American men and women in uniform on their way to Bosnia.[4]

Some observers called the Republican leader's change of heart an act of political courage that strengthened the credibility of American leadership in the world. Others criticized him for caving in to a flawed policy. But whatever one's view of the substantive issue, the senator's switch highlighted Congress's continuing timidity in foreign policy.

As the U.S.-led NATO peacekeeping operation unfolded, it appeared that the effort might have benefited from the kind of broad-based deliberation a responsible Congress would have provided. Key policy makers acknowledged they had given insufficient attention to civilian matters that President Clinton considered "absolutely essential to making the peace endure."[5] Even Assistant Secretary of State for European Affairs Richard Holbrooke, the principal architect of the Bosnia peace accords, lamented their "ambiguities" and "undeniable shortcomings."[6] The main difficulties concerned the realization of specific provisions for the return of refugees, preservation of human rights, prosecution of war criminals, and conduct of free and fair elections. Underlying these problems was the absence of steps towards confidence-building among the formerly warring parties.[7] Yet the Congressional debate on U.S. intervention had hardly touched upon these critical issues.

The outcome of 1995's political confrontation over Bosnia suggested the persistence of Congress's 50 year old culture of deference in foreign policy—notwithstanding the sea change in partisan control of the legislature.

ILLUSIONS OF POTENCY

Earlier, Congress had been complicit in the failure of the United States to develop an effective policy toward the bloodletting in Bosnia and the former Yugoslavia (see pp. 7–10). Over nearly five years, its major foreign policy committees had held relatively few public hearings, refrained from calling upon the leading academic experts on the region, published but a single staff report on the issues (on "ethnic cleansing" in 1992), and authored virtually no legislation.

But in mid-1995, as the Clinton administration struggled to cope with the Bosnian Serbs' brutal attacks on United Nations "safe areas" for Muslims and their taking of U.N. peacekeepers as hostages, Bosnia became a leading preoccupation of the new Republican legislature. And it appeared that the members were responding with a new assertiveness. During the summer, the House and Senate defied the president by passing a bill—co-authored by Senator Dole—unilaterally lifting the U.N. arms embargo against the militarily disadvantaged Bosnian government. Moreover, the legislation garnered better than two-thirds majorities in each house, bipartisan coalitions with the potential to override a presidential veto.

In the fall, both houses expressed strong skepticism regarding the President's intention to deploy 20,000 ground troops as part of a NATO plan to enforce a developing U.S.-mediated peace accord. More important, they demanded prior congressional debate and approval of any such deployment. "Should an agreement be reached," Senator Dole and House Speaker Newt Gingrich cautioned the president, its mere existence will not constitute sufficient reason for the deployment of American forces simply because you had previously made such a commitment. Among other considerations, you will need to demonstrate to the Congress and the American people that the mission to Bosnia is vital to our national interests, it is well-defined and achievable, and that it is the best option available.[8]

The Republican leaders were fortified by opinion polls showing that a majority of Americans were opposed to sending troops to Bosnia.

In the end though, the "revolutionary" Republican Congress largely backed down. The administration persuaded NATO to retaliate strongly against the Bosnian Serbs from the air and launched a new peace initiative; after those events, Congress did not even attempt to override President Clinton's veto of the arms embargo bill. And when the administration eventually brokered a Bosnian peace agreement, Congress canceled its demand for advance approval of troop deployment by waiting three weeks before beginning its deliberations. By then the president had authorized the dispatch of the first 700 U.S. troops and they had begun to arrive in eastern Bosnia.

Following debate, the Senate passed a resolution co-authored by Dole which, "notwithstanding reservations", acceded to the deployment with minimal conditions on the ground that the President "has decided" and "begun" it, and "preserving United States credibility is a strategic interest."[9] This was a direct repudiation of Dole's previous position that a "presidential commitment" was not "sufficient reason for the deployment of American forces." The House adopted a different, nonbinding resolution reiterating "serious concerns and opposition" to the deployment while expressing "pride and admiration for the soldiers involved."[10] The upshot of these contrasting decisions was that the President was left free to pursue his course in Bosnia without any congressional authorization or conditions to bind him.

Many members of Congress groused that they had been hemmed in by President Clinton. He had failed, they said, to consult them in advance concerning his initiatives. And he had maneuvered them into voting on an unwise intervention at the very moment the troops were arriving. It would have been dishonorable and politically imprudent to cut off their support. What was omitted from this account was Congress's own lethargy.

A DEARTH OF POLICY

In retrospect, the transient strength of the congressional challenge to the President's military prerogatives had masked Congress's enduring weakness in Bosnia policy making. As in Vietnam, the Persian Gulf, and Somalia, Congress would not have been confronting a unilateral presidential military commitment if it had been previously involved in formulating and bargaining for its own policy preferences. But like its Democratic predecessors, the Republican Congress never developed a coherent strategy toward Bosnia, one that aimed to achieve defined goals by influencing regional political circumstances. It was this failure that seemed to be at the heart of the 104th Congress's cave-in to the President. Lacking a full-fledged policy of its own, Congress was constantly thrown on the defensive by the administration's initiatives: retreating from its insistence on arming the Bosnian government, asking "questions" about (rather than offering alternatives to) the President's plans, almost begging him to make a "convincing case" for the troop deployment. When it finally yielded to him, it cited the weakest of foreign policy arguments—the need to defend the credibility of U.S. leadership and support American troops regardless of the wisdom of the underlying approach.

In five years of consideration the only significant suggestion Congress came up with on Bosnia was to unilaterally lift the arms embargo. Yet, as Senator Sam Nunn (D.-Ga.) pointed out during the summer 1995 debate, this was "far from [a] complete and coherent [policy]."[11] In fact, lifting the embargo was mainly a gesture of moral outrage in the face of Bosnian Serb atrocities that (as one senator put it) "made us cry at night"[12] and transparent aggression on the part of Serbia. Legislators offered not even a general vision of the kind of political solution they hoped to achieve by arming Bosnia, provided no indication of the types of weapons and training they might supply, and evaded the critical question of whether neighboring Croatia would cooperate in the effort. Nor did they take account of the ongoing Western diplomacy in the region, including offers to suspend economic sanctions against Serbia if it would formally recognize Bosnia, and expanding U.S. diplomatic and military cooperation with Croatia.

In short, while Congress identified some national values at stake in Bosnia, and even some geopolitical interests (preventing the spread of warfare and responding to the concerns of key Muslim states), it failed to define its political objectives and spell out the means for achieving them. Rep. Henry Hyde (R-Ill.) expressed the moral as opposed to political essence of Congress's action:

> This is not the time or the place to discuss the incredibly complicated problems of peace in the Balkans. It is incredibly difficult. But before we get to that problem we ought to understand genocide cannot be tolerated. We cannot remain indifferent to it.[13]

This helps explain why it was so easy for the administration to overwhelm the embargo-lifting proposal by simply showing it was "doing something" against evil through two weeks of air strikes and a new peace initiative. Congress does not normally bury a bill that gets two-thirds-plus majorities, even a foreign policy bill. If the President lines up more than a third of the members to sustain his veto, a majority can still try to tack an amendment onto an appropriations bill the administration needs. But on Bosnia, Congress was less interested in making real policy than in satisfying its moral impulse. The President's new activism sufficed to meet that need.

Benefiting from NATO's new military leverage with all the parties to the conflict, the administration pursued its peace initiative for over three months, culminating in a difficult but successful negotiation with the Bosnian leaders at the Dayton (Ohio) Air Force Base in November. However the general outline of the settlement was visible almost from the beginning. Bosnia would be effectively split in half between the minority Serbs (31 percent of the population) and a federation of the Muslims and Croats. There would be a very weak central government. Still, efforts would be made to ensure the human rights of all and rejuvenate a multiethnic Bosnia. And NATO would send in a peace implementation force to which U.S. ground troops would make an important contribution.

During this long gestation period, Congress made no real effort to present its own view of the general requirements for a just and stable peace and an appropriate U.S. military role. Instead, Dole, other senators, and Gingrich sent long letters to the President posing largely informational questions about his policy. Majorities in both houses asked to be consulted, and promised they would be heard before final decisions were taken. But when their advice was not sought, they declined to advance substantive recommendations on their own. By remaining silent Congress dissipated its potential influence over the U.S.-led peace process. Uncertain of congressional and public support, the administration would have had a strong incentive to pay attention to congressional input. Indeed one of the major ingredients in Clinton's decision to strengthen his policy in Bosnia had been his fear that Congress might lift the arms embargo over his veto.

Even the final Dayton agreement contained enough ambiguity to allow for significant congressional clarifications of U.S. policy. Dole, for example, was able to persuade the administration to somewhat sharpen its promised "defensive" military support for the Bosnian government, albeit within the context of a peace agreement which that government had only reluctantly accepted. During the climactic mid-December congressional debates a number of the President's supporters pointed out the need to further clarify the agreement's delimitation of military tasks to avoid the risks of "mission creep." Many also emphasized the need to add a "post-exit" diplomatic and military strategy to keep the peace after the troops withdrew. But they made no specific proposals to remedy these deficiencies.

Thus, through a considerable absence of policy, Congress largely abandoned the field to the President. Although the resulting reinforcement of the constitutional imbalance between the President and Congress immediately harmed the Republican majority, there would inevitably be a fallout for future Democratic Congresses as well. In addition, Democrats as well as Republicans might consider the real possibility that a more responsible Congress would have helped to foster a sounder and more sustainable policy. Significantly, even some of the President's most important and respected allies expressed major reservations about his course.

"Two bad choices is no choice at all," lamented Senator Joseph Biden (D.-Del.), one of the best-informed legislators on Bosnia. Biden was one of the only senators who had specifically addressed the details of an earlier peace proposal that foreshadowed the veiled partition of the Dayton agreement. For him the "best choice" would have been to lift the arms embargo, conduct air strikes, "wait while it is being done, and let the Bosnian Government establish itself," and thereby create a balance of power "essential for maintaining a lasting peace."[14] His view was given some credence by the aftermath of two weeks of NATO air strikes as Bosnian government forces (with Croatian assistance) recovered nearly a third of their territory.

Senator Bill Bradley (D.-N.J.) considered the administration's decision to commit ground forces "a prime example of the reigning ad hocism" in foreign policy. In his own scheme of international priorities, Bosnia was not a "strategic interest" and would have had no claim to American troops except for the President's public commitment. Other "grave problems" with the policy included a one-year exit date that invited "delayed violations" of the agreement, an underestimation of the ambitions of Bosnian Croatians and Serbs to "carve up" the country, and an overestimatation of the West's capacity to begin to overcome "ethnic hatreds" and "create one federated Bosnian state" in a year's time.[15] A few months later Carl Bildt, High Representative for Bosnian civil affairs under the Dayton agreement, confirmed that "the forces for ethnic separation are at present proving stronger than the forces of national re-integration," and called for "a seriously renewed commitment from us in the international community."[16]

A PERSISTENT CULTURE

The new Congress's weak performance on Bosnia demonstrated that the web of customs promoting deference in foreign policy had survived both the Republican transition and the large influx of new members in the House of Representatives. Most evident perhaps was the legislators' continuing tendency to give the President "the benefit of the doubt" in a new and urgent situation. By leading NATO and the Bosnians toward a peace accord and quickly deploying advance troops, President Clinton was able to create just that kind of situation.

More fundamentally, Congress continued to fail to deploy its resources to develop a fully independent perspective on policy. The major foreign policy committees—House International Relations and Senate Foreign Relations—did not even begin to hold public hearings on Bosnia until mid-October, and then only with administration witnesses. The House panel belatedly heard from former Republican officials and humanitarian agency representatives as well. But neither committee ever summoned the leading U.S. and international academic experts on Bosnia and the former Yugoslavia, or on international conflict resolution. Nor did they publish any staff analyses of the issues. (Perhaps this helped explain why a gross oversimplification of history—that the Bosnian conflict flowed from 500 years of ethnic hatred—flourished on the House and Senate floors, and why the congressional debate gave so little attention to means of lessening conflict.) Finally, the committees failed to nurture significant legislation on Bosnia. All the important bills and resolutions debated on the House and Senate floors arrived directly from individual members. The great structural lesson of the Bosnia episode was that individual travel, press statements, and bills cannot substitute for a systematic and collaborative committee process oriented to producing authentic foreign policies with solid political support.

Congress also continued to display a weak inclination to make and uphold binding law. When the going got tough, it abandoned the embargo-lifting legislation it had worked on for years. It shunned opportunities to help guide the peace process, preferring to pepper the President with questions and hollow warnings. Following belated and separate actions regarding troop deployment, the House and Senate made no effort to enact common legislation that could hold the administration to some minimal conditions.

There was an alternative path for Congress on Bosnia, one of participation and partnership with the President in policy making. As we have seen, in the last decade alone exceptional congressional leaders have succeeded in promoting peaceful democratic change in the

Philippines, South Africa, and El Salvador. Departing from the culture of deference, they and their colleagues undertook the tasks of developing broadly supported policies to shape events on the ground, enacting legislation to guide the executive, and limiting the President's leeway in not-so-urgent "crises."

Certainly there were risks in attempting to bring Congress in as a responsible partner in foreign policy. However, in Indochina, Somalia, the former Yugoslavia, and other areas of the world, the cumulative costs of congressional deference were also apparent. In the spring of 1996 though, it seemed that a lot more chickens would have to come home to roost before Congress would be ready to fully resume its constitutional responsibilities in foreign affairs.

Notes

Unfortunately, there is not a single directory, or even a limited number of indexes, to aid researchers attempting to locate declassified and other publicly released government documents such as those cited in this book. To my knowledge, among the major foreign policy agencies, only the State Department produces a public listing of releases, but this appears monthly and it is not cumulative.

Nor can researchers search for these records themselves in one, or even a few, central locations. A significant exception is the treasure trove of documents relating to human rights in El Salvador that were released in response to congressional requests in 1993. State Department records are accessible through the Department's Freedom of Information Office; CIA and Defense Department materials may be consulted at the Library of Congress. Many of these documents have been utilized in the preparation of chapters 2 and 5.

Other documents employed in this study were obtained through Freedom of Information Act (FOIA) requests by the author, the generous sharing of materials by previous individual requestors, and by courtesy of the main institutional requestor, the National Security Archive in Washington, D.C. In addition to its central holdings, the Archive has also become a repository of many individual collections. The Archive's resources on Iran-contra, Nicaragua, El Salvador, and the Philippines (including the individual collection of Raymond Bonner) were particularly useful for this project.

I plan to donate the FOIA materials I personally accumulated in the preparation of this volume to the Archive in the near future.

CHAPTER 1. A CONGRESSIONAL CULTURE

1. *Congressional Record* (Sept. 9, 1993): S11264.

2. Ibid., S11264 and S11270.

3. Carroll J. Doherty, "Foreign Policy: Is Congress Still Keeping Watch?" *Congressional Quarterly Weekly Review*, Aug. 21, 1993: 2267.

4. Ibid., pp. 2267–69.

5. Carnegie Endowment for International Peace National Commission, *Changing Our Ways: America and the New World* (Washington, D.C.: Carnegie Endowment for International Peace, 1992).

6. John Stuart Mill, *On Liberty,* ed. David Spitz (New York: Norton, 1975), p. 21.

7. Morton Halperin, "The Way to Pick a Fight: Democratizing the Debate on Using Force Abroad," *Washington Post*, Jan. 10, 1993, p. C4.

8. Arthur M. Schlesinger, Jr., *The Imperial Presidency* (New York: Popular Library, 1973), p. 287.

9. U.S. Congress, House Select Committee to Investigate Covert Arms Transactions with Iran and Senate Select Committee on Secret Military Assistance to Iran and the Nicaraguan Opposition, *The Iran-Contra Affair*, 100th Cong., 1st Sess., Nov. 13, 1987, 12 (hereafter cited as Report of the Congressional Committees). On the undermining of future support for the contras, see Cynthia J. Arnson, *Crossroads: Congress, the President, and Central America 1976–1993*, 2d ed. (University Park: Pennsylvania State University Press, 1993), pp. 218–26.

10. Report of the Congressional Committees, p. 11.

11. Ann Devroy and R. Jeffrey Smith, "Clinton Reexamines a Foreign Policy Under Siege," *Washington Post*, Oct. 17, 1993, pp. A28–29.

12. Eric Schmitt, "Somalia War Casualties May Be 10,000," *New York Times*, Dec. 8, 1993, p. A14.

13. Daniel Williams and Ann Devroy, "U.S. Limits Peacekeeping Role," *Washington Post*, Nov. 25, 1993, p. A60. See also Anthony Lake, "The Limits of Peacekeeping," *New York Times*, Feb. 6, 1994, sec. IV, p. 17; and Elaine Sciolino, "New U.S. Peacekeeping Policy Emphasizes Role of the U.N.," *New York Times*, May 6, 1994, pp. A1, A7.

14. *Congressional Record* (Oct. 14, 1993): S13424–79; *Congressional Record* (Nov. 9, 1993): H9839–62.

15. Michael Wines, "Bush Outlines a Somalia Mission to 'Save Thousands,'" *New York Times*, Dec. 5, 1992, p. 4.

16. *Congressional Record* (Feb. 4, 1993): S1363–68; Walter Pincus, "Senate Authorizes Troops to Somalia," *Washington Post*, Feb. 5, 1993, p. A10; Barton Gellman, "U.S., U.N. Differ Over Best Way to Silence Somalia's Many Guns," *Washington Post*, Dec. 23, 1992, p. A19.

17. *Congressional Record* (May 25, 1993): H27444–65.

18. *Congressional Record* (Sept. 9, 1993): S11274.

19. Anonymous, telephone interview with author, January 16, 1994; and Adwoa Dunn, telephone interview with author, Jan. 16, 1994.

20. Steven J. Woehrel and Julie Kim, "Yugoslavia Crisis and U.S. Policy," CRS Issue Brief, Congressional Research Service, Library of Congress, July 11, 1994, p. CRS-7.

21. David Gompert, "How to Defeat Serbia," *Foreign Affairs* 73 (July/Aug. 1984): 31.

22. Don Oberdorfer, "A Bloody Failure in the Balkans," *Washington Post*, Feb. 8, 1993, pp. A1, A14; Statement of General Galvin in House Committee on Armed Services, *The Policy Implications of U.S. Involvement in Bosnia: Hearings before the Committee on Armed Services,* 103rd Cong., 1st sess., May 25 and 26, 1993, 4–5.

23. Anthony Lewis, "Do What It Takes," *New York Times*, Apr. 15, 1994, p. A31. See also similar comments by Secretary of State Warren Christopher in Hearing of the Subcommittee on Commerce, Justice, State, and Judiciary of the House Appropriations Committee Concerning the Fiscal Year 1995 International Affairs Budget Request, 103d Cong., 2d sess., Mar. 17, 1994, Federal News Service Transcript.

24. John M. Goshko, "In the Foreign Service, Complaints Grow about Clinton's Team," *Washington Post*, June 20, 1994, p. A13. See also Daniel Williams, "U.S. Bosnia Policy Cited in Another Resignation," *Washington Post*, Aug. 9, 1993, p. A12.

25. Elaine Sciolono, "As U.S. Sought a Bosnian Policy, the French Offered a Good Idea," *New York Times*, Feb. 14, 1994, pp. A1, A6; Daniel Williams, "U.S. Policy Shift Puts Pressure on Muslims," *Washington Post*, Feb. 11, 1994, p. A35.

26. The following discussion is based on a review of all congressional hearings and all statements and debate in the *Congressional Record*

on the former Yugoslavia from 1991 through July 1, 1994, as well as selected anonymous congressional staff interviews.

27. *Congressional Record* (May 13, 1994): S5729. See also Helen Dewar, "Conflicting Directives in Senate on Bosnia," *Washington Post*, May 13, 1994, pp. A1, A43; and Steven Greenhouse, "October Deadline Is Cited to End Bosnian Arms Embargo," *New York Times*, Aug. 12, 1994, p. A3.

28. House Committee on Banking, Finance, and Urban Affairs, *Banca Nazionale Del Lavoro (BNL) Scandal and the Department of Agriculture's Commodity Credit Corporation (CCC) Program for Iraq: Hearing before the Committee on Banking, Finance, and Urban Affairs*, pt. 1, 100th Cong., 2d sess., May 21, 1992, 65.

29. Kenneth Katzman, Clyde R. Mark, and Alfred Prados, "U.S. Policy Toward Iraq: 1980–1990," CRS Report for Congress, Congressional Research Service, Library of Congress, June 26, 1992.

30. Pamela Fessler, "Congress's Record on Saddam: Decade of Talk, Not Action," *Congressional Quarterly Weekly Report* (Apr. 27, 1991): 1068, 1072–74. Former Senate Foreign Relations Committee staff member Peter Galbraith says that if the legislation had passed, Iraq "would have understood that there were consequences to relations for illegal behavior and quite possibly would not have invaded Kuwait" (telephone interview by author, Feb. 1994).

31. Fessler, "Congress's Record on Saddam," pp. 1074–77.

32. Thomas E. Mann and Norman T. Ornstein, *Renewing Congress: A First Report* (Washington, D.C.: American Enterprise Institute and Brookings Institution, 1992), p. 11.

33. Dante Fascell, interview by author, Jan. 27, 1994.

34. Walter Lippmann, *Public Opinion* (New York: Free Press, 1965), p. 154.

35. Richard Sobel, ed., *Public Opinion in U.S. Foreign Policy: The Controversy over Contra Aid* (Lanham, Md.: Rowman and Littlefield, 1993), pp. ix, 12.

36. Eugene R. Wittkopf, "Elites and Masses: Another Look at Attitudes Towards America's World Role," *International Studies Quarterly* 3 (June 1987): 131–59.

37. Benjamin I. Page and Robert Y. Shapiro, *The Rational Public: Fifty Years of Trends in America's Policy Preferences* (Chicago: University of Chicago Press, 1992), pp. 172–284; Sobel, *Public Opinion in U.S. Foreign Policy*, p. 8.

38. For an interesting discussion regarding Nicaragua policy, see Sobel, *Public Opinion in U.S. Foreign Policy*, pp. 241–65. Charles W. Kegley, Jr., and Eugene Wittkopf, *American Foreign Policy: Pattern and Process*, 3d ed. (New York: St. Martin's Press, 1987), p. 305, concludes, "Policy formation does not derive from the simple preferences of an uninformed, uninterested, unstable, acquiescent, and manipulable 'public voice.'"

39. Dave McCurdy, interview by author, Jan. 26, 1994.

40. Stephen Solarz, interview by author, Oct. 27, 1993.

41. Charles Percy, interview by author, Nov. 9, 1994; William Goodling, interview by author, Mar. 21, 1994. Percy's positions on the Middle East, perceived by some as insufficiently pro-Israel, also ended up hurting him in the election with a portion of his Jewish constituency (one of the few constituencies in foreign affairs).

42. Floyd Fithian, interview by author, Nov. 4, 1994.

43. Elliott Abrams, *Undue Process: A Story of How Political Differences Are Turned into Crimes* (New York: Free Press, 1993), p. 171.

44. Michael Clough, *U.S. Policy Toward Africa and the End of the Cold War* (New York: Council on Foreign Relations Press, 1992), p. 82; Richard Moose, interview by author, May 10, 1993.

45. House Committee on Foreign Affairs, Subcommittee on Africa, *Reprogramming of Military Aid to Somalia: Hearing before the Subcommittee on Africa*, 96th Cong., 2d sess., Aug. 26, 1980, 17.

46. George C. Wilson, "Indian Ocean Bases Plan Hits Snag," *Washington Post*, Aug. 28, 1980, p. A10.

47. Moose, interview.

48. Lannon Walker, interview by author, Apr. 16, 1993.

49. Frank Crigler, interview by author, Apr. 14, 1993.

50. Sissela Bok, *Lying: Moral Choice in Public and Private Life* (New York: Vintage, 1989), p. 32. On Abrams's October 1991 admission of legal guilt for responding to specific congressional requests for information by "unlawfully, willfully and knowingly" withholding facts he "well knew," see U.S. Court of Appeals for the District of Columbia, Division for the Purpose of Appointing Independent Counsel, Division No. 86-6, *Final Report of the Independent Counsel for Iran/Contra Matters, Vol. II: Indictments, Plea Agreements, Interim Reports to the Congress, and Administrative Matters, Aug. 4, 1993* (Washington: Government Printing Office, 1994), pp. 395–414.

51. Ibid., p. xxi.

52. Alexander Hamilton, James Madison, and John Jay, *The Federalist Papers* (New York: New American Library, 1961), p. 82 (Federalist 10).

53. Matthew McHugh, interview by author, Nov. 30, 1993.

54. Wyche Fowler, interview by author, May 23, 1993.

55. Anonymous, interview by author, date withheld.

56. Peter W. Morgan, "The Undefined Crime of Lying to Congress: Ethics Reform in the Rule of Law," *Northwestern University Law Review* 86 (Winter 1992): 253.

57. Information flows more freely, however, to those committees and members that are supportive of the administration's policy.

58. Michael Barnes, interview by author, Nov. 24, 1993.

59. Senator Richard G. Lugar, *Letters to the Next President* (New York: Simon and Schuster, 1988), p. 63.

60. Solarz, interview.

61. Richard Armitage (former high-ranking foreign-policy official), interview by author, Sept. 22, 1993.

62. John Carbaugh, interview by author, Nov. 1, 1993.

63. Anonymous, interview by author, Oct. 31, 1993.

64. George Ingram, interview by author, Dec. 9, 1993; Gary Bombardier, interview by author, Oct. 22, 1993; also anonymous, interview by author, Oct. 31, 1993.

65. William Woodward, interview by author, Sept. 24, 1993.

66. Dick Clark, interview by author, Sept. 21, 1993.

67. Ibid.

68. Gregory Craig, interview by author, Sept. 27, 1993; and McCurdy, interview.

69. Fascell, interview.

70. Victor C. Johnson, "Congress and Foreign Policy: The House Foreign Affairs and Senate Foreign Relations Committees" (Ph.D. diss., Political Science, University of Wisconsin—Madison, 1975), 102.

71. McHugh, interview.

72. Ibid.

73. Kay Lehman Schlozman and John T. Tierney, *Organized Interests and American Democracy* (New York: Harper and Row, 1986), pp. ix, 289–317, 400. This note also refers to the discussion in the following two sentences.

74. Solarz, interview.

75. Howard Marlowe, interview by author, Sept. 24, 1993.

76. Stuart Sweet, interview by author, Oct. 21, 1993.

77. Paul Manafort, interview by author, Nov. 17, 1993.

78. Frank J. Smist, Jr., *Congress Oversees the United States Intelligence Community 1947–1989* (Knoxville: University of Tennessee Press, 1990), p. 238.

79. The definition is taken from Public Law 102-88, the Intelligence Authorization Act, Fiscal Year 1991, Section 503 (e). Leslie H. Gelb, "Overseeing of C.I.A. by Congress Has Produced Decade of Support," *New York Times*, July 7, 1986, pp. A1, A10; Patrick E. Tyler and David B. Ottoway, "Casey Enforces Reagan Doctrine with Reinvigorated Covert Action," *Washington Post*, Mar. 9, 1986, pp. A1, A10; Gregory F. Treverton, *Covert Action: The Limits of Intervention in the Postwar World* (New York: Basic Books, 1987), p. 14.

80. Smist, *Congress Oversees the United States Intelligence Community*, p. 238.

81. Hamilton, Madison, and Jay, *The Federalist Papers*, pp. 320–23 (Federalist 51).

82. Louis Henkin, "Foreign Affairs and the Constitution," *Foreign Affairs* 66 (Winter 1987/88): 286–90.

83. See Concurring Opinion in *Youngstown Sheet and Tube v. Sawyer,* 343 U.S. Reports, 635–38 (1952).

84. Schlesinger, *The Imperial Presidency*, pp. 47–105; on Theodore Roosevelt and Panama, see Thomas A. Bailey, *A Diplomatic History of the American People*, 9th ed. (Englewood Cliffs, N.J.: Prentice-Hall, 1974), p. 497.

85. Roger H. Brown, *The Republic in Peril: 1812* (New York: Norton, 1971), pp. 284–300.

86. Walter LaFeber, *The New Empire: An Interpretation of American Expansion 1860–1898* (Ithaca, N.Y.: Cornell University Press, 1963), pp. 400–406; Bailey, *A Diplomatic History*, pp. 451–64.

87. Bailey, *A Diplomatic History*, pp. 563–94, 711–26; Selig Adler, *The Uncertain Giant: American Foreign Policy Between the Wars* (New York: Macmillan, 1965), pp. 2, 8–9, 161–65, 199–205, 221–24, 238–43.

88. LaFeber, *The New Empire*, pp. 147, 50, 38–39; Bailey, *A Diplomatic History*, pp. 614–23.

89. Bailey, *A Diplomatic History*, pp. 700–703, 713–15.

90. Brown, *The Republic in Peril: 1812*.

91. LaFeber, *The New Empire*, pp. 400–406; Bailey, *A Diplomatic History*, pp. 451–64.

92. Bailey, *A Diplomatic History*, pp. 563–94, 711–26; Adler, *The Uncertain Giant*, pp. 2, 8–9, 161–65, 199–205, 221–24, 238–43.

93. Schlesinger, *Imperial Presidency*, pp. 340, 317–57.

94. Thomas M. Franck and Edward Weisband, *Foreign Policy by Congress* (New York: Oxford University Press, 1979), pp. 6–7.

95. Ibid., pp. 61–155.

96. Robert A. Katzmann, "War Powers: Toward a New Accommodation," in *A Question of Balance: The President, the Congress and Foreign Policy*, ed. Thomas E. Mann (Washington, D.C.: Brookings Institution, 1990), p. 46.

97. Barry M. Blechman, *The Politics of National Security: Congress and U.S. Defense Policy* (New York: Oxford University Press, 1990), p. 193.

98. Fessler, "Congress' Record on Saddam," p. 1069.

99. Andrew Hacker, *The End of the American Era* (New York: Atheneum, 1972); Richard Alba, *Ethnic Identity: The Transformation of White America* (New Haven, Conn.: Yale University Press, 1990).

100. On arms control, for example, see Douglas C. Waller, *Congress and the Nuclear Freeze: An Inside Look at the Politics of a Mass Movement* (Amherst: University of Massachusetts Press, 1987); and David S. Meyer, *A Winter of Discontent: The Nuclear Freeze and American Politics* (New York: Praeger, 1990).

CHAPTER 2. GIVING THE PRESIDENT THE BENEFIT OF THE DOUBT:
THE CONGRESSIONAL OPPOSITION AND U.S. POLICY TOWARD
EL SALVADOR, 1980–1984

1. Central Intelligence Agency (CIA) cable, Mar. 25, 1980.

2. Certification of Extraditability and Order of Commitment, In Re: Extradition of Alvaro Rafael Saravia, United States District Court, Southern District of Florida, Case No. 87-3598 CIV-Extradition-Johnson, pp. 4, 10–11, 13–14.

3. CIA, "El Salvador: Assassination of Archbishop Romero."

4. K. Larry Storrs, "El Salvador Highlights, 1960–1990: A Summary of Major Turning Points in Salvadoran History and U.S. Policy," CRS Report for Congress, Congressional Research Service, Library of Congress, Mar. 13, 1990, pp. 11–13. Benjamin Schwarz, *American Counterinsurgency Doctrine and El Salvador: The Frustrations of Reform and the Illusions of Nation Building* (Santa Monica, Calif.: RAND, 1991), p. 2, estimates total aid as about $6 billion if

one includes "$850 million in unsubsidized credits and an estimated CIA investment of over $500 million."

5. Thomas Carothers, *In the Name of Democracy: U.S. Policy Toward Latin America During the Reagan Years* (Berkeley: University of California Press, 1991), p. 21.

6. Thomas Quigley, interview by author, Feb. 9, 1994.

7. Bill Keller, "Interest Groups Focus on El Salvador Policy," *Congressional Quarterly Weekly Report* (Apr. 24, 1982): 895–900; and Cynthia Buhl, interview by author, October 19, 1994. See also statement by Rep. Matthew McHugh on p. 40; and statements of Senators Charles Percy and Claiborne Pell in Senate Committee on Foreign Relations, *Certification Concerning Military Aid to El Salvador: Hearing before the Committee on Foreign Relations,* 97th Cong., 2d sess., Feb. 8 and Mar. 11, 1982, 1, 5–6.

8. The best analysis of the areas of agreement and disagreement, which were discussed in numerous congressional hearings, is provided by Cynthia J. Arnson, *Crossroads: Congress, the President, and Central America 1976–1993,* 2d ed. (University Park: Pennsylvania State University Press, 1993), esp. pp. 265–89. See also Carothers, *In the Name of Democracy,* pp. 17–30. The reference in the previous paragraph to "slow and arduous" military reform is from the deputy director of the Central Intelligence Agency, "Statement on El Salvador—Certification Issues," Senate Committee on Foreign Relations, Aug. 2, 1982; the phrase also applies to other political and economic reforms.

   Some areas of formal agreement were subject to practical dispute. For example, critics of U.S. policy complained that the administration arbitrarily excluded hundreds of members of the U.S. military mission, medical trainers, private U.S. contractors, and reconnaissance personnel from the official total of fifty-five U.S. military trainers in El Salvador. See Sen. Mark Hatfield, Rep. George Miller, and Rep. Jim Leach, *U.S. Aid to El Salvador: An Evaluation of the Past, A Proposal for the Future,* Report to the Arms Control and Foreign Policy Caucus, Washington, D.C., February 1985, pp. 23–24.

9. *International Security and Development Cooperation Act of 1981,* Conf. Rept. to accompany S. 1696, 97th Cong., 1st sess., Dec. 15, 1981, Conference Print 97-58, 85–86.

10. Carothers, *In the Name of Democracy,* p. 44; Arnson, *Crossroads,*

pp. 270–72, 288, 292–94; Schwarz, *American Counterinsurgency Doctrine and El Salvador*, pp. 62–70, 81–84.

11. Schwarz, *American Counterinsurgency Doctrine and El Salvador*, p. xii.

12. House Committee on Appropriations, Subcommittee on Foreign Operations, *Foreign Assistance and Related Programs Appropriations for 1981: Hearings before the Subcommittee on Foreign Operations,* pt. 1, 96th Cong., 2d sess., 426.

13. Ibid., pp. 367–68; American Embassy, San Salvador (1122), to Secretary of State, "Subj: Text of Archbishop's Letter to President Carter," Feb. 19, 1980, pp. 2–3.

14. House Subcommittee on Foreign Operations, *Foreign Assistance and Related Programs Appropriations for 1981*, pp. 434, 430–31, 433.

15. Matthew McHugh, interview by author, Nov. 30, 1993.

16. House Subcommittee on Foreign Operations, *Foreign Assistance and Related Programs Appropriations for 1981*, pp. 432–33, 380.

17. House Committee on Appropriations, Subcommittee on Foreign Operations, *Foreign Assistance and Related Programs Appropriations for 1982: Hearings before the Subcommittee on Foreign Operations,* pt. 1, 97th Cong., 1st sess., 10, 253–80.

18. Ibid., 293.

19. Arnson, *Crossroads,* pp. 68, 56.

20. House Subcommittee on Foreign Operations, *Foreign Assistance and Related Programs Appropriations for 1982*, pp. 299–301.

21. House Committee on Appropriations, Subcommittee on Foreign Operations, *Foreign Assistance and Related Programs Appropriations for 1984: Hearings before the Subcommittee on Foreign Operations,* pt. 2, 98th Cong., 1st sess., 59–61.

22. Ibid., 59.

23. Report of the United Nations Commission on the Truth for El Salvador, *From Madness to Hope: The 12-Year War in El Salvador*, United Nations Security Council, S/25500, Apr. 1, 1993, p. 11

24. Douglas Farah, "Salvadorans Vote in Peace Despite Delays," *Washington Post*, Mar. 21, 1994, p. A1; and "Salvadoran Ex-Rebels Now Targeting Voters Show Power in Polls," *Washington Post*, Feb. 19, 1994, p. A23.

25. Commission on the Truth, *From Madness to Hope*, pp. 194–200.

26. From *Anexos,* tomo 1, no. 5, of ibid., cited in "El Salvador: Accountability and Human Rights: The Report of the United Nations Com-

mission on the Truth for El Salvador," *Americas Watch* 5 (Aug. 10, 1993): 15n 50.

27. Commission on the Truth, *From Madness to Hope*, pp. 43–44, 132.

28. Michael Barnes, interview by author, Nov. 24, 1993.

29. Michael Ross, "Probe Is Sought of Salvador Ties," *Los Angeles Times* (Washington Edition), Mar. 19, 1993, p. A2.

30. United Nations Commission on the Truth, "Summary", n.d., document submitted in connection with House Committee on Foreign Affairs, Subcommittee on Western Hemisphere Affairs, *The Peace Process in El Salvador: Hearing before the Subcommittee on Western Hemisphere Affairs,* 103d Cong., 1st sess., Mar. 16, 1993, 1, 3.

31. Commission on the Truth, *From Madness to Hope*, pp. 131, 135–36, 127–28. Concerning U.S. opposition to D'Aubuisson's ascendancy, see Arnson, *Crossroads*, pp. 96–98; on D'Aubuisson's continuing influence on Salvadoran policy, see Schwarz, *American Counterinsurgency Doctrine and El Salvador*, esp. pp. 26–27, 46–48, 59–60.

32. Senate Committee on Foreign Relations, *The Situation in El Salvador: Hearings before the Committee on Foreign Relations*, 97th Cong., 1st sess., Mar. 18 and Apr. 9, 1981, 116–58.

33. Commission on the Truth, *From Madness to Hope*, p. 129.

34. House Permanent Select Committee on Intelligence, Subcommittee on Oversight and Evaluation, *U.S. Intelligence Performance on Central America: Achievements and Selected Instances of Concern*, staff report, 97th Cong., 2d sess., Sept. 22, 1982, pp. 12–14.

35. Robert White, interview by author, Dec. 20, 1993.

36. Norman Parker to Dwight Ink, "Subject: Report and Update of Your Human Rights Testimony Before the Obey Committee (HAC) on April 21, 1987," U.S. Agency for International Development memorandum, Mar. 22, 1988, p. 3.

37. House Committee on Appropriations, Subcommittee on Foreign Operations, *Foreign Assistance and Related Appropriations for 1983: Hearing before the Subcommittee on Foreign Operations,* pt. 1, 97th Cong., 2d sess., 127.

38. The reply to Percy is quoted in Clifford Krauss, "U.S. Aware of Killings, Kept Ties to Salvadoran Rightists, Papers Suggest," *New York Times*, Nov. 9, 1993, p. A9; on the Foreign Affairs Committee secret session, see House Committee on Foreign Affairs, *Directing the Secretary of State to Provide to the House of Representatives Certain Information Concerning Roberto D'Aubuisson*, 97th Cong., 2d

sess., H.R. 955, official transcript (May 26, 1982; declassified 1994): 24. The CIA informed Senator Robert F. Byrd that there "has never been any definitive information regarding those responsible for [Romero's] death," in CIA Chief Legislative Liaison to Mr. Richard McCall, Senate Democratic Policy Committee, Feb. 23, 1982.

39. Laurie Becklund, "Lots Reportedly Drawn to Kill Salvador Arch-bishop," *Los Angeles Times*, Apr. 15, 1983, p. 1.

40. Powell A. Moore, Assistant Secretary of State for Legislative and Intergovernmental Affairs to the Honorable Tom Corcoran, House of Representatives, Aug. 3, 1983.

41. House Committee on Foreign Affairs, Subcommittees on Human Rights and International Organizations and Western Hemisphere Affairs, *The Situation in El Salvador: Hearings before the Subcom-mittees on Human Rights and International Organizations and Western Hemisphere Affairs,* 98th Cong., 2d sess., Jan. 26, Feb. 6, 1984, 50–51.

42. House Committee on Foreign Affairs, Subcommittee on Western Hemisphere Affairs, *Foreign Assistance Legislation for Fiscal Year 1985: Hearings before the Subcommittee on Western Hemisphere Affairs* (and markup), pt. 6, 98th Cong., 2d sess., Feb. 8, 21, 22, 23, and Mar. 1, 1984, 121–23. See also W. Tapley Bennett, Jr., Assistant Secretary of State for Legislative and Intergovernmental Affairs to the Honorable Tom Tauke, House of Representatives, Apr. 11, 1984: "The information contained in the cables is limited and incomplete and no definitive conclusions regarding D'Aubuisson's involvement can be drawn from it. We have received other intelli-gence reports on the Romero assassination which contradict the charges in these two cables."

43. Thomas Enders, interview by author, Oct. 1, 1993.

44. House Subcommittee on Western Hemisphere Affairs, *Foreign Assistance Legislation for Fiscal Year 1985*, 42.

45. White, interview.

46. Carl Gettinger, interview by author, Jan. 25, 1994.

47. Ibid., and American Embassy, San Salvador (1212), to Secretary of State, "Subject: (S) Conversation with National Guard Officer," Nov. 19, 1980.

48. American Embassy, San Salvador (5121), to Secretary of State, "Subject: Rightist Doings," Aug. 14, 1981; American Embassy, San Salvador (3083), to Secretary of State, "Subject: Security Force Officer Comments on Sheraton Murders, Other Rightist Vio-lence," Apr. 23, 1981, p. 3.

49. American Embassy, San Salvador (9718), to Secretary of State, "Subject: Assassination of Archbishop Romero," Dec. 21, 1980.

50. Gettinger, interview; American Embassy, San Salvador (3048), to Secretary of State, "Subject: More Suspects in Killings of U.S. Churchwomen," Apr. 22, 1981, p. 3.

51. Carl Gettinger, interview by author, Mar. 14, 1994; U.S. Department of State, "Report of the Secretary of State's Panel on El Salvador," July 1983, p. 22; Tom Enders to the Secretary of State, "Subject: Suspects in Killings of U.S. Churchwomen," Department of State memorandum, Apr. 16, 1981.

52. Elliott Abrams and Michael Newlin to Ambassador Armacost, "Subject: Entry of Roberto D'Aubuisson into the U.S.," Department of State action memorandum, Aug. 2, 1985, p. 1.

53. Todd Greentree, interview by author, Jan. 13, 1994.

54. Deane Hinton, interview by author, Mar. 3, 1994.

55. CIA cable, "Subject: Background on Assassination of Archbishop Romero," May 28, 1987; CIA cable, "Subject: Romero Murder Case," Aug. 3, 1984; CIA cable, Mar. 10, 1984; CIA cable, "Subject: Allegation by Chief of the Nationalist Republican Alliance (ARENA) Paramilitary Unit that a National Guard Officer Assassinated Archbishop Romero in 1980," Apr. 22, 1983; CIA cable, "Subject: Existence of a Rightist Death Squad Within the Salvadoran National Police; Location of Clandestine Prison Used by the Death Squad," Mar. 19, 1983; CIA biographical sheet on Detective Edgardo Sigifredo Perez Linares, n.d.

56. CIA Directorate of Intelligence, "El Salvador: D'Aubuisson's Terrorist Activities," Mar. 2, 1984, p. 3.

57. Greentree, interview.

58. White, interview.

59. American Embassy, San Salvador (5121), Aug. 14, 1981; American Embassy, San Salvador (9718), Dec. 21, 1981.

60. Gettinger, interview, Jan. 25, 1994.

61. Victor Johnson, interviews by author, July 6, 1993, and Feb. 15, 1994; Robert Kurz, interviews by author, June 11, 1993, and Feb. 14, 1994.

62. Chairman Clement Zablocki, House Foreign Affairs Committee, to the Honorable George Shultz, Secretary of State, Apr. 19, 1983.

63. Johnson, interviews, July 6, 1993, and Feb. 15, 1994; Kurz, interviews, June 11, 1993, and Feb. 14, 1994.

64. Commission on the Truth, *From Madness to Hope*, pp. 114–21.

65. American Embassy, San Salvador (0164), to Secretary of State, "Subject: Alleged Morazan Massacre," Jan. 8, 1982.

66. "Massacre of Hundreds Reported in Salvador Village," *New York Times*, Jan. 27, 1982, pp. A1, A10; "Salvadoran Peasants Describe Mass Killing," *Washington Post*, Jan. 7, 1982, pp. A1, A16.

67. For example, see Senate Committee on Foreign Relations, *Certification Concerning Military Aid to El Salvador*, p. 21.

68. House Subcommittee on Oversight and Evaluation, *U.S. Intelligence Performance on Central America*, 18–19. The critical cable is: American Embassy, San Salvador (0773), to Department of State, "Subject: Report on Alleged Massacre," Jan. 31, 1982.

69. Mark Danner, "The Truth of El Mozote," *New Yorker*, Dec. 6, 1993, p. 50.

70. American Embassy, San Salvador (7683), to Secretary of State, "Subject: Chat with General Garcia," Feb. 1, 1982.

71. American Embassy, San Salvador (7684), to Secretary of State, "Subject: Allegations of Massacre in Morazan," Feb. 1, 1982.

72. Hinton, interview; and Kenneth Bleakley, interview by author, Mar. 8, 1994.

73. American Embassy, San Salvador (7683), Feb. 1, 1982.

74. Johnson, interviews, July 6, 1993, and Feb. 15, 1994; Kurz, interviews, June 11, 1993, and Feb. 14, 1994.

75. American Embassy, Tegucigalpa (6688), to Secretary of State, "Subject: Reports of Alleged Massacre by the Salvadoran Army," Feb. 17, 1982.

76. Department of State, "Report of the Secretary of State's Panel on El Salvador," p. 59; Department of State, "Discussions with Socorro Juridico About El Mozote and Follow Up" and "Discrepancies in Socorro Letter," n.d. (written by Todd Greentree).

77. Todd Greentree, interview by author, Feb. 9, 1994.

78. Kurz, interview, Feb. 14, 1994.

79. Hinton, interview.

80. CIA cable, Mar. 19, 1983, (see n. 55 to this chapter); CIA cable, Apr. 17, 1984 ("Brief backgrounder" on ARENA and its association with right-wing death squad activity); CIA "Special Analysis"—"El Salvador: Threat from the Right," 1983 (date on copy unclear). See also CIA, "Briefing Paper on Right-Wing Terrorism in El Salvador," Oct. 27, 1983, which notes, among other things, that the death squads' "official protection from prosecution or governmental interference is primarily the result of personal alliances between key government officials and group leaders"(p. 3). House *Report on the Activities of the Permanent Select Commit-*

tee on Intelligence During the 98th Congress, 98th Cong., 2d sess., Jan. 2, 1985, p. 19.

81. William Woodward, interview by author, Sept. 24, 1993; Kurz, interview, Feb. 14, 1994; and Johnson, interview, Feb. 15, 1994.

82. Kurz, interview, Feb. 14, 1994.

83. Johnson, interview, Feb. 15, 1994.

84. Dante Fascell, interview by author, Jan. 27, 1994.

85. Johnson, interview, Feb. 15, 1994.

86. Kurz, interview, Feb. 14, 1994.

87. Arnson, *Crossroads*, pp. 268, 90–91, 153–62.

88. Enders, interview.

89. Barnes, interview.

90. Kurz, interview, June 11, 1993; and Johnson, interview, July 6, 1993.

91. McHugh, interview.

92. Stephen Solarz, interview by author, Oct. 28, 1993.

93. "U.S. Policy in Central America and Cuba Through FY 1984, Summary Paper," Apr. 1982, in *New York Times*, Apr. 7, 1983, p. 16.

94. Carothers, *In the Name of Democracy*, pp. 25–27; Arnson, *Crossroads*, pp. 95–98.

95. Arnson, *Crossroads*, pp. 99–100.

96. Tom Enders to Walter J. Stoessel, Jr., "Subject: Your Luncheon for President José Napoleon Duarte of El Salvador, 12:30 p.m., September 21, at the State Department—Scope Paper," Department of State briefing memorandum, Sept. 19, 1981, p. 5.

97. Arnson, *Crossroads*, p. 140.

98. Senate Committee on Foreign Relations to Secretary of State George P. Shultz, Mar. 24, 1983; Senate Committee on Appropriations to Secretary of State George P. Shultz, Mar. 23, 1983.

99. Interagency task force working paper for NSC. Cited in Philip Taubman, "U.S. Said to Weigh 40 Percent Increase in Military Funds for Latin Allies," *New York Times*, July 17, 1983, p. 10.

100. American Embassy, San Salvador (11567), to Secretary of State, "Subject: Vice-President Bush's Meetings with Salvadoran Officials," Dec. 14, 1983, pp. 1–2.

101. House Committee on Foreign Affairs, *Congress and Foreign Policy 1984*, pp. 22–23.

102. *Congressional Record* (May 10, 1984): H11807–76

103. Arnson, *Crossroads*, p. 283.

104. Senate Committee on Foreign Relations, and House, Committee on Foreign Affairs, "Joint Conference 1982 Foreign Assistance Authorization Act," Monday, Dec. 14, 1981, typewritten transcript, p. 67, National Archives, Washington, D.C.

105. Ibid., pp. 41, 51–52.

106. Ibid., pp. 41–42, 62. For a similar House view of the meaning of the provision, see statement of Michael Barnes, *Congressional Record* (Dec. 16, 1981): 31702

107. See, for example, House Committee on Foreign Affairs, Subcommitee on Inter-American Affairs, *Presidential Certification on El Salvador: Hearings before the Subcommittee on Inter-American Affairs,* pt. 1, 97th Cong., 2d sess., Feb. 2, 23, 25, and Mar. 2, 1982, 28, 97–98.

108. House Subcommittee on Oversight and Evaluation, *U.S. Intelligence Performance on Central America*, 5–7. CIA, National Foreign Assessment Center, "Arms Trafficking in Central America," n.d. (between July and Sept. 1980), p. 12, stated, "On balance, therefore, it seems likely that the Sandinista leadership has provided the Salvadoran insurgents with at least some tangible support and assistance—probably in modest quantities."

109. House Committee on Foreign Affairs, Subcommittee on Inter-American Affairs, *Review of the Presidential Certification of Nicaragua's Connection to Terrorism: Hearing before the Subcommittee on Inter-American Affairs*, 96th Cong., 2d sess., Sept. 30, 1980, 26. Former NSC staff member Robert Pastor wrote that the State Department legal advisor established the "standard of proof" (Pastor to the author, Sept. 15, 1993).

110. Ibid., pp. 11, 19.

111. C. W. Bill Young, interview by author, Feb. 10, 1994.

112. Steve Weissman to Howard Wolpe, "Re: Pending FY 1983 Foreign Aid Supplemental Appropriation on the Floor This Week," memorandum, n.d. (Apr. or May 1983).

113. Steve Weissman to Howard Wolpe and Steve Solarz, "Tomorrow Morning's HFAC Meeting on El Salvador and the Pending Foreign Aid Bill," memorandum, Sept. 28, 1983.

114. Steve Weissman to Howard Wolpe and Steve Solarz, "Re: Avoiding Disaster on the Foreign Aid Bill Next Week," memorandum, May 1, 1984.

115. Carothers, *In the Name of Democracy*, p. 43.

CHAPTER 3. THE POLITICS OF LOBBYING:
U.S. POLICY TOWARD ZAIRE, 1979–1990

1. Stephen R. Weissman, "CIA Covert Action in Zaire and Angola," *Political Science Quarterly* 94 (Summer 1979): 263–86; U.S. government documents shown to author in the mid-1970s.

2. Stephen R. Weissman, *American Foreign Policy in the Congo 1960–1964* (Ithaca, N.Y.: Cornell University Press, 1974), p. 142n.

3. Crawford Young, "The Zairian Crisis and American Foreign Policy," in Gerald J. Bender, James S. Coleman, and Richard L. Sklar, eds., *African Crisis Areas and U.S. Foreign Policy* (Berkeley: University of California Press, 1985), pp. 209–24; David J. Gould, *Bureaucratic Corruption and Underdevelopment in the Third World: The Case of Zaire* (New York: Pergamon, 1980); and Michael G. Schatsberg, *The Dialectics of Oppression in Zaire* (Bloomington: Indiana University Press, 1988).

4. See, for example, House Committee on Foreign Affairs, Subcommittee on Africa, *Foreign Assistance Legislation for Fiscal Years 1980–81: Hearings before the Subcommittee on Africa* (and markup), pt. 6, 96th Cong., 1st sess., Feb. 13, 14, 21, 22, 27, 28, Mar. 5, 6, 7, 12, 1979, 353–70 (Testimony of Richard M. Moose, Assistant Secretary of State for African Affairs); House Committee on Foreign Affairs, Subcommittee on Africa, *Foreign Assistance Legislation for Fiscal Years 1984–85: Hearings before the Subcommittee on Africa* (and markup), pt. 8, 98th Cong., 1st sess., Mar. 17, 22, Apr. 13, 1983, pp. 120–21, 182–83 (Testimony of Chester A. Crocker, Assistant Secretary of State for African Affairs); and House Committee on Foreign Affairs, Subcommitee on Africa, *Foreign Assistance Legislation for Fiscal Years 1986–87: Hearings before the Subcommittee on Africa,* pt. 7, 99th Cong., 1st sess., Mar. 5, 7, and 19, 1985, 90–92 (Testimony of Frank Wisner, Deputy Assistant Secretary of State for African Affairs). On U.S. intelligence-sharing with Zaire to bolster Mobutu's rule, see Weissman, "CIA Covert Action in Zaire and Angola," p. 273; and Jack Anderson, "CIA Helps Zaire Leader Crush Plot," *Washington Post*, Nov. 22, 1984, p. E15.

5. House Committee on Foreign Affairs, *The Impact of U.S. Foreign Policy on Seven African Countries*, report prepared by a congressional study mission to Ethiopia, Zaire, Zimbabwe, Ivory Coast, Algeria, and Morocco, Aug. 6–25, 1983 and a staff study mission to

Tunisia, Aug. 24–27, 1983, 98th Cong., 2d sess., Mar. 9, 1984, 35–36.

6. Interagency Intelligence Memorandum, "The Outlook for the Zairian Economy," Nov. 3, 1982, p. 12; Department of State, Bureau of Intelligence and Research, "Zaire: Mobutu No Longer an Alternative to Chaos," *Africa Trends* (July 26, 1991): 5.

7. House Committee on Foreign Affairs, Subcommittee on Africa, *Foreign Assistance Legislation for Fiscal Year 1981: Hearings before the Subcommittee on Africa*, pt. 7 (and markup), 96th Cong., 2d sess., Feb. 7, 12, 13, 20, 25, 26, 27, 28, and Mar. 5 and 6, 1980, xiii–xvi; House Subcommittee on Africa, *Foreign Assistance Legislation for Fiscal Years 1984–85*, pp. xvi–xvii.

8. House Committee on Foreign Affairs, *The Impact of U.S. Foreign Policy on Seven African Countries*, 35–36.

9. House Subcommittee on Africa, *Foreign Assistance Legislation for Fiscal Year 1981*, 527–28.

10. The congressional resolutions may be found in *Congressional Record* (Nov. 19, 1991): H10581–82; and *Congressional Record* (Mar. 18, 1992): S3862; Herman J. Cohen, "The Situation in Zaire," statement before the Subcommittee on Africa of the Committee on Foreign Affairs of the House of Representatives, Oct. 26, 1993; Testimony of Assistant Secretary of State George Moose before the Subcommittee on Africa, U.S. House of Representatives, Oct. 26, 1993.

11. House Committee on Foreign Affairs, Subcommittees on Human Rights and International Organizations and Africa, *The Human Rights Situation in South Africa, Zaire, the Horn of Africa, and Uganda: Hearings before the Subcommittees on Human Rights and International Organizations and Africa*, 98th Cong., 2d sess., June 21, Aug. 9, 1984, 34.

12. House Committee on Foreign Affairs, *The Impact of U.S. Foreign Policy on Seven African Countries*, 27–36.

13. Ibid.

14. Jay Ross, "Capitol Hill Takes Its Bickering to Africa," *Washington Post*, Aug. 18, 1983, p. A22.

15. *Salongo* (Kinshasa, Zaire), Aug. 11, 1987.

16. Tape recording of a meeting in December 1987 between Rep. Mickey Leland and Zaire opposition leader Etienne Tshisekedi (courtesy of reporter Richard Sokolow).

17. Ibid.

18. Edward T. Pound, "Congo Drums," *Wall Street Journal*, Mar. 7, 1990, pp. A1, A4; Dan Morgan, *Merchants of Grain* (New York: Viking, 1979), pp. 295–310; Charles R. Babcock, "The Corporate King of Honoraria," *Washington Post*, Mar. 20, 1990, p. A9; Brooks Jackson, *Honest Graft: Big Money and the American Political Process* (Washington, D.C.: Farragut Publishers, 1990), pp. 137–38, 210–11; Timothy S. Robinson, "U.S. Rice Exporter to Korea Is Indicted," *Washington Post*, May 27, 1978, p. A9; Agnes T. Gottlieb, *Associated Press*, Apr. 17, 1979.

19. U.S. House of Representatives, Committee on Standards of Official Conduct, George Thomas Leland, Financial Disclosure Statements for 1986, 1987, and 1988.

20. Federal Election Commission (computer printout).

21. Connell Rice and Sugar spent approximately $347,000 in honoraria from 1986–89, almost all of it on Democrats. See Babcock, "The Corporate King of Honoraria," pp. A1, A9; Pound, "Congo Drums," p. A4; and Charles R. Babcock, "Controversial Rice Broker Provides Plentiful Hill Speech Fees," *Washington Post*, July 11, 1989, p. A5.

22. Federal Election Commission (computer printout). Mr. and Mrs. Connell spent $280,000 on campaign contributions, close to the legal maximum, during 1985–90; almost all went to Democratic candidates for Congress.

23. Connell Rice and Sugar donated $200,000 over four years (around the mid-1980s), according to Babcock, "The Corporate King of Honoraria," p. A9.

24. Ibid.; information provided by U.S. Department of Agriculture, June 10, 1994.

25. Edward T. Pound, "Connell Loses Lucrative Contract to Supply a Mining Firm in Zaire," *Wall Street Journal*, Nov. 26, 1990, p. B5.

26. Babcock, "The Corporate King of Honoraria," p. A9.

27. Howard Wolpe, interview by author, Nov. 18, 1993.

28. Randy Katsoyannis, interview by author, Nov. 14, 1993.

29. Wolpe, interview; and Katsoyannis, interview.

30. House Subcommittee on Africa, *Foreign Assistance Legislation for Fiscal Years 1980–81*, 40, 351.

31. Ibid., 399–400, 382.

32. Gould, *Bureaucratic Corruption and Underdevelopment in the Third World*, pp. 49, xiii.

33. David Lamb, "Zaire Near Brink of Collapse Under Pro-West

Despot," *Los Angeles Times*, Mar. 4, 1979, p. 5. While the rice was technically not a gift, it was made available by a loan at highly concessional rates and with delayed maturity. Due to repeated debt reschedulings for Zaire, the rice aid may turn out to be all or almost all "gift."

34. David J. Gould, "The Problem of Seepage in International Development Assistance: Why United States Aid to Zaire Goes Astray," n.d., p. 17, typescript.

35. House Subcommittee on Africa, *Foreign Assistance Legislation for Fiscal Years 1980–81*, 430–31, 531, 368–69; U.S. Department of State, "Executive Branch Position Paper: Transfer of Rice Provided Under the Zaire PL-480 Title I Program to Title II," 1979.

36. U.S. Department of Agriculture, "1991 Rice: List Ranking for Harvested Areas."

37. David Bowen, telephone interview by author, Nov. 16, 1993.

38. Federal Election Commission (computer printouts).

39. Bowen, telephone interview.

40. Susan B. Epstein and Jasper Womach, "Agricultural Trade: The United States and Selected Developed and Developing Countries," Congressional Research Service, Library of Congress, Mar. 6, 1987, p. CRS-34; U.S. Agency for International Development, "PL 480 Title I Rice Programs, 1978–80."

41. Bowen, telephone interview.

42. House Committee on Foreign Affairs, *Foreign Assistance Legislation for Fiscal Years 1980–81*, pt. 8, Markup, 96th Cong., 1st sess., Mar. 20, 21, 22, 27, 28, and 29, 1979, pp. 179–92.

43. *Congressional Record* (Apr. 5, 1979): 7366–74; U.S. Department of Agriculture, "1991 Rice: List Ranking for Harvested Areas;" Telephone communication from representative of Tony Coelho, May 23, 1994.

44. Bowen, telephone interview.

45. George A. Chauncey, Interreligious Taskforce on U.S. Food Policy, Mar. 30, 1979, to members of the House of Representatives.

46. *Elima* (Kinshasa, Zaire), Apr. 3, 1979 (author's translation), p. 4.

47. Comptroller General of the United States, General Accounting Office, *Search for Options in the Troubled Food-For-Peace Program in Zaire*, report prepared for the Subcommittee on Africa of the House Committee on Foreign Affairs, Feb. 12, 1989 (ID 80-25), esp. pp. 9–25.

48. House Subcommittee on Africa, *Foreign Assistance Legislation for Fiscal Year 1981*, pp. 544–45.

49. U.S. Agency for International Development, "FY 1983 Annual Budget Submission: PL-480 Narrative (Zaire)," p. 34; House Subcommittee on Africa, *Foreign Assistance Legislation for Fiscal Years 1986–87*, p. 126; Bowen, telephone interview.

50. Senate Committee on Foreign Relations, "To Markup S584 to Amend the Foreign Assistance Act of 1961 and the Arms Export Control Act, and for Other Purposes," May 3, 1979, pp. 93–97, typewritten transcript, National Archives, Washington, D.C.; George McGovern, interwiew by author, Nov. 22, 1993; and Pauline Baker, interview by author, Aug. 5, 1993.

51. McGovern, interview; and Baker, interview.

52. Senate Committee on Foreign Relations, "To Markup S584 . . . ," pp. 96, 94.

53. Senate Committee on Foreign Relations and House Committee on Foreign Affairs, "Joint Conferees, H.R. 3173, International Security Assistance Act of 1979," July 31, 1979, pp. 20–33, typewritten transcript, National Archives, Washington, D.C.

54. Senate Committee on Banking, Housing, and Urban Affairs, Subcommittee on International Finance, *U.S. Loans to Zaire: Hearing before the Subcommittee on International Finance*, 96th Cong., 1st sess., May 24, 1979, esp. 6–7, 18, 37–42, 55–68; Katherine Dixon, "The Inga-Shaba Project: Disaster for Development Banks in Zaire," *Country Notes*, Center for Development Policy, Washington, D.C., Apr. 26, 1982; Young, "The Zairian Crisis and American Foreign Policy," pp. 216–17; *Time*, Jan. 10, 1983, p. 48.

55. Mike Wetherell, telephone interview by author, Nov. 1, 1993; and Peter Fenn, telephone interview by author, Nov. 2, 1983.

56. Leroy Ashby, telephone interview by author, Aug. 25, 1993.

57. Fenn, telephone interview.

58. The sixteen "principal American [academic] specialists on Zaire" who wrote Senator Church and other members of the Foreign Relations Committee that "further military aid would be counterproductive" (letter of Apr. 27, 1979) did not comprise a political constituency.

59. Floyd Fithian, interview by author, Nov. 4, 1993.

60. House Subcommittee on Africa, *Foreign Assistance Legislation for Fiscal Year 1981*, pp. 83, 652.

61. House Committee on Foreign Affairs, *Foreign Assistance Legislation for Fiscal Year 1981*, pt. 9, Markup, 96th Cong., 2d sess., March 11, 12, 13, 18, 19, 20, 25, 26, and 27, 1980, pp. 143–54; U.S. Congress, Senate Committee on Foreign Relations and House

Committee on Foreign Affairs, "Joint Conferees HR 6924," Nov. 19, 1980 (morning sess.), pp. 23–35, typewritten transcript, National Archives, Washington, D.C.

62. House Committee on Foreign Affairs, Subcommittee on Africa, *Political and Economic Situation in Zaire—Fall 1981: Hearing before the Subcommittee on Africa,* 97th Cong., 1st sess., Sept. 15, 1981; Barbara Crossette, "Leader in Exile Pleads His Case in the Capital," *New York Times,* Sept. 28, 1981, p. B12.

63. Don Oberdorfer, "Zaire, Stung By Criticism, To Renounce U.S. Aid," *Washington Post,* May 14, 1982, p. A20.

64. Senate Committee on Foreign Relations, *Zaire: A Staff Report,* 97th Cong., 2d sess., July 1982.

65. Paris, *Agence France Presse* (Foreign Broadcast Information Service translation), May 13, 1982; see also Alan Cowell, "Superstition Deepens Mobutu's Fear and Isolation," *New York Times,* June 18, 1982, p. A2.

66. House Committee on Foreign Affairs, *Foreign Assistance Legislation for Fiscal Year 1983,* pt. 8, Markup, 97th Cong., 2d sess., May 4, 5, 6, 11, 12, and 13, 1982, 188.

67. Mitchell Geoffrey Bard, *The Water's Edge and Beyond* (New Brunswick, N.J.: Transaction, 1991), p. 301.

68. Ibid., pp. 7–13; Hedrick Smith, *The Power Game: How Washington Works* (New York: Ballantine, 1988), pp. 215–29; David Howard Goldberg, *Foreign Policy and Ethnic Interest Groups: American and Canadian Jews Lobby for Israel* (New York: Greenwood Press, 1991), pp. 17–27. See also n. 69, this chapter.

69. Anonymous, telephone interview by author, Apr. 8, 1994; Anonymous, telephone interview by author, Apr. 13, 1994; and author discussions with AIPAC officials at the time.

70. U.S. Department of Justice, Foreign Agents Registration Statement, Hampton-Windsor Corporation, Aug. 17, 1981; Zev Furst, telephone interview by author, Apr. 15, 1994.

71. Don Oberdorfer, "Limit Involvement with Mobutu, Senate Staff Report Urges U.S.," *Washington Post,* June 4, 1982, p. A20; Edward Tivnan, *The Lobby: Jewish Political Power and American Foreign Policy* (New York: Simon and Schuster, 1987), pp. 189–91.

72. Erwin Blumenthal, "Zaire: Report on Her International Financial Credibility," confidential, Apr. 7, 1982, p. 19, typescript.

73. Anonymous, telephone interview by author, Apr. 10, 1994; Anonymous, telephone interview by author, Apr. 15, 1994.

74. U.S. Department of Justice, Foreign Agents Registration Final Statement, Hampton-Windsor Corporation, period ending June 30, 1983, p. 3; Furst, telephone interview; Federal Election Commission, itemized receipts, Robert Torricelli for Congress Campaign Committee, Inc., 1983–84.

75. House Committee on Foreign Affairs, *Foreign Assistance Legislation for Fiscal Years 1984–85*, pt. 9, Markup, 98th Cong., 1st sess., Apr. 19, 26, 27, May 3, 9, 10, 11, 12, 1983, 388.

76. Ibid., 386–95.

77. House Committee on Foreign Affairs, *Foreign Assistance Legislation for Fiscal Years 1986–87*, pt. 8, Markup, 99th Cong., 1st sess., Mar. 26, 27, Apr. 1, 2, 3, 1985, 192.

   I observed congressional reaction to AIPAC's tactics at the time. AIPAC's resulting retreat was suggested by a participant (Anonymous, telephone interview by author, Apr. 13, 1994). Furst described his departure from lobbying for Zaire in telephone interview (Apr. 14, 1994).

78. House Committee on Foreign Affairs, Subcommittee on Africa, *Foreign Assistance Legislation for Fiscal Year 1985: Hearing before the Subcommittee on Africa,* pt. 7, Markup, 98th Cong., 2d sess., Feb. 23, 1984, viii.

79. House Committee on Foreign Affairs, *Foreign Assistance Legislation for Fiscal Years 1984–85*, 394.

80. U.S. House of Representatives, Committee on Standards of Official Conduct, Mervyn M. Dymally, Financial Disclosure Statement for 1988, Attachment 2B (letter of Feb. 9, 1988).

81. Rep. Robert J. Mrazek and colleagues to President Mobutu Sese Seko, Feb. 2, 1988.

82. Mervyn M. Dymally to Honorable Robert J. Mrazek, Feb. 3, 1988.

83. Robert J. Mrazek to Honorable Mervyn M. Dymally, Feb. 10, 1988.

84. Pound, "Congo Drums," p. A4.

85. Ibid.; Government of the District of Columbia, Department of Consumer and Regulatory Affairs, Business Regulation, Certificate of Incorporation, Zaire-American Research Institute, Mar. 1, 1988; Anonymous, interview by author, Apr. 7, 1994; and Anonymous, interview by author, Apr. 15, 1994.

86. Press releases, Congressman Mervyn M. Dymally and Zaire-American Research Institute, Sept. 29, 1988.

87. Tshisekedi wa Mulumba, National Secretariat, Union for Democracy

and Social Progress, to Nancy Ross, Rainbow Lobby, Dec. 3, 1988.

88. William Harrop, interview by author, July 26, 1993.

89. Pound, "Congo Drums," p. A4.

90. Mervyn Dymally, telephone interview by author, June 3, 1994; Federal Election Commission (computer printout); Anonymous, interview by author, Apr. 7, 1994; and Anonymous, interview by author, Apr. 15, 1994.

91. Harrop, interview.

92. Howard S. Abramson and Rose A. Horowitz, "Rep. Dymally Defends Letter to Uganda," *Journal of Commerce*, June 16, 1989, pp. A1, A10.

93. Ibid., p. A10.

94. Pound, "Congo Drums," p. A4; Jonathan Kapstein, "Can Mobutu Persuade the West to Bail Out Zaire?" *Business Week*, Dec. 12, 1983, p. 10; "Zaire: Unrest at the Top," *Africa Confidential* (London) 25 (May 23, 1984): 7–8; "Zaire: High Life," *Africa Confidential* (London) 27 (Sept. 17, 1986): 5–6; "Belgium/Zaire: Radio Trottoir," *Africa Confidential* 29 (Dec. 2, 1988): 8; Guy Bouten, "Deval," *Trends* (Brussels) (Mar. 3, 1988): 17–19; Anonymous, interview by author, Apr. 7, 1994; and Anonymous, interview by author, Apr. 15, 1994.

95. Pound, "Congo Drums," p. A4; "Favored Few Tap Zaire Wealth," *Africa News*, Jan. 29, 1990, p. 10.

96. "Favored Few"; Abramson and Horowitz, "Rep. Dymally Defends Letter to Uganda," p. A10; Pound, "Congo Drums," p. A4; Jim McGee, "Peace Corps Worker Alleges Rep. Savage Assaulted Her," *Washington Post*, July 19, 1989, pp. A1, A8.

97. Dymally, telephone interview; Jim McGee, "Rep. Dymally's Contacts Raise Issues of Public Trust, Private Interests," *Washington Post*, Jan. 2, 1990, p. A15.

98. Federal Election Commission (computer printouts).

99. "Favored Few . . . ," pp. 3, 11; McGee, "Rep. Dymally's Contacts," p. A15.

100. McGee, "Rep. Dymally's Contacts," p. A15. Dymally (telephone interview) confirmed that it was "true" that "little money [from the telethon] got to the kids."

101. Ibid.; Rose A. Horowitz and Howard S. Abramson, "California Congressman Said to Press Uganda on Choice of Agent," *Journal of Commerce*, June 15, 1989, pp. A1, A8. On Dymally's emphasis, as Chairman of the House Africa Subcommittee, on promoting African-American businesspeople in Africa, see House Committee

on Foreign Affairs, *Congress and Foreign Policy 1992*, 103rd Cong., p. 83.

102. Dymally, telephone interview; Abramson and Horowitz, "Rep. Dymally Defends Letter to Uganda," p. A1.

103. HR 3355, 100th Cong., 1st sess.; Mrazek and colleagues to President Mobutu Sese Seko; Michael Klein, "Capitol Hill Scrap Over Zaire," *National Alliance*, Feb. 19, 1988, p. 4.

104. Nancy Ross, interview by author, Apr. 4, 1994; Deborah Green, telephone interviews by author, Apr. 8 and 29, 1994; Nancy Ross, "The Impact of the Anti-Mobutu Lobby and the Emergence of the Pro-Mobutu Lobby," presentation to the African Studies Association, Atlanta, Georgia, 1989, typescript; *Deborah Green's International Democracy Report* 1 (February 1993); *Rainbow Lobby Quarterly Alert* 2: 1, 1988.

105. For example, see Olive Vassell, "Dymally Blasts Group," *Washington Afro-American*, Feb. 20, 1988; U.S.-Congo Friendship Committee, statement by Gloria Strickland (Joint Press Conference with Rainbow Lobby), Feb. 11, 1988; Rainbow Lobby, "Response to Dymally 1990" (statement) (Washington, D.C.: Rainbow Lobby, n.d.).

106. Ross, "The Impact of the Anti-Mobutu Lobby," p. 4.

107. Bob Brauer, telephone interview by author, Apr. 15, 1994.

108. Stephen Goose, interview by author, Nov. 8, 1993.

109. See, for example, "The New Alliance Party: A Study in Deception," ADL Research Report, 1990; and Glenn R. Simpson, "Under the Other Rainbow," *City Paper* (Washington, D.C.), Aug. 17, 1990. Rainbow Lobby responses include: Deborah Green to Mr. Jeffrey Sinensky, director, Civil Rights Division, Anti-Defamation League, May 30, 1990; and statement of Deborah Green, Tufts University, Nov. 21, 1989.

110. Pound, "Connell Loses Lucrative Contract."

111. Two former U.S. officials (anonymous), interviews by author, May 24, 1993, April 15, 1994, and date withheld.

112. Pound, "Connell Loses Lucrative Contract."

113. Two former U.S. officials (anonymous), interviews.

114. Pound, "Connell Loses Lucrative Contract"; World Bank Report No. P-5052 ZR, "Memorandum and Recommendation of the President of the International Development Association to the Executive Directors on a Proposed Credit of SDR 15.4 million to the Republic of Zaire for a Second Gécamines Technical Assistance Project,"

June 8, 1989, p. 2 referred to "excessive fees paid to agents [by Gécamines]"; John Russell, Public Affairs, Justice Department, telephone interview by author, Nov. 28, 1994.

115. Pound, "Congo Drums," p. A4.

116. Anonymous, interview by author, date withheld.

117. Harrop, interview; Anonymous, interview by author, May 24, 1993.

118. Pound, "Congo Drums," p. A4; "Favored Few," p. 10; Babcock, "The Corporate King of Honoraria," pp. A1, A9; Federal Election Commission (computer printout).

119. Pound, "Congo Drums," p. A4; Anonymous U.S. official, interview by author, date withheld.

120. House Subcommittee on Africa, *Foreign Assistance Legislation for Fiscal Years 1990–91: Hearings before the Subcommittee on Africa*, pt. 6, Markup, 101st Cong., 1st sess., Mar. 8, 9, and Apr. 25, 1989, 104.

121. Clifford Krauss, "House Democrats Challenge Bush by Seeking to Reduce Aid to Zaire," *New York Times*, Apr. 11, 1990, p. A2.

122. Based on author conversation at the time with a staff aide to Rep. Torricelli.

123. Goose, interview.

CHAPTER 4. THE SECRET CONGRESS: THE INTELLIGENCE COMMITTEES AND U.S. COVERT ACTION IN NICARAGUA AND ANGOLA

1. Senate Select Committee to Study Governmental Operations with Respect to Intelligence Activities, *Supplementary Detailed Staff Reports on Foreign and Military Intelligence*, bk. 4, 94th Cong., 2d sess., Apr. 23, 1976, 35–36; Patrick E. Tyler, "U.S. Says Hussein Is Purging Military," *New York Times*, July 6, 1992, p. A6; Elaine Sciolino, "Clinton to Scale Down Program to Oust Iraq Leader," *New York Times*, Apr. 10, 1993, p. I3; and Chris Hedges, "Rebels Have Little to Show for Efforts to Topple Saddam Hussein," *New York Times*, July 3, 1994, p. 8.

2. Gregory F. Treverton, *Covert Action: The Limits of Intervention in the Postwar World* (N.Y.: Basic Books, 1987), pp. 13–14; The Twentieth Century Fund Task Force on Covert Action and American Democracy, *The Need To Know* (New York: The Twentieth Century Fund Press, 1992), pp. 38–39, 63–64.

3. Leslie H. Gelb, "Overseeing of CIA by Congress Has Produced Decade of Support," *New York Times*, July 7, 1986, pp. A1, A10; David B. Ottoway and Patrick E. Tyler, "Casey Enforces Reagan

Doctrine with Reinvigorated Covert Action," *Washington Post*, Mar. 9, 1986, pp. A1, A10; Selig S. Harrison, "Afghanistan: Soviet Intervention, Afghan Resistance, and the American Role," in Michael T. Klare and Peter Kornbluh, eds., *Low-Intensity Warfare: Counterinsurgency, Proinsurgency, and Antiterrorism in the Eighties* (New York: Pantheon, 1987), pp. 184, 199–203.

4. The Twentieth Century Task Force on Covert Action and American Democracy, *The Need To Know*, pp. 40–41, 49.

5. Ibid., pp. 67–71.

6. The best general analysis of the oversight process is Frank J. Smist, Jr., *Congress Oversees the United States Intelligence Community, 1947–89* (Knoxville: University of Tennessee Press, 1990).

7. Lee H. Hamilton, "A View from the House," *Extracts from Studies in Intelligence*, Sept. 1987 (Langley, Va.), p. 69.

8. Cynthia J. Arnson, *Crossroads: Congress, the President, and Central America 1976–93*, 2d ed. (University Park: Pennsylvania State University Press, 1993), pp. 79–81, 106–12, 123–36, 163–72, 178–80; Wyche Fowler, interview by author, May 23, 1993; Robert Kastenmeier, interview by author, Nov. 23, 1993; Dave McCurdy, interview by author, Jan. 26, 1994; William Goodling, interview by author, Mar. 21, 1994; Michael O'Neil, interview by author, July 18, 1993; Anonymous House Intelligence Committee staffer, interviews by author, July 15–16, 1993; and Robert Simmons, interview by author, Dec. 16, 1993.

9. *Congressional Record* (June 15, 1987): H4693 (Boland's statement of July 28, 1983, cited in legislative history of Boland Amendment).

10. Barry M. Goldwater with Jack Caserly, *Goldwater* (New York: Doubleday, 1988), pp. 306–08.

11. Arnson, *Crossroads*, p. 179.

12. Anonymous, interview by author, date withheld.

13. Robert Parry, Associated Press, June 10, 1985; Alfonso Chardy, "U.S. Found to Skirt Ban on Contras," *Miami Herald*, June 24, 1985, pp. 1A, 7A; Joel Brinkley, "Nicaraguan Rebels Getting Advice from White House on Operations," *New York Times*, Aug. 8, 1985, pp. A1, A9; Joanne Omang, "White House Defends Legality of NSC Contact with Contras," *Washington Post*, Aug. 9, 1985, pp. A1, A18; and "McFarlane Aide Facilitates Policy," *Washington Post*, Aug. 11, 1985, pp. A1, A18; Alfonso Chardy, "Colonel's Actions May Have Broken Contra Aid Ban," *Miami Herald*, Apr. 30, 1986, p. 8A; Alfonso Chardy, "Despite Ban, U.S. Helping Contras,"

Miami Herald, June 8, 1986, pp. 1A, 26A; Alfonso Chardy, "Sources: White House OK'd Contra Supply Network," *Miami Herald*, June 22, 1986, p. 26A; and Robert Parry and Brian Barger, Associated Press, June 10, 1986.

14. Report of the Congressional Committees, pp. 31–153, 387–407; United States Court of Appeals for the District of Columbia Circuit, Division for the Purpose of Appointing Independent Counsel, Division No, 86-6, *Final Report of the Independent Counsel for Iran/Contra Matters, Volume I: Investigations and Presentations, Aug. 4, 1993* (Washington, D.C.: Government Printing Office, 1994), esp. pp. 1–10, 63–68.

15. Report of the Congressional Committees, pp. 122–42; Jonathan Fuerbinger, "McFarlane Backs Aide on Contra Role," *New York Times*, Sept. 6, 1985, p. A3. Although it has not been reported, former Senate Intelligence Committee staff director Bernard McMahon and former Rep. Dave McCurdy recall committee meetings with Poindexter at this time (Bernard McMahon, interview by author, June 1, 1994; and McCurdy, interview).

16. Simmons, interview.

17. Anonymous, interview by author, July 15, 1993.

18. Smist, *Congress Oversees the Intelligence Community, 1947–1989*, p. 265; Michael Barnes, interview by author, Nov. 24, 1993; United States District Court for the District of Columbia, *United States of America versus Oliver L. North*, Docket No. CR 88-80, vol. 11, Feb. 22, 1989, pp. 1822–23 (transcript).

19. McMahon, interview.

20. O'Neil, interview.

21. Matthew McHugh, interview by author, Nov. 30, 1993.

22. United States District Court for the District of Columbia, *United States of America vs. Clair Elroy George*, Docket Number: CR 91-521 and CR 92-215, Aug. 4, 1992, p. 1749 (transcript).

23. Dan Finn, interview by author, June 8, 1994.

24. McMahon, interview.

25. Finn, interview; McHugh, interview; and Kastenmeier, interview.

26. Kastenmeier, interview.

27. McHugh, interview.

28. Senate, *Report of the Senate Select Committee on Intelligence, Jan. 1, 1983–Dec. 1, 1984*, 98th Cong., 2d sess., Oct. 10, 1984, p. 2.

29. Kastenmeier, interview. McHugh agreed (interview).

30. William Goodling, interview by author, Mar. 21, 1994.

31. McCurdy, interview.

32. McMahon, interview; and Anonymous, interview by author, May 9, 1994.

33. McHugh, interview; Treverton, *Covert Action*, p. 255.

34. U.S. District Court for the District of Columbia, *United States of America vs. Clair Elroy George*, pp. 1779, 1749.

35. McCurdy, interview; Steven Berry, Associate Counsel, House Permanent Select Committee on Intelligence, Memo to the Files: Aug. 6, 1986, White House Situation Room, p. 2, in Peter Kornbluh and Malcolm Byrne, *The Iran-Contra Scandal: The Declassified History* (New York: New Press, 1993), pp. 211–12.

36. Anonymous, interview, May 9, 1994; and McMahon, interview.

37. Fuerbinger, "McFarlane Backs Aide on Contra Role."

38. McMahon, interview.

39. This was noted, in interviews by the author, by several members of the House Committee as well as staff of the Senate Committee.

40. House Select Committee to Investigate Covert Arms Transactions with Iran and Senate Select Committee on Secret Military Assistance to the Nicaraguan Opposition, *Testimony of Robert C. McFarlane, Gaston J. Sigur, Jr. and Robert W. Owen: Hearings before the House Select Committee to Investigate Covert Arms Transactions with Iran and Senate Select Committee on Secret Military Assistance to the Nicaraguan Opposition,* 100–2, 100th Cong., 1st sess., May 11, 12, 13, 14, and 19, 1987, pp. 546–47, 553–55. (Hereafter cited as House and Senate Investigating Committees); Report of the Congressional Investigating Committees, pp. 122–30; U.S. District Court of Appeals for the District of Columbia, *Final Report of the Independent Counsel for Iran-Contra Matters*, pp. 83–87.

41. Michael Barnes, interview by author, Nov. 24, 1993; and Robert Kurz, interview by author, June 11, 1993.

42. John L. Jackley, *Hill Rat: Blowing the Lid Off Congress* (Washington, D.C.: Regnery Gateway, 1992), p. 152.

43. Victor Johnson, interview by author, July 6, 1993; and Kurz, interview.

44. Barnes, interview.

45. House and Senate Investigating Committees, pp. 553–55.

46. Jackley, *Hill Rat*, pp. 150–56.

47. Lee H. Hamilton, chairman, to Ronald D. Coleman, Aug. 12, 1986.

48. An extremely valuable analysis of the rise and fall of the Clark Amendment is June Sager Speakman, "Congress and Policy

Change: The Case of Angola" (Ph.D. diss., Political Science, City University of New York, 1994); on the factors accounting for passage of the Amendment, see esp. 95–221.

49. Dick Clark, "Clark Amendment," June 1993 (typescript provided by the author); see also John Stockwell, *In Search of Enemies: A CIA Story* (New York: Norton, 1978), p. 230. The nub of the lie was that the CIA was not simply replacing arms sent by Zaire to Angola but also supplying the Angolan factions directly.

50. The difference was subsequently underlined by the CIA's Office of General Counsel: "Unlike the Clark Amendment, this section limits all funds rather than all assistance and it could be thought, therefore, to permit certain activities precluded under the Clark Amendment." See Office of General Counsel for General Counsel, "Subject: HR 5399–Section 107, Prohibition on Covert Assistance for Military Operations in Nicaragua," memorandum, Aug. 23, 1984, in Senate Select Committee on Secret Military Assistance to Iran and the Nicaraguan Opposition and House Select Committee to Investigate Covert Arms Transactions with Iran, *Iran-Contra Investigation, Testimony of Dewey R. Claridge, C/CATF, and Clair George: Joint Hearings in Executive Sess.* (as declassified), 100-11, 100th Cong., 1st sess., Aug. 4, 5, and 6, 1987, 977.

51. Senate Committee on Foreign Relations, *International Security Assistance and Arms Export Control Act of 1976–77, Report on S 3439*, 94th Cong., 2d sess., May 14, 1976, 55; and House Committee on International Relations, *International Security Assistance Act of 1976: Report*, 94th Cong., 2d sess., Feb. 24, 1976, 40. See also earlier discussions of the legislation in Senate Committee on Foreign Relations, Subcommittee on Foreign Assistance, *Foreign Assistance Authorization: Arms Sales Issues: Hearings before the Subcommittee on Foreign Assistance,* 94th Cong., 1st sess., June 17, 18, Nov. 19, 21, and Dec. 4, 5, 1975, 540, 542; Senate Committee on Foreign Relations, *Restrictions on Assistance to Angola, Report to Accompany S.J. Res. 156*, 94th Cong., 1st sess., Dec. 18, 1975, 4–5; and House Committee on International Relations, *International Security Assistance Act of 1976: Hearings before the Committee on International Relations,* 94th Cong., Nov. 1975–Feb. 1976 (numerous dates), 735, 739, 742–43, 761–62.

52. Dick Clark, interview by author, Sept. 21, 1993; and Pauline Baker, interview by author, Aug. 5, 1993. See also Walter Pincus and Robert Kaiser, "Clark Fears Revived Role in Angola," *Washington Post*, May 24, 1978, pp. A1, A16.

53. SCC (Special Coordination Committee) Meeting on Horn of Africa, National Security Council, Mar. 2, 1978, White House Situation Room, p. 13.

54. Albert R. Hunt and Thomas J. Bray, "An Interview with Ronald Reagan," *Wall Street Journal*, May 6, 1980, p. 26.

55. "The Return of the Portuguese to Angola is Fundamental," *O Tempo* (Lisbon), Jan. 21, 1982 (translated by Congressional Research Service Language Service, Library of Congress).

56. American Embassy, Lisbon (1049) to Secretary of State, "UNITA Denies Receiving U.S. Aid Despite Clark Amendment," Feb. 3, 1982.

57. "Uneasy Over a Secret War," *Time*, May 16, 1983, p. 12; "America's Secret Warriors," *Newsweek*, Oct. 10, 1983, p. 42; "CIA, State Hedge on Story About Clandestine Aid," *Washington Times*, Oct. 4, 1983, p. 7A.

58. Robert J. Rosenthal, "Angola Rebels Press Military Drive, Seek to Force Government into Talks," *Washington Post*, Aug. 28, 1984, p. A12; House Committee on Foreign Affairs, Subcommittee on Africa, *Foreign Assistance Legislation for Fiscal Years 1986–87: Hearings before the Subcommittee on Africa,* pt. 7, Markup, 99th Cong., 1st sess., Mar. 5, 7, and 19, 1985, 294.

59. Richard Allen, telephone interview by author, May 5, 1993.

60. Anonymous, interview by author, date withheld.

61. Robert Neuman, interview by author, Oct. 20, 1993; and Anonymous, interviews by author, July 1 and 28, 1987.

62. Chester Crocker, interview by author, Oct. 5, 1993.

63. Anonymous, interview by author, June 15, 1993.

64. Secretary of State to American Embassies: Rabat, Nairobi, Libreville, Abidjan, Dakar (33122), "Subject: Message to Chief of State on Savimbi Visit to the U.S.," Dec. 15, 1981.

65. Chester A. Crocker, *High Noon in Southern Africa: Making Peace in a Rough Neighborhood* (New York: Norton, 1992), pp. 227, 286.

66. House Committee on Foreign Affairs, Subcommittee on Africa, *Namibia: Internal Repression and United States Diplomacy: Hearing before the Subcommittee on Africa,* 99th Cong., 1st sess., Feb. 21, 1985, 23. A similar assurance was provided to Senator Daniel Moynihan in a letter from Powell A. Moore, Assistant Secretary for Congressional Relations, Department of State, May 17, 1982.

67. A U.S. businessman told Chairman Howard Wolpe and his Africa Subcommittee staff on June 23, 1987, that he had learned, in conversation with CIA analyst Keith Moore sometime in 1980–81, that

U.S. military trainers were involved, in an undefined way, with Moroccan military training of UNITA. This businessman was known to the Subcommittee as a reliable source. Testimony from another American businessman on possible CIA coordination with Saudi and Moroccan assistance to UNITA is found in House Committee on Foreign Affairs, Subcommittee on Africa, *Possible Violation or Circumvention of the Clark Amendment: Hearing before the Subcommittee on Africa*, 100th Cong., 1st sess., July 1, 1987. Seymour M. Hersh, *The Samson Option* (New York: Random House, 1991), p. 13n., cites Israeli sources revealing a "joint intelligence operation" including "economic/military support to UNITA" said to have been "put in motion" by CIA Director Casey in early 1981.

68. Howard Wolpe, chairman, to Honorable Lee Hamilton, May 14, 1985.

69. Lee H. Hamilton, chairman, to Honorable Howard Wolpe, May 31, 1985.

70. Arnson, *Crossroads*, p. 282.

71. *Congressional Record* (July 10, 1985): H18496.

72. Crocker, *High Noon in Southern Africa*, pp. 279–303.

73. House Committee on Foreign Affairs, Subcommittee on Africa, *Angola: Intervention or Negotiation: Hearings before the Subcommittee on Africa,* 99th Cong., 1st sess., Oct. 31, Nov. 12, 1985, 70–72.

74. Crocker, *High Noon in Southern Africa*, pp. 295–300, 302; *Congressional Record* (Sept. 17, 1986): H7042.

75. Neil A. Lewis, "Administration Decides that Aid to UNITA Rebels Will Continue," *New York Times*, June 11, 1987, pp. A1, A9; Andrew Alexander, "U.S. Aid to Angola Rebels Would Be Almost Tripled Under White House Plan," *Atlanta Constitution*, Mar. 15, 1988, p. A3; George Lardner, Jr., "Angola Lobbies to Cut CIA Aid to Savimbi's Rebels," *Washington Post*, Sept. 12, 1990, p. 9. See also George P. Shultz, *Turmoil and Triumph: My Years as Secretary of State* (New York: Charles Scribner's Sons, 1993), p. 1124, which confirms funding to UNITA of $18 million in 1987 and $40 million in 1988.

76. Crocker, *High Noon in Southern Africa*, pp. 290–302; *Congressional Record* (Oct. 17, 1990): esp. H10042–44, H10057–58.

77. Howard Wolpe, "Seizing Southern African Opportunities," *Foreign Policy* 73 (Winter 1988–89): 60–75; *Congressional Record* (Oct. 17, 1990): H10035–70.

78. John A. Marcum, "Angola: War Again," *Current History* 92 (May 1993): 218–23; Fred Bridgland, "Angola's Secret Bloodbath," *Washington Post,* Mar. 29, 1992, pp. C1, C4; Clifford Krauss, "Angola Rebel Lays Killing to CIA Plot," *New York Times*, May 5, 1992, p. A7; Stuart Sweet, interview by author, Oct. 21, 1993; and Art Roberts, interview by author, Nov. 8, 1993.

79. Howard Wolpe, "More U.S. Aid for Savimbi?" *New York Times*, June 10, 1989, p. 27; David B. Ottoway, "Bush Assures Savimbi of U.S. Support," *Washington Post*, Jan. 12, 1989, pp. A1, A30. The author learned at the time of Assistant Secretary-Designate Cohen's abortive initiative.

80. McHugh, interview.

81. Anonymous, interviews by author, May 9–10, 1994.

82. Kastenmeier, interview.

83. O'Neil, interview.

84. McHugh, interview.

85. Crocker, interview.

86. Bill Richardson, interview by author, Jan. 26, 1994.

87. Christopher Lehman, interview by author, Aug. 10, 1993.

88. Peter Kelly, interview by author, Apr. 5, 1994.

89. Sweet, interview.

90. McMahon, interview.

91. Anonymous, interview by author, May 9, 1994.

92. McMahon, interview.

93. Chester Crocker, telephone interview by author, June 13, 1994.

94. Paul Manafort, interview by author, Nov. 17, 1993; Lehman, interview; and Anonymous, interview by author, Aug. 11, 1993.

95. Lehman, interview.

96. "Lobbyists Active in Presidential Campaign," *Africa News* (Oct. 17, 1988): 3–5; "Lobby Gets Results for Savimbi," *Africa News* 32 (Nov. 1989): 1–3.

97. Paul Manafort explained the strategic role of BMSK for the whole lobbying effort (interview). For detailed information on the finances, personnel, and activities of the foreign-supported components of the UNITA lobby during the period discussed, see U.S. Department of Justice, Foreign Agents Registration Act Statements for Black, Manafort, Stone and Kelly Public Affairs Company (1985–90), TKC International (1986–90), and UNITA (1986–90). See also Thomas B. Edsall, "Profit and Presidential Politics," *Washington Post,* Aug. 12, 1989, pp. A1, A6; Patrick E.

Tyler and David B. Ottoway, "The Selling of Jonas Savimbi: Success and a $600,000 Tab," *Washington Post*, Feb. 9, 1986, pp. A1, A8; Peter H. Stone, "Black, Manafort Takes Africa," *Legal Times*, Aug. 6, 1990, pp. 1, 14; Louis M. Peck, "Wired to Washington," *Hartford Monthly* (Nov. 1989): 46ff.

98. John Spicer Nichols, "The Power of the Anti-Fidel Lobby," *Nation*, Oct. 24, 1988, pp. 389–90; Scott Sleek, "Mr. Mas Goes to Washington," *Common Cause Magazine* (Jan./Feb. 1991): 37–41; Carla Anne Robbins, "Dateline Washington: Cuban-American Clout," *Foreign Policy* 88 (Fall 1992): 162–82; Peter H. Stone, "Cuban Clout," *National Journal* (Feb. 20, 1993): 449–52; and Sweet, interview.

99. House Subcommittee on Africa, *Angola: Intervention or Negotiation*, p. 70.

100. Sweet, interview; and Kelly, interview. Federal Election Commission (computer printout).

101. Kelly, interview.

102. Manafort, interview.

103. Lehman, interview.

104. Kelly, interview; Federal Election Commission (computer printout).

105. Kelly, interview; and Peter Kelly, telephone interview by author, June 16, 1994.

106. Sweet, interview; Manafort, interview.

107. Manafort, interview.

108. Sweet, interview.

109. McCurdy, interview.

110. Senator Dennis DeConcini and thirty-six other senators to President Ronald Reagan, May 12, 1988 (see also "Senators Urge Reconciliation in Angolan Civil War," in *Christian Science Monitor*, May 19, 1988, p. 6); Kelly, interview, Apr. 5, 1994; and Art Roberts, interview by author, Nov. 8, 1993. On the impact of Dodd's actions, see Rowland Evans and Robert Novak, "Liberals Reassess Savimbi," *Washington Post*, July 1, 1988, p. A23.

111. Manafort, interview; Federal Election Commission (computer printout).

112. U.S. Department of Justice, Foreign Agents Registration Act Supplemental Statements, Black, Manafort, Stone and Kelly Public Affairs Company, July 14, 1988, pp. 22, 24, 28, 32–33, 40, 43–44; and Dec. 14, 1988, pp. 2, 6.

113. Manafort, interview.

114. Dante Fascell, interview by author, Jan. 27, 1994.

115. Nichols, "The Power of the Anti-Fidel Lobby"; George Lardner, "How Lobbyists Briefed a Rebel Leader," *Washington Post*, Oct. 8, 1990, p. A21; and Federal Election Commission (computer printout).

116. Fascell, interview.

117. Anonymous, interviews by author, during the period of the events.

118. Roberts, interview; and Richardson, interview. Richardson discussed his disillusionment with Savimbi in House Committee on Foreign Affairs, Subcommittee on Africa, *New Reports of Human Rights Violations in the Angolan Civil War: Hearing before the Subcommittee on Africa,* 101st Cong., 1st sess., Apr. 12, 1989, 7.

119. Steve Morrison and Steve Weissman to Howard Wolpe, "Re: Revised Strategy on Angola," memorandum, July 28, 1989; Steve Morrison and Steve Weissman to Howard Wolpe, "Re: Your Meeting at Noon with Randall Robinson," memorandum, Sept. 14, 1989; House Committee on Foreign Affairs, Subcommittee on Africa, *A Review of United States Policy Towards Political Negotiations in Angola: Hearing before the Subcommittee on Africa,* 101st Cong., 1st sess., Sept. 27, 1989. The author was involved in Wolpe's discussions with Angolan officials.

120. *Congressional Record* (Oct. 17, 1990): H10035–70.

121. Herman Cohen, interview by author, Nov. 17, 1993.

CHAPTER 5. TRANSCENDING THE CULTURE: CONGRESSIONAL LEADERSHIP AND EL SALVADOR, THE PHILIPPINES, AND SOUTH AFRICA

1. Representative J. J. Pickle to Secretary of State James Baker III, Dec. 15, 1989, p. 1. Similar expressions were sent by many other congresspeople including, significantly, a letter to President George Bush by Republican representatives John Miller, Benjamin Gilman, Doug Bereuter, Rod Chandler, Tom Ridge, and Steve Gunderson, Nov. 21, 1989, and a letter to Secretary Baker by Republican senator Arlen Specter, Dec. 1, 1989.

2. Cynthia J. Arnson, *Crossroads: Congress, the President, and Central America 1976–93,* 2d ed. (University Park: Pennsylvania State University Press, 1993), p. 246.

3. Bernard Aronson, interview by author, Jan. 13, 1984.

4. Cited in Rep. John Miller et al. to President George Bush.

5. "Interim Report of the Speaker's Task Force on El Salvador," Apr. 30, 1990, p. 1.

6. William Walker, interview by author, Dec. 13, 1993.

7. Aronson, interview.

8. Bernard Aronson, interview by author, Mar. 1, 1994; Arnson, *Crossroads*, pp. 229–30.

9. Walker, interview.

10. William Woodward, interview by author, Sept. 24, 1993.

11. Jim McGovern, telephone interview by author, July 11, 1994.

12. Woodward, interview; and Joseph Moakley, interview by author, Aug. 2, 1994; McGovern, telephone interview; and Michael O'Neil, telephone interview by author, July 11, 1994.

13. McGovern, telephone interview.

14. Moakley, interview.

15. McGovern, telephone interview; William Walker, interviews by author, Dec. 13, 1993, and Jan. 3, 1994; and Moakley, interview.

16. Walker, interview, Dec. 13, 1993.

17. Ibid.; Leónel Gomez, interview by author, Mar. 11, 1994; Walker, interview, Jan. 3, 1994; and Teresa Whitfield, *Paying the Price: Ignacio Ellacuría and the Murdered Jesuits of El Salvador* (Philadelphia: Temple University Press, 1994), p. 165.

18. The following discussion is largely based on interviews by the author cited in notes 10–17 to this chapter. In addition, the delay in responding to task force questions is discussed in Secretary of State (046164) to American Embassy, San Salvador, "Subject: Official/Informal-Moakley Task Force," Feb. 12, 1990, p. 1. On the major's withheld affidavit, see American Embassy, San Salvador (2043) to Secretary of State, "Subject: Official/Informal," Feb. 12, 1990. On Moakley's threat of a subpoena and its impact, see Robert Henry Michael, Republican Leader, to Honorable John Joseph Moakley, March 6, 1990; and Terrence O'Donnell, General Counsel of the Secretary of Defense, to Honorable John Joseph Moakley, March 9, 1990. On the issue of withheld cables, see Pat Butenis, ARA (CEN) to Steve Berry, H, Department of State memorandum, Apr. 27, 1990, with handwritten notations. Moakley's view is found in Clifford Krauss, "Religion and Politics Become Fused in Congressman's District, and Heart," *New York Times*, Aug. 23, 1990, p. A20. Also on Moakley's activities and style, see Whitfield's very perceptive *Paying the Price,* esp. pp. 164–69, 184–87, 286–87, 368–72.

19. "Interim Report of the Speaker's Task Force on El Salvador," Apr. 30, 1990. The Embassy's views are expressed in American

Embassy, San Salvador (4907) to Secretary of State, "Subject: Jesuit Case: An Assessment," Apr. 7, 1990.

20. Janet G. Mullins-H and Bernard Aronson-ARA to the Acting Secretary, "Subject: El Salvador: Statement by Rep. Joe Moakley on the Jesuits' Case," Department of State Information memorandum, Aug. 16, 1990.

21. Gomez, interview.

22. Report of the Commission on the Truth for El Salvador, *From Madness to Hope: The 12-Year War in El Salvador*, United Nations Security Council, S/25500, Apr. 1, 1993, pp. 53, 24.

23. American Embassy, San Salvador (10791) to Secretary of State, "Subject: The Jesuit Case, Another Big Jolt," Aug. 13, 1990.

24. Early examples of the State Department taking a tough position with the military and wielding the threat of a congressional aid cutoff can be found in American Embassy, San Salvador (15668) to Secretary of State, "Subject: The Importance of the Jesuit Case Emphasized to the High Command," Dec. 5, 1989; and Secretary of State (142303) to American Embassy, San Salvador, "Subject: Moving the Jesuit Case," May 3, 1990. The impact of the Moakley inquiry on the Salvadoran government is recognized in U.S. Department of State, "Report of the Secretary of State's Panel on El Salvador," p. 19.

25. American Embassy, San Salvador (10914) to Secretary of State, "Subject: Jesuit Case: Proposed Measures to Evaluate Information, Increase Pressure on ESAF," Aug. 14, 1990; American Embassy, San Salvador (11127) to Secretary of State, "Subject: Ambassador's Demarche to President Cristiani on the Jesuit Case," Aug. 18, 1990.

26. Moakley, interview; "Statement of Representative Joe Moakley, Chairman of the Speaker's Task Force on El Salvador, Nov. 18, 1991."

27. American Embassy, San Salvador (14598) to Secretary of State, "Subject: Moakley Statement–What's New?" Nov. 22, 1991, p. 3. The most important partially declassified embassy reports on higher-level complicity in the murders include the following from the CIA: untitled, July 10, 1991; "El Salvador," June 6, 1991; "Subject: The Jesuit Case: Claims of Colonel Guillermo Benavides," n.d.; untitled, memorandum, Sept. 19, 1990; "Subject: Social Evening in Guatemala City," memorandum for the Record, May 22, 1990; and "Subject: Report on Activities of Embassy Task

Force on the Jesuit Killings," memorandum, Dec. 10, 1989. Also useful are USDAO, San Salvador (11532) to Ruek/JCS/DIA, "Young Turk Talks Turkey on Tandona and Jesuit Case," Aug. 27, 1990; USDAO, San Salvador (11533) to Ruek/JCS/DIA, "ESAF 'Graybeard' Talks Turkey on Tandona and Jesuit Case,"Aug. 27, 1990; and American Embassy, San Salvador (1206) to Secretary of State, "Subject: Jesuit Update: Alleged Espinoza Letter May Implicate Bustillo and Others," Sept. 20, 1991.

A 1984 CIA memorandum for Vice President Bush indicated that Colonels Ponce and Zepeda, the two leading members of the high command in 1989, were among right-wing extremist Roberto D'Aubuisson's "most notorious associates" in allegedly violent actions, and reportedly mentored junior officers "involved in death squad and other illegal activities." (CIA, Directorate of Intelligence to George Bush, "El Salvador: D'Aubuisson's Terrorist Activities," memorandum, Mar. 2, 1984.)

28. Walker, interview, Dec. 13, 1993.
29. *Congressional Record* (May 22, 1990): H2698–99; Arnson, *Crossroads*, pp. 253–56; William Woodward, telephone interview by author, July 25, 1994. For discussion and debate on the Senate floor, see *Congressional Record* (Aug. 2, 1990): S11934–37; and *Congressional Record* (Oct. 19, 1990): S16137–58, S16171–92.
30. *Congressional Record* (May 22, 1990): H2712–13; Thomas Quigley, interview by author, Feb. 9, 1994; Cynthia Buhl, interview by author, Oct. 19, 1994; Woodward, interview; Moakley, interview; Woodward, telephone interview; and McGovern, telephone interview.
31. Arnson, *Crossroads*, p. 254.
32. *Congressional Record* (May 22, 1990): H2701.
33. American Embassy, San Salvador (01650) to Secretary of State, "Subject: Ambassador Points Out Damage ESAF Errors Causing GOES, USG Policy," Feb. 7, 1990.
34. Woodward, interview; Moakley, interview; McGovern, telephone interview. Bernard Aronson also recalls that Murtha "felt strongly" about the Jesuit case (interview by author, Mar. 1, 1994).
35. K. Larry Storrs, "El Salvador Under Cristiani: U.S. Foreign Assistance Decisions," CRS Issue Brief, Congressional Research Service, Library of Congress, Mar. 26, 1991, p. CRS-14.
36. Arnson, *Crossroads*, p. 257.
37. American Embassy, San Salvador (00939) to Secretary of State,

"Subject: Congressman Murtha's Discussions with Cristiani, MOD Ponce," Jan. 22, 1991.

38. Arnson, *Crossroads*, p. 258.

39. Department of State, "President's Meeting with Salvadoran President Alfredo Cristiani: Scenesetter," n.d. (Sept. 1991)

40. Secretary of State (088663) to American Embassy, San Salvador, "Subject: Jesuit Update—Ponce Initiative Creates New Options," Mar. 20, 1991, p. 1.

41. "Remarks of U.S. Rep. Joe Moakley, Chairman of the Speaker's Task Force on El Salvador, University of Central America–San Salvador, El Salvador, July 1, 1991."

42. American Embassy, San Salvador (08579) to Secretary of State, "Subject: Moakley Presses Cristiani on Jesuits and Peace Talks," July 6, 1991; Gomez, interview; McGovern, telephone interview.

43. Arnson, *Crossroads,* pp. 260–61. Similar views were expressed in McGovern, telephone interview; Gomez, interview; and Woodward, interview.

44. Arnson, *Crossroads*, p. 260.

45. Walker, interview, Jan. 3, 1994.

46. Arnson, *Crossroads*, p. 243; Bernard Aronson, interviews by author, Jan. 13 and Mar. 1, 1994.

47. Walker, interviews, Dec. 13, 1993, and Jan. 3, 1994; Aronson, interviews, Jan. 13 and Mar. 1, 1994; Gomez, interview; and McGovern, telephone interview.

48. American Embassy, San Salvador (10914) to Secretary of State, "Subject: Jesuit Case: Proposed Measures to Evaluate Information, Increase Pressure on ESAF," Aug. 14, 1990, p. 9.

49. American Embassy, San Salvador (15710) to Secretary of State, "Subject: ESAF Puts Forward Go-Between on Jesuit Case," Nov. 26, 1990; American Embassy, San Salvador (15850) to Secretary of State, "Subject: Walking the Jesuit Tightrope—Military Cooperation," Nov. 27, 1990. See also American Embassy, San Salvador (16120) to Secretary of State, "Subject: Jesuit Case," Dec. 3, 1990.

50. Aronson, interview, Mar. 1, 1994; Arnson, *Crossroads*, pp. 262–63. Department of State, "Meeting with President Cristiani: Points to be Made,", n.d. (Sept. 1991), indicates President Bush's awareness that the Congressional "consensus" for military aid "is eroding" due to the Jesuit murders.

51. George P. Shultz, *Turmoil and Triumph: My Years as Secretary of State* (New York: Charles Scribner's Sons, 1993), pp. 633–34; notes

from "Notebook" of Charlie Hill, Executive Assistant to Secretary of State Shultz (transcript from recording courtesy of Stanley Karnow).

52. William E. Kline and James Worthen, "The Fall of Marcos," Case Program, John F. Kennedy School of Government, Harvard University, 1992, pp. 1–18; Stanley Karnow, *In Our Image: America's Empire in the Philippines* (New York: Random House, 1989), pp. 404–6; and Senate Committee on Foreign Relations, *The Situation in the Philippines*, staff report, 98th Cong., 2d sess., Oct. 1984, p. 15.

53. American Embassy, Manila (10344) to Secretary of State, "Subject: Final Thoughts on the Philippines," Apr. 17, 1984 (by Ambassador Michael Armacost).

54. The White House, National Security Decision Directive Number 163, "United States Policy Towards the Philippines," Feb. 20, 1985. This document was declassified with some deletions. The well-known formulation, "part of the problem . . . part of the solution," and the discussion of chastisement, are taken from an earlier draft that was leaked: Department of State, "NSDD: U.S. Policy Towards the Philippines: Executive Summary," Nov. 2, 1984. These aspects were confirmed to have been part of the final policy by former policymakers in interviews. See also Raymond Bonner, *Waltzing with a Dictator: The Marcoses and the Making of American Policy* (New York: Vintage, 1988), pp. 366–68.

55. House Committee on Foreign Affairs, *Assessing America's Options in the Philippines*, report of a workshop sponsored by the Subcommittee on Asian and Pacific Affairs, the Woodrow Wilson International Center for Scholars, and the Congressional Research Service, 99th Cong., 2d sess., Feb. 3, 1986, 112.

56. *Congressional Record* (Sept. 18, 1986): 23872.

57. Gaston Sigur, interview by author, Oct. 25, 1993.

58. Richard Armitage, interview by author, Sept. 22, 1993.

59. Paul Wolfowitz, interview by author, Jan. 25, 1994.

60. Sigur, interview.

61. Stephen Bosworth, interview by author, Sept. 30, 1993.

62. Armitage, interview.

63. Ibid.

64. American Embassy, Manila (18668), to Secretary of State, "Subj: Congressman Solarz' Visit to the Philippines," Dec. 1, 1976; Bosworth, interview.

65. In addition to the public record of Committee hearings and meetings and published opinion pieces, Stephen Solarz, interviews by author, Sept. 28 and Oct. 27, 1993, and Stanley Roth, interview by author, June 23, 1993, were very helpful.

66. Stanley Karnow, "Interview with Steve Solarz, Philippines Project," n.d., pp. 2–3; Solarz, interview, Sept. 28, 1993.

67. House Committee on Foreign Affairs, *Foreign Assistance Legislation for Fiscal Year 1985*, pt. 8, Markup, 98th Cong., 2d sess., Feb. 28, 29; Mar. 1, 6, 7, 14, 1984, pp. 46–47, 108–13; and Committee on Foreign Affairs, *Foreign Assistance Legislation for Fiscal Years 1986–87*, pt. 8, Markup, 99th Cong., 1st sess., Mar. 26, 27; Apr. 2, 3, 1985, pp. 13–15, 310–14.

68. Senate Committee on Foreign Relations, *International Security and Development Cooperation Act of 1984*, Report, 98th Cong., 2d sess., Apr. 18, 1984, pp. 19–20; Fred Brown, interview by author, Sept. 8, 1993; and Bosworth, interview.

69. Senate Committee on Foreign Relations, *The Situation in the Philippines*, p.1.

70. Ibid., p. 4.

71. Department of State, "NSDD: U.S. Policy Towards the Philippines"; Brown, interview.

72. Brown, interview; and Richard Lugar, interview by author, Aug. 2, 1994.

73. Brown, interview; Graeme Bannerman, interview by author, Sept. 27, 1993; and Philip Christenson, interview by author, Sept. 27, 1993.

74. Bernard Gwertzman, "Senator Planning Sweeping Hearings on Foreign Policy," *New York Times*, Dec. 9, 1984, p. 1.

75. Ibid., p. 20.

76. Senate Committee on Foreign Relations, *Security and Development Assistance: Hearings before the Senate Committee on Foreign Relations,* 99th Cong., 1st sess., Mar. 15, 20, 21, 22, and 26, 1985, pp. 620–33 (quote is at 623).

77. U.S. Congress, Senate Committee on Foreign Relations, "Markup of Foreign Assistance for Fiscal Year 1986," Mar. 27, 1985 (Afternoon sess.), p. 146, typewritten transcript, National Archives, Washington, D.C.; U.S. Congress, Senate Committee on Foreign Relations and House Committee on Foreign Affairs, "Joint Conferees, S 960, The Foreign Assistance Bill," July 25, 1985, p. 156, typewritten transcript, National Archives, Washington, D.C.

78. Senate Committee on Foreign Relations, *Visit to the Philippines, Aug. 2–15, 1985*, staff report, 99th Cong., 2d sess., Apr. 1986, pp. 1, 16.

79. Senate Committee on Foreign Relations, *Administration Review of U.S. Policy Towards the Philippines: Hearings before the Senate Committee on Foreign Relations,* 99th Cong., 1st sess., Oct. 30, 1985, p. 6.

80. Lugar, *Letters to the Next President*, p. 105.

81. Senate Committee on Foreign Relations, *Administration Review of U.S. Policy Towards the Philippines*, pp. 66–67, 58–61.

82. Roth, interview.

83. Senate Committee on Foreign Relations and House Committee on Foreign Affairs, "Joint Conferees, S 960, The Foreign Assistance Bill," pp. 156, 197–205.

84. Senate Committee on Foreign Relations, *Administration Review of U.S. Policy Towards the Philippines*, p. 67.

85. Bosworth, interview.

86. This was particularly noted by a prominent Filipino democrat, Mariano Quesada, in National Endowment for Democracy, *The Challenge of Democracy*, proceedings of a conference on efforts underway to advance the cause of democracy throughout the world, Washington, D.C., May 18 and 19, 1987, p. 40.

87. See Karnow, *In Our Image*, p. 413; and Sheila J. Coronel, "Dateline Philippines: The Lost Revolution," *Foreign Policy* 84 (Fall 1991): 179.

88. Brown, interview.

89. Philippine Task Force—John Finney, Director, to the Secretary [of State], "Subject: Your Meeting with Congressional Leaders Monday Feb. 24 at 1: 45 pm," Department of State briefing memorandum, Feb. 24, 1986. While Laxalt and Ambassador Bosworth differ about whether the snap election was raised at the time of Laxalt's visit (the former says it was), it appears that Laxalt did at least discuss this with Marcos during subsequent telephone conversations. See Bonner, *Waltzing with a Dictator,* p. 391; and Paul Laxalt to the author, Nov. 3, 1993, pp. 1–2. Bonner (pp. 376–77) indicates Casey did not broach a snap election with Marcos during his own visit in May 1985, but a high U.S. official who wishes to remain anonymous told the author that in this period, "I believe Casey proposed early elections. We didn't think it was a good idea. Many were appalled" (interview by author, date withheld). Laxalt states that Casey told him he had "raised" the idea of a snap election with Marcos (Laxalt to the author, p. 1).

90. Bosworth, interview; Armitage, interview; Sigur, interview; Nayan Chanda, "A Word In Your Ear," *Far Eastern Economic Review*, Jan. 31, 1985, p. 31; Department of State, "Themes for a Meeting of Presidential Envoy with President Marcos," Aug. 19, 1985.

91. Bosworth, interview; see also Bonner, *Waltzing with a Dictator*, p. 387.

92. Secretary of State (337854) to USDEL Secretary, "Subject: Highlights of Sunday Morning Talk Shows, 11/3/85," Nov. 3, 1985, p. 1; Bill Keller, "Laxalt Reports Pledges By Marcos on Political and Military Changes," *New York Times*, Oct. 23, 1985, p. A1.

93. Paul Laxalt to the author, p. 2.

94. Senator Paul Laxalt, "My Conversations with President Ferdinand Marcos: A Lesson in Personal Diplomacy," *Policy Review* 37 (Summer 1986): 2.

95. American Embassy, Manila (34979), to Secretary of State, "Subject: Marcos' Motivations for Snap Elections," Nov. 9, 1985.

96. Roth, interview; and Solarz, interview, Sept. 28, 1993.

97. Recounted in Lugar, *Letters to the Next President*, pp. 53, 56–9.

98. House *International Security and Development Cooperation Act of 1985*, Conference Report, 99th Cong., 1st sess., July 29, 1985, p. 81.

99. *Congressional Record* (Nov. 14, 1985): S15670–75; Lugar, *Letters to the Next President*, p. 109.

100. EAP-Paul Wolfowitz to the Secretary, "Subject: Early Presidential Elections and Our Philippine Policy," Department of State action memorandum, Nov. 6, 1985; House Committee on Foreign Affairs, Subcommittee on Asian and Pacific Affairs, *Recent Events in the Philippines: Hearings before the Committee on Foreign Affairs and the Subcommittee on Asian and Pacific Affairs*, 99th Cong., Markup, 1st sess., Nov. 12 and 13, 1985, p. 64.

101. Laxalt, "My Conversations with President Marcos," p. 4; Keller, "Laxalt Reports Pledges by Marcos on Political and Military Changes," p. A1; and Secretary of State (337854) to USDEL Secretary, p. 2.

102. EAP-Paul Wolfowitz to the Secretary, pp. 2–3.

103. Lugar, *Letters to the Next President*, p. 117.

104. Ibid. pp. 110–11; Senate Committee on Foreign Relations, *Presidential Election Process in the Philippines*, report prepared by the Center for Democracy, Boston University, Boston, Massachusetts and Washington, D.C., 99th Cong., 2d sess., Jan. 1986.

105. Lugar, *Letters to the Next President*, pp. 116–18.

106. Ibid., pp. 121–23.

107. Solarz, interview, Sept. 28, 1993; and Roth, interview.

108. Brown, interview; Lugar, interview; Sen. Richard G. Lugar to the president, Jan. 31, 1986 (cf. "Philippine Elections," statement by the president, Jan. 30, 1986, in *Weekly Compilation of Presidential Documents,* Feb. 3, 1986, pp. 110–11); and Lugar, *Letters to the Next President*, pp. 118–26, 146–47.

109. Shultz, *Turmoil and Triumph*, p. 626; Lugar, *Letters to the Next President*, pp. 149–50; Bernard Weinraub, "Reagan Praises Two-Party System of Philippines," *New York Times*, Feb. 11, 1986, p. A1.

110. Lugar, *Letters to the Next President*, pp. 148, 152.

111. Shultz, *Turmoil and Triumph*, pp. 627–28.

112. Ibid., p. 628.

113. Ibid.; Stanley Karnow, "Phil Habib Interview, 10/7/86," pp. 1, 2, 8.

114. Shultz, *Turmoil and Triumph*, p. 630.

115. Bosworth, interview; Wolfowitz, interview. See also Shultz, *Turmoil and Triumph*, pp. 629–30.

116. Sigur, interview.

117. Karnow, "Phil Habib Interview, 10/7/86," pp. 6, 19.

118. Lugar, interview.

119. Don Oberdorfer, "U.S. Adds to the Pressures," *Washington Post*, Feb. 23, 1986, pp. A1, A21; Karnow, *In Our Image*, p. 412.

120. Roth, interview.

121. Lugar, interview. Compare Bonner, *Waltzing with a Dictator*, p. 427. Laxalt to the author, p. 3.

122. Lugar's important public role is highlighted in stories on the Philippines appearing in both the *Washington Post* and *New York Times* from Feb. 8–23, 1986; see for example, Don Oberdorfer and Joanne Omang, "Lugar Says Fraud Could Halt Manila Aid," *Washington Post*, Feb. 13, 1986, p. A1. See also Hedrick Smith, *The Power Game* (New York: Ballantine Books, 1988), pp. 17, 43–4, 81.

123. House Committee on Foreign Affairs, Subcommittee on Asian and Pacific Affairs, *The Philippine Election and the Implications for U.S. Policy: Hearings before the Subcommittee on Asian and Pacific Affairs,* 99th Cong., Markup, 2d sess., Feb. 19 and 20, 1986.

124. The White House, National Security Decision Directive Number 215, "Philippines," Feb. 23, 1986. According to notes provided to the author from a private meeting of the Council on Foreign Relations in New York City, Feb. 18, 1986, Wolfowitz opposed a mili-

tary aid cut because the Philippine army was in bad shape, and this would help the NPA. Expressing fear of a rapid transition, he said "The parties need to get together" and the U.S. should not cut off contacts with Marcos and "drive him into a corner." See also Bonner, *Waltzing with a Dictator*, pp. 437–38.

125. Solarz, interview, Sept. 28, 1993.

126. Laxalt to the author, p. 2.

127. U.S. Department of Justice, Foreign Agents Registration and Supplemental Statements (No. 3600), Black, Manafort, Stone, and Kelly Public Affairs Company, Nov. 25, 1985, Dec. 14, 1985, and June 14, 1986; Paul Manafort, telephone interview by author, July 11, 1994; and Bonner, *Waltzing with a Dictator*, pp. 403, 420–22.

128. L. E. S. de Villiers, "U.S. Sanctions Against South Africa: A Historical Analysis of the Sanctions Campaign and its Political Implications 1946–1993" (Ph.D. diss., History, University of Stellenbosch, South Africa, 1994), 408–9.

129. Quoted in *Southscan* (London), Sept. 6, 1991, p. 274.

130. de Villiers, "U.S. Sanctions Against South Africa," p. 409.

131. American Embassy, Lusaka (01011) to Secretary of State, "Subject: CODEL Gray Meeting with Nelson Mandela and National Executive Committee of the ANC," Mar. 5, 1990.

132. Department of State, "Report to the Congress Pursuant to Section 501 of the Comprehensive Anti-Apartheid Act of 1986," Oct. 1, 1990, p. 7.

133. "Envoy Backs U.S. Sanctions Against South Africa," *Washington Post*, June 21, 1987, p. A15.

134. Lugar, interview.

135. de Villiers, "U.S. Sanctions Against South Africa," p. 420, notes that in 1991 the South African Foreign Trade Organization estimated at R3 Billion (approximately $1.2 billion) the combined annual cost of "export market closures, re-routing export shipments on detours, backhanders to middlemen and special price cuts as sweeteners to overseas buyers—so-called 'sanctions premiums'."

136. On the impact of sanctions, Assistant Secretary of State for African Affairs Herman Cohen said, "Sanctions are having a major impact on the psychology of the white community. There is no capital inflow. There is disinvestment. . . . People worry about the future" (quoted in Anthony Lewis, "South Africa Possibilities," *New York Times*, June 25, 1989, p. IV27). See also Roger Thurow, "South Africa Facing a No-Growth Future," *Wall Street Journal*, July 26,

1988, p. 21, regarding South African business perspectives. On the way South African leaders factored sanctions into their ultimate political decisions, see de Villiers, "U.S. Sanctions Against South Africa," pp. 441–42.

137. Chester A. Crocker, "South Africa: Strategy for Change," *Foreign Affairs* 59 (Winter 1980/81): 33; see also the citation in Pauline H. Baker, *The United States and South Africa: The Reagan Years* (New York: Ford Foundation-Foreign Policy Association, 1989), p. 117.

138. Crocker, "South Africa: Strategy for Change," pp. 347–49; Senate Committee on Foreign Relations, *U.S. Policy Toward South Africa: Hearings before the Senate Committee on Foreign Relations,* Apr. 24, May 2, and May 22, 1985, p. 62.

139. Ibid., p. 38.

140. Stephen R. Weissman, "Dateline South Africa: The Opposition Speaks," *Foreign Policy* 58 (Spring 1985): 167.

141. Richard Cohen, "To Reporters, Quit South Africa," *New York Times,* Aug. 31, 1987, p. A19.

142. Howard Wolpe, interview by author, Nov. 18, 1993.

143. Ibid.

144. Pam Valery, Case Program, John F. Kennedy School of Government, Harvard University, "The United States and South Africa: The Sanctions Debate of 1985," 1988, pp. 9–11; Baker, *The United States and South Africa,* pp. 29–30; and Susan Rasky, "Anti-Apartheid Protest Gains Ground," *New York Times,* Sept. 15, 1985, p. 16.

145. David Hoffman, "Americans Back S. African Blacks," *Washington Post,* Sept. 25, 1985, p. A28; "44% in Survey Want U.S. to Press Pretoria," *New York Times,* Nov. 18, 1985, p. A3. Six years earlier, a majority opposed such measures, as reported in James E. Baker, J. Daniel O'Flaherty, and John de St. Jorre, "Full Report: Public Opinion Poll on American Attitudes Toward South Africa," Carnegie Endowment for International Peace, 1979.

146. Anonymous, interview by author, Oct. 20, 1993; Anonymous, interview by author, date withheld; and William Gray III, interview by author, Dec. 17, 1993.

147. Gray, interview.

148. Ibid.; Anonymous, interview, Oct. 20, 1993; and Anonymous, interview, date withhheld.

149. William Finnegan, "Coming Apart Over Apartheid," *Mother Jones* (Apr.–May 1986): 19–21; Rasky, "Anti-Apartheid Protest Gains Ground"; Robert Walker, interview by author, Feb. 2, 1994.

150. South African government and business agents in the United States and their political activities are discussed in detail in Richard Leonard, "South African Propaganda in the United States and the Impact of South African Censorship and Media Control," a report prepared for the United Nations Centre Against Apartheid, draft, Aug. 1988, pp. 22–28.

151. Wolpe, interview; Gray, interview; and Lugar, interview. The quotation is from a "senior House Republican" cited less specifically in Crocker, *High Noon in Southern Africa*, p. 319 (Chester Crocker, interview by author, Oct. 5, 1993).

152. Crocker, *High Noon in Southern Africa*, p. 319.

153. Wolpe, interview; Christenson, interview; Anonymous, interview, Oct. 20, 1993; and Anonymous, interview by author, date withheld. This point was also confirmed by the author's own observations.

154. Ken Zinn, Associate Director, Washington Office on Africa, to House and Senate Aides, "Re: National Citizens Lobby Day," memorandum, May 1, 1985. The observation about TransAfrica is based on the author's experience and on anonymous interviews with several former TransAfrica staff members over the past several years.

155. Solarz, interview, Oct. 27, 1993; Wolpe, interview; and Lugar, interview.

156. *Congressional Record* (Oct. 27, 1993): H8744.

157. Ibid.

158. Gray, interview.

159. Wolpe, interview.

160. Senate Democratic staff continually stressed to the author and other House staff the importance of early House action as a pressure on the Senate to move.

161. Gray, interview; and Subcommittee on Africa vote estimates at the time, based on canvassing members' offices.

162. Robert Walker, interview.

163. Mark Siljander, telephone interview by author, Nov. 1, 1993.

164. Robert Walker, interview.

165. Lugar, *Letters to the Next President*, pp. 212–13; Lugar, interview.

166. Christenson, interview; and Bannerman, interview.

167. Lugar, *Letters to the Next President*, pp. 217, 208, 210.

168. Ibid., p. 217; and Valery, "The United States and South Africa: The Sanctions Debate of 1985," p. 28.

169. A useful comparison of Lugar's proposal and that of Senate Democrats is found in *Congressional Record* (July 28, 1986):

S9776–77. Lugar also proposed two notable political sanctions, restricting visas to South African officials and prohibiting South African airplanes from landing in the U.S. See also Lugar, *Letters to the Next President*, pp. 223–27.

170. Lugar, interview.

171. Steve Weissman to Interested House Members and Staff, "Why Senate Passed Foreign Relations Committee Bill (S 995)," memorandum, July 12, 1985. Compare Lugar, *Letters to the Next President*, p. 218, which neglects the Democrats' practical political reasons for going along with his strategy.

172. U.S. Congress, Senate Committees on Foreign Relations and Banking, Housing and Urban Affairs and House Committees on Foreign Affairs and Banking, Finance and Urban Affairs, "Joint Conferees, H.R. 1460, The Anti-Apartheid Act of 1985, July 31, 1985," typewritten transcript, National Archives, Washington, D.C.; Richard G. Lugar, "This is Not a Disinvestment Bill," *Washington Post*, Sept. 6, 1985, p. A23.

173. Lugar, *Letters to the Next President*, p. 221.

174. Ibid., pp. 221–23.

175. Ibid., pp. 222–23.

176. Weissman, "Why Senate Passed Senate Foreign Relations Bill."

177. Lugar, *Letters to the Next President*, pp. 234–35; Bannerman, interview; and Gray, interview. The author was also aware of these developments from attending meetings at the time.

178. Christopher Madison, "Solarz's Brash Style Tempers His Quest for Influence in the Foreign Policy Arena," *National Journal*, Oct. 26, 1985, p. 2413.

179. Krauss, "Religion and Politics Become Fused in Congressman's District, and Heart."

180. Lugar, interview.

181. Ibid.

CHAPTER 6. TOWARD CONGRESSIONAL REVIVAL

1. This is the notable conclusion of a study that draws a distinction between congressional "activism" and influence. See Randall B. Ripley and James M. Lindsay, *Congress Resurgent: Foreign and Defense Policy on Capitol Hill* (Ann Arbor: University of Michigan Press, 1993), p. 280. Lindsay's thorough and insightful *Congress and Nuclear Weapons* (Baltimore, Md.: Johns Hopkins University

Press, 1991) comes to similar conclusions, and notes the contribu-
tion of norms of deference: see pp. 116–21, 145–59. See also
Harold Hongju Koh, *The National Security Constitution: Sharing
Power after the Iran-Contra Affair* (New Haven, Conn.: Yale Uni-
versity Press, 1990); and Barbara Hinckley, *Less Than Meets the
Eye: Foreign Policy Making and the Myth of the Assertive Congress*
(Chicago: University of Chicago Press, 1994).

2. Hinckley, *Less Than Meets the Eye*, pp. 171–76.

3. Ibid., pp. 47–48.

4. House Committee on Foreign Affairs, Subcommittee on Africa,
*Enforcement of the United States Arms Embargo Against South
Africa: Hearing before the Subcommittee on Africa*, 97th Cong., 2d
sess., Mar. 30, 1982, 41–92.

5. William Scott Malone, David Halevy, and Sam Hemingway, "The
Guns of Saddam," *Washington Post*, Feb. 10, 1991, pp. C1, C4;
Michael Z. Wise, "4 Austrians Convicted of Arms Sales to Iran,"
Washington Post, Feb. 2, 1991, p. A14; Douglas Frantz, "Untan-
gling the Threads of Iraq's Arms Network," *Los Angeles Times*,
Nov. 22, 1992, pp. A1, A28, A29; Trevor Rowe, "Iraq Gives U.N.
Evidence of Supergun," *Washington Post*, July 20, 1991, pp. A14,
A17.

6. Malone et al., "The Guns of Saddam," p. C4. The main evidence
regarding the U.S. origin of the artillery technology is detailed in
Lawrence Curtis, Special Agent in Charge, U.S. Customs Service,
Derby Line, Vermont, to [deleted], Arms Licensing Division,
Office of Munitions Control (OMC), Department of State, Sept.
19, 1984; and in "Space Research Corporation, Phoenix Engineering: Chronology," n.d., U.S. Customs Service. OMC officials' general acceptance of this evidence is indicated in House
Subcommittee on Africa, *Enforcement of the United States Arms
Embargo Against South Africa*, p. 16; Office of Munitions Control
to Mr. Lawrence Curtis, Apr. 22, 1985; Secretary of State (179936)
to American Embassy, Ottawa, "Subject: China to Receive 155
mm. Cannons," July 10, 1982; and Joseph Smaldone (former chief
of OMC's Licensing Division), interview by author, June 30, 1993.
On the U.S. technological contribution to the supergun, see also
Great Britain, House of Commons, Trade and Industry Committee, Second Report, *Exports to Iraq: Project Babylon and Long
Range Guns*, report together with the Proceedings of the Committee, Mar. 13, 1992, p. xx.

7. INR/PMA/AT-"Pat" Miller to T-Mr. Steven Saboe, "Staunch" Committee, "Subject: Austrian Field Guns Via Libya to Iran: Talking Points," Department of State memorandum, Feb. 6, 1986.

8. See interview in *Montreal Gazette*, Mar. 21, 1981.

9. "Space Research Corporation, Phoenix Engineering: Chronology."

10. Ibid.; Malone et al., "The Guns of Saddam," p. C4; Senate Committee on Banking, Housing and Urban Affairs, *United States Export Policy Toward Iraq Prior to Iraq's Invasion of Kuwait: Hearing before the Senate Committee on Banking, Housing and Urban Affairs,* 102d Cong., 2d sess., Oct. 27, 1992, p. 161; Smaldone, interview.

11. Senate Committee on Banking, Housing and Urban Affairs, *United States Export Policy Toward Iraq Prior to Iraq's Invasion of Kuwait*, pp. 168, 219.

12. Seymour M. Hersh, "U.S. Secretly Gave Aid to Iraq Early in Its War Against Iran," *New York Times*, Jan. 26, 1992, pp. 1, 12; Murray Waas, "Gulfgate: How the U.S. Secretly Armed Iraq," *Village Voice*, Dec. 18, 1990, pp. 26–37; Alan Friedman, *Spider's Web: The Secret History of How the White House Illegally Armed Iraq* (New York: Bantam, 1993), esp. pp. 3–55; and Friedman, "The President Was Very, Very Mad," *New York Times*, Nov. 7, 1993, p. IV15.

13. House Committee on Foreign Affairs, *Report of the Task Force on Foreign Assistance*, 101st Cong., 1st sess., Feb. 1989, pp. 32, 27.

14. House Committee on Foreign Affairs, *Structural Adjustment in Africa: Insights from the Experiences of Ghana and Senegal*, Report of a Staff Study Mission to Great Britain, Ghana, Senegal, Cote d'Ivoire, and France, Nov. 29–Dec. 20, 1988, esp. pp. 20–21, 9, 12, 15.

15. George Ingram, interview by author, Dec. 9, 1993.

16. Dante Fascell, interview by author, Jan. 27, 1994.

17. House Committee on Foreign Affairs, *Report of the Task Force on Foreign Assistance*, p. 33.

18. Ingram, interview.

19. James M. Lindsay, *Congress and the Politics of U.S. Foreign Policy* (Baltimore, Md.: Johns Hopkins University Press, 1994), pp. 183–84, 162.

20. Koh, *The National Security Constitution*, pp. 167–76; Edmund S. Muskie, Kenneth Rush, and Kenneth W. Thompson, *The President, the Congress and Foreign Policy* (Lanham, Md.: University Press of America, 1986), pp. 4, 29; Thomas E. Mann and Norman T. Ornstein, *Renewing Congress: A Second Report* (Washington,

D.C.: American Enterprise Institute and Brookings Institution, 1993), p. 81; Robert A. Katzmann, "War Powers: Toward a New Accommodation," in Thomas E. Mann, ed., *A Question of Balance: The President, the Congress and Foreign Policy* (Washington, D.C.: The Brookings Institution, 1990), pp. 65–69.

21. On the reforms undertaken by the new 1995 House, see Michael Wines, "Republicans Seek Sweeping Changes in House Rules," *New York Times*, Dec. 8, 1994, pp. A1, B21. On the overall congressional reform movement, see Mann and Ornstein, *Renewing Congress* (First and Second Reports); Janet Hook, "Senate Members OK Panel Cuts, Two-Year Budget Cycle," *Congressional Quarterly Weekly Review* (Nov. 13, 1993): 3094–96; Janet Hook and Beth Donovan, "Reform Panel Mirrors Issues Rather Than Mends Them," *Congressional Quarterly Weekly Review* (Nov. 20, 1993): 3171–72; Thomas Geoghegan, "The Dole Filibuster," *Washington Post*, Sept. 4, 1994, pp. C1, C4.

22. Morton Halperin, "The Way to Pick a Fight: Democratizing the Debate on Using Force Abroad," *Washington Post*, Jan. 10, 1993, pp. C1, C4.

23. Gregory F. Treverton, "Intelligence: Welcome to the American Government," in Mann, *A Question of Balance*, p. 108.

24. Fascell, interview.

25. Compare Koh, *The National Security Constitution*, pp. 169–75.

26. House Committee on Foreign Affairs, *American Public Attitudes Towards Foreign Policy: Hearing before the Committee on Foreign Affairs*, 103d Cong., 2d sess., July 27, 1994; Andrew H. Kohut and Robert C. Toth, "Arms and the People," *Foreign Affairs* 73 (Nov.–Dec. 1994): 47–61; and John Rielly, ed., *American Public Opinion and U.S. Foreign Policy*, Reports for 1975, 1979, 1983, 1987, 1991 (Chicago: Chicago Council on Foreign Relations, 1976, 1980, 1984, 1988, 1992).

27. This section is partly based on interviews by the author during September and November 1994 with representatives of more than a dozen nongovernmental interest groups and several informed observers.

28. House Permanent Select Committee on Intelligence, *Compilation of Intelligence Laws and Related Laws and Executive Orders of Interest to the National Intelligence Community, As Amended Through Mar. 1, 1985*, 99th Cong., 1st sess., July 1985, 390–91.

29. See the following articles by Steven Greenhouse: "Republicans

Plan to Guide Foreign Policy by Purse String," *New York Times*, Nov. 13, 1994, p. I12; "Russian Aid Under Siege by G.O.P.," *New York Times*, Nov. 25, 1994, p. A15; "On the Hill, Foreign Policy Splits G.O.P.," *New York Times*, Dec. 11, 1994, p. I23; "A G.O.P. House Leader Presses Attack on Clinton Foreign Policy," *New York Times*, Dec. 9, 1994, p. A5; and "G.O.P. Senate Bill Would Slash Foreign Aid for Africa," *New York Times*, Dec. 13, 1994, p. A9. Note too R. Jeffrey Smith, "House Foreign Panel Chief Vows Scrutiny," *Washington Post*, Dec. 9, 1994, p. A20.

30. See Helen Dewar, "Senate Foreign Relations Panel Founders," *Washington Post*, Oct. 10, 1989, pp. A1, A12; Tim Weiner, "Man With His Own Foreign Policy," *New York Times*, Dec. 7, 1994, p. A10; Cynthia Arnson, *Crossroads: Congress, the President, and Central America 1976–1993,* 2d ed. (University Park: Pennsylvania State University Press, 1993), pp. 158, 332; Bruce W. Jentleson, "Diplomacy," in Mann, ed., *A Question of Balance*, pp. 175–76; Helen Dewar, "Helms Rekindles a Furor Trying to Put One Out," *Washington Post*, Nov. 23, 1994, pp. A1, A14; and Helen Dewar, "Saying Helms Vows to Hold His Tongue, Dole Won't Deny Him Chairmanship," *Washington Post*, Nov. 24, 1994, p. A25.

31. Smith, "House Foreign Panel Chief Vows Scrutiny"; Greenhouse, "A G.O.P. House Leader Presses Attack."

EPILOGUE: THE NEW REPUBLICAN CONGRESS AND BOSNIA

1. *Congressional Record* (Dec. 12, 1995): S18431.

2. *Congressional Record* (Dec. 13, 1995): S18459.

3. "Bosnia Update," Press Release from Senator Bob Dole, Sept. 26, 1995.

4. "Bosnia and U.S. Troops," Press Release from Senator Bob Dole, Nov. 30, 1995.

5. "Clinton's Words on Mission to Bosnia: The Right Thing to Do," *New York Times*, Nov. 28, 1995, p. A14.

6. John Pomfret, "Balkan Leaders Meet to Salvage Peace Accords," *Washington Post*, Feb. 18, 1996, p. A32.

7. See Carl Bildt, "Keeping Bosnia in One Peace," *Washington Post*, Mar. 31, 1996, p. C2; Anthony Borden, "Moving Dayton to Bosnia," *Nation*, Mar. 25, 1996, pp. 18–22; Misha Glenny, "The Price of Peace in Bosnia," *New York Times*, Mar. 3, 1996, Sec. IV, p. 15; John Pomfret, "Muslims Return Home as Bosnia Pact Viola-

tions Alleged," *Washington Post*, Mar. 13, 1996, p. A16; "Muslims Seem to Discard Dream of Multiethnic Bosnia," *Washington Post*, Mar. 17, 1996, p. A22; and "New Muslim-Croat Federation Falling Apart," *Washington Post*, Mar. 27, 1996, pp. A1, A26; Philip Shennon, "Pentagon Report Predicts Bosnia Will Fragment Without Vast Aid," *New York Times*, Mar. 20, 1996, pp. A1, A12; Craig R. Whitney, "In Bosnia, Securing a Peaceful Future Now Depends on Roads, Refugees and Elections," *New York Times*, Mar. 26, 1996, p. A10.

8. Letter from Newt Gingrich, Speaker of the House, and Bob Dole, Senate Majority Leader, to President Bill Clinton, Nov. 10, 1995.

9. *Congressional Record* (Dec. 13, 1995): S18552.

10. *Congressional Record* (Dec. 13, 1995): H14847.

11. *Congressional Record* (July 26, 1995): S10690–91.

12. *Congressional Record* (July 25, 1995): S10630.

13. *Congressional Record* (Aug. 1, 1995): H8103.

14. *Congressional Record* (Dec. 13, 1995): S18497.

15. *Congressional Record* (Dec. 13, 1995): S18528–29.

16. Bildt, "Keeping Bosnia in One Peace."

Index